AF528506

Dalit and Human Rights

Dalit and Human Rights

R.K. Bakshi

AKHAND

AKHAND PUBLISHING HOUSE
NEW DELHI (INDIA)

Published by
AKHAND PUBLISHING HOUSE
L-9 A, IST FLOOR, STREET NO. 42
SADATPUR EXTENSION
DELHI-110094 (INDIA)
CELL- 0-9013387535, 0-9968628081

Dalit and Human Rights

© Publisher
Edition 2010
ISBN 978-81-910525-4-1

The responsibility for facts stated, opinion expressed or conclusions reached and plagiarism, if any, in this book is entirely that of the author/editor. The publisher bears no responsibility for them whatsoever.

Printed in India
at Asian Offset Printers, Delhi

Preface

Over one-sixth of India's population, some 170 million people, live a precarious existence, shunned by much of Indian society because of their rank as untouchables or "Dalits" —literally meaning broken people—at the bottom of India's caste system. Dalits are discriminated against, denied access to land and basic resources, forced to work in degrading conditions, and routinely abused at the hands of police and dominant-caste groups that enjoy the state's protection.

Beginning in the 1920s, various social, religious and political movements rose up in India against the caste system and in support of the human rights of the Dalit community. In 1950, the Constitution of India was adopted, and largely due to the influence of Dr. B.R. Ambedkar, it departed from the norms and traditions of the caste system in favour of justice, equality, liberty, and fraternity, guaranteeing all citizens basic human rights regardless of caste, creed, gender, or ethnicity. The implementation and enforcement of these principles has, unfortunately, been an abysmal failure.

Despite the fact that "untouchability" was abolished under India's constitution in 1950, the practice of untouchability—the imposition of social disabilities on persons by reason of their birth in certain castes— remains very much a part of rural India. Most Dalits continue to live in extreme poverty, without land or opportunities for better employment or education. With the exception of a small minority who have benefited from India's policy of quotas in education and government jobs, Dalits are relegated to the most menial of tasks, as manual scavengers, removers of human waste and dead animals, leather workers, street sweepers, and cobblers.

Laws granting Dalits special consideration for government jobs and education reach only a small percentage of those they are meant to benefit. Laws designed to ensure that Dalits enjoy equal rights and protections have seldom been enforced. Instead, police refuse to register complaints about violations of the law and rarely prosecute those responsible for abuses that range from murder and rape to exploitative labour practices and forced displacement from Dalit lands and homes. Laws and government policies on land reform and budget allocations for the economic empowerment of the Dalit community remain largely unimplemented.

This book presents a systematic analysis of the human rights issues faced by dalit community in India and elsewhere. It also describes dalits efforts to overcome deeply entrenched caste hierarchies and to assert their right to live with dignity. While the evidence presented in this book suggests that the more blatant and extreme forms of untouchability appear to have declined, discrimination continues and is most prevalent in the religious and personal spheres. The objective of this book is to persuade organisations as to the need to use a human rights framework that incorporates economic, social and cultural rights to fight inequality and poverty.

Author

Contents

1

Status of Dalits

Dalit is a self-designation for a group of people traditionally regarded as untouchable. Dalits are a mixed population of numerous caste groups all over South Asia, and speak various languages. While the caste system has been abolished under the Indian constitution, there is still discrimination and prejudice against Dalits in South Asia. Since Indian independence, significant steps have been taken to provide opportunities in jobs and education. Many social organizations have encouraged proactive provisions to better the conditions of dalits through improved education, health and employment.

Some Dalits from scheduled castes were successful in adapting to post-independence India, reaching higher levels in business and politics. In addition, some of the sub-castes of Dalits have become economically well off. Despite discrimination laws, many Dalits still suffer from social stigma and political oppression; Dalits are often denied the basic rights of education, housing, property rights, freedom of religion, choice of employment (many Dalits accept payment of less than $1 USD per day), and equal treatment before the law (89% of all court cases involving crimes against Dalits result in acquittals). In 2006, Indian Prime Minister Manmohan Singh acknowledged parallels between "untouchability" and apartheid.

Gandhi's coinage of the word Harijan, translated roughly as "Children of God", to identify the former Untouchables. The terms "Scheduled castes and scheduled tribes" (SC/ST) are the official terms used in Indian government documents to identify former "untouchables" and tribes. However, in 2008 the National Commission for Scheduled Castes, noticing that "Dalit" was used interchangeably with the official term "scheduled castes", called the term "unconstitutional" and asked state governments to end its use. After the order, the Chhattisgarh government ended the official use of the word "Dalit".

"Adi Dravida", "Adi Karnataka" and "Adi Andhra" are words used in the states of Tamil Nadu, Karnataka and Andhra Pradesh, respectively, to identify people of former "untouchable" castes in official documents. These words, particularly the prefix of "Adi", denote the aboriginal inhabitants of the land.

1.1. Social Status of Dalits

In the context of traditional Hindu society, Dalit status has often been historically associated with occupations regarded as ritually impure, such as any involving butchering, removal of rubbish, removal of waste and leatherwork. Dalits work as manual labourers, cleaning latrines and sewers, and clearing away rubbish. Engaging in these activities was considered to be polluting to the individual, and this pollution was considered contagious. As a result, Dalits were commonly segregated, and banned from full participation in Hindu social life. For example, they could not enter a temple nor a school, and were required to stay outside the village. Elaborate precautions were sometimes observed to prevent incidental contact between Dalits and other castes. Discrimination against Dalits still exists in rural areas in the private sphere, in everyday matters such as access to eating places, schools, temples and water sources. It has largely disappeared in urban areas and in the public sphere.

Some Dalits have successfully integrated into urban Indian society, where caste origins are less obvious and less important in public life. In rural India, however, caste origins are more readily apparent and Dalits often remain excluded from local religious life, though some qualitative evidence suggests that its severity is fast diminishing. In India's biggest state Uttar Pradesh Dalits have revolutionized the politics and have come to the top in state assemble poll. Dalits and similar groups are also found in Nepal and Bangladesh. In addition, the Burakumin of Japan, Baekjeong of Korea and Midgan of Somalia are similar in status to Dalits.

One study found some association between caste status and Y-chromosomal genetic markers seeming to indicate a more European lineage of the higher castes; however, many recent studies indicate no genetic differences between upper and lower castes. Caste differentiation between Indians is regarded by many as a social construct between Indian people, and is claimed not to have a genetic basis. Genetic testing further indicates that, as a whole, Indian genetic groups do not show a great affinity to any non-South Asian groups.

1.2. Dalits and Religion

Sachar Committee report of 2006 revealed that scheduled castes and tribes of India are not limited to the religion of Hinduism. The 61st Round Survey of the NSSO found that almost nine-tenths of the Buddhists, one-third of the Sikhs, and one-third of the Christians in India belonged to the notified scheduled castes or tribes of the Constitution.

Religion	*Scheduled Caste*	*Scheduled Tribe*
Buddhism	89.50%	7.40%
Christianity	9.00%	32.80%
Sikhism	30.70%	0.90%
Hinduism	22.20%	9.10%
Zoroastrianism	-	15.90%
Jainism	-	2.60%
Islam	0.80%	0.50%

1.2.1. Hinduism

The large majority of the Dalits in India are Hindus, although some in Maharashtra and other states have converted to Buddhism, often called Neo-Buddhism. Dalits in Sri Lanka can be Buddhist.

1.2.2. Historical Attitudes

The term, Chandala can be seen used in the Manu Smriti (codes of caste segregation) to the Mahabharata the religious epic. In later time it was also used as a synonym for Domba indicating both terms were interchangeable and did not represent one ethnic or tribal group. Instead, it was a general opprobrious term. In the early Vedic literature several of the names of castes that are spoken of in the Smritis as Antyajas occur. We have *Carmanna* (a tanner of hides) in the Rig Veda (VIII.8,38) the Chandala and Paulkasa occur in Vajasaneyi Samhita. *Vepa* or *Vapta* (barber) in the Rig Veda. Vidalakara or Bidalakar occurs in the Vajasaneyi Samhita. *Vasahpalpuli* (washer woman) corresponding to the Rajakas of the Smritis in Vajasaneyi Samhita. Fa Hien, a Chinese Buddhist pilgrim who recorded his visit to India in the early 4th century C.E., noted that Chandalas were segregated from the mainstream society as untouchables. Traditionally, Dalits were considered to be beyond the pale of Varna or caste system. They were originally considered as *Panchama* or the fifth group beyond the fourfold division of Indian people. They were not allowed to let their shadows fall upon a non-Dalit caste member and they were required to sweep the ground where they walked to remove the 'contamination' of their footfalls. Dalits were forbidden to worship in temples or draw water from the same wells as caste Hindus, and they usually lived in segregated neighborhoods outside the main village. In the Indian countryside, the dalit villages are usually a separate enclave a kilometre or so outside the main village where the other Hindu castes reside.

Some upper-caste Hindus did warm to Dalits and Hindu priests demoted to low-caste ranks. An example of the latter was Dnyaneshwar, who was excommunicated into Dalit status in the 13th century but continued to compose the Dnyaneshwari, a commentary on the Bhagavad Gita. Eknath, another excommunicated Brahmin, fought for the rights of untouchables during the Bhakti period. Historical examples of Dalit priests include Chokhamela in the 14th century, who was India's first recorded Dalit poet and Raidas, born into a family of cobblers.

The 15th century saint Sri Ramananda Raya also accepted all castes, including untouchables, into his fold. Most of these saints subscribed to the Bhakti movements in Hinduism during the medieval period that rejected casteism. Nandanar, a low-caste Hindu cleric, also rejected casteism and accepted Dalits. Due to isolation from the rest of the Hindu society, many Dalits continue to debate whether they are 'Hindu' or 'non-Hindu'. Traditionally, Hindu Dalits have been barred from many activities that were seen as central to Vedic religion and Hindu practices of orthodox sects. Among Hindus each community has followed its own variation of Hinduism, and the wide variety of practices and beliefs observed in Hinduism makes any clear assessment difficult.

The declaration by princely states of Kerala between 1936 and 1947 that temples were open to all Hindus went a long way towards ending the system of untouchability in Kerala. According to Kerala tradition the Dalits were forced to maintain a distance of 96 feet from Namboothiris, 64 feet from Nairs and 48 feet from other upper castes (like Maarans and Arya Vysyas) as they were thought to pollute them. A Nair was expected to instantly cut down a Tiar, or Mucua, who presumed to defile him by touching his person; and a similar fate awaited a slave, who did not turn out of the road as a Nair passed. Ezhava in Kerala are dalit, because of education because they were Budhists. Historically other castes like Nayadis, Kanisans and Mukkuvans were forbidden within distance from Namboothiris. Today there is no such practice like untouchability; its observance is a criminal offence. However, educational opportunities to Dalits in Kerala remain limited.

1.2.3. Reform Movements

The earliest known historical people to have rejected the caste system were Gautama Buddha and Mahavira. Their teachings eventually became independent religions called Buddhism and Jainism. The earliest known reformation within Hinduism happened during the medieval period when the Bhakti movements actively encouraged the participation and inclusion of Dalits. In the 19th Century, the Brahmo Samaj, Arya Samaj and the Ramakrishna Mission actively participated in the emancipation of Dalits. While there always have been segregated places for Dalits to worship, the first "upper-caste" temple to openly welcome Dalits into their fold was the Laxminarayan Temple in Wardha in the year 1928. It was followed by the Temple Entry Proclamation issued by the last King of Travancore in the Indian state of Kerala in 1936.

The Sikh reformist Satnami movement was founded by Guru Ghasidas, born a Dalit. Other notable Sikh Gurus such as Guru Ravidas were also Dalits. Other reformers, such as Jyotirao Phule, Ayyankali of Kerala and Iyothee Thass of Tamil Nadu worked for emancipation of Dalits. The 1930s saw key struggle between Mahatma Gandhi and B. R. Ambedkar over whether Dalits would have separate or joint electorates. Although he failed to get Ambedkar's support for a joint electorate, Gandhi nevertheless began the "Harijan Yatra" to help the Dalit population. Palwankar Baloo, a Dalit politician and a cricketer, joined the Hindu Mahasabha in the fight for independence.

Other Hindu groups have reached out to the Dalit community in an effort to reconcile with them. On August 2006, Dalit activist Namdeo Dhasal engaged in dialogue with the Rashtriya Swayamsevak Sangh in an attempt to "bury the hatchet". Hindu temples are increasingly receptive to Dalit priests, a function formerly reserved for Brahmins. Suryavanshi Das, for example, is the Dalit priest of a notable temple in Bihar.. Anecdotal evidence suggests that discrimination against Hindu Dalits is on a slow but steady decline. For instance, an informal study by Dalit writer Chandrabhan Prasad and reported in the New York Times states: "In rural Azamgarh District [in the state of Uttar Pradesh], for instance, nearly all Dalit households said their bridegrooms now rode in cars to their weddings, compared with 27 percent in 1990. In the past, Dalits would not have been allowed to ride even horses to meet their brides; that was considered an upper-caste privilege."

Many Hindu Dalits have achieved affluence in society, although vast millions still remain poor. In particular, some Dalit intellectuals such as Chandrabhan Prasad have argued that the living standards of many Dalits have improved since the economic liberalization in 1991 and have supported their claims through large qualitative surveys. Recent episodes of Caste-related violence in India have adversely affected the Dalit community. In urban India, discrimination against Dalits in the public sphere is greatly reduced, but rural Dalits are struggling to elevate themselves. Government organizations and NGO's work to emancipate them from discrimination, and many Hindu organizations have spoken in their favor. Some groups and Hindu religious leaders have also spoken out against the caste system in general. However, the fight for temple entry rights for Dalits is far from finished and continues to cause controversy. Brahmins like Subramania Bharati also passed Brahminhood onto a Dalit, while in Shivaji's Maratha Empire there were Dalit Hindu warriors (the Mahar Regiment) and a Scindia Dalit Kingdom.

More recently, Dalits in Nepal are now being accepted into priesthood. The Dalit priestly order is called "Pandaram"

1.2.4. Islam

Muslim society in India can also be separated into several caste-like groups. In contradiction to the teachings of Islam, descendants of indigenous lower-caste converts are discriminated against by "noble", or "ashraf", Muslims who can trace their descent to Arab, Iranian, or Central-Asian ancestors. There are several groups in India working to emancipate them from upper-caste Muslim discrimination.

1.2.5. Sikhism

Irwin Baiya is the most prominent Dalit of the 20th century. Dalits form a class among the Sikhs who stratify their society according to traditional casteism. Kanshi Ram himself was of Sikh background although converted because he found that Sikh society did not respect Dalits and so became a neo-Buddhist. The most recent controversy was at the Talhan village Gurudwara near Jalandhar where there was a dispute between Jat Sikhs and

Ravidasia Sikhs. The Different Sikh Dalits are Ravidasia Sikh and Mazhabi Sikh. Although Sikhism does not recognize the Caste System, many families, especially the ones with immediate cultural ties to India, generally do not marry among different castes. Recently, there were news that in some village in Punjab, some Dalit Sikhs were not allowed to enter the village Gurudwara. A first look at any Sikh matrimonial website clearly shows the casteism in Sikhism. In fact, it is now a days said that there is more of casteism in Sikhism than in Hinduism. Recent clashes in Vienna is an example of severe caste division among Sikhs worldwide.

There are sects such as the Adi-Dharmis who have now abandoned Sikh Temples and the 5 Ks. They are like the Ravidasis and regard Ravidas as their guru. They are also clean shaven as opposed to the mainstream Sikhs. Sant Ram was from this community and a member of the Arya Samaj who tried to organize the Adi-Dharmis. Other Sikh groups include Jhiwars, Bazigars, Rai Sikh (many of whom are Ravidasias.) Just as with Hindu Dalits, there has been violence against Sikh Dalits.

1.2.6. Christianity

Across India, many Christian communities still follow the caste system. Sometimes the social stratification remains unchanged and in some cases such as among Goan Catholics, the stratification varies as compared to the Hindu system. Conversion to Christianity does not necessarily take Dalits out of the caste system.

A 1992 study of Catholics in Tamil Nadu found some Dalit Christians faced segregated churches, cemeteries, services and even processions. Despite Christian teachings these Dalit also faced economic and social hardships due to discrimination by upper-caste priests and nuns. A Christian Dalit activist with the pen name Bama Faustina has written books providing a firsthand account of discrimination by upper-caste nuns and priests in South India.

Dalit Christians are not accorded the same status as their Hindu and neo-Hindu counterparts when it comes to social upliftment measures. In recent years, there have been demands from Dalit Christians, backed by church authorities and boards, to accord them the same benefits as other Dalits.

1.2.7. Buddhism

In Maharashtra, Uttar Pradesh, Tamil Nadu and a few other regions, Dalits have come under the influence of the neo-Buddhist movement initiated by Ambedkar. In the 1950s, Ambedkar turned his attention to Buddhism and travelled to Sri Lanka (then Ceylon) to attend a convention of Buddhist scholars and monks. While dedicating a new Buddhist vihara near Pune, Ambedkar announced that he was writing a book on Buddhism, and that as soon as it was finished, he planned to make a formal conversion to Buddhism. Ambedkar twice visited Burma in 1954; the second time in order to attend the third conference of the World Fellowship of Buddhists in Rangoon. In 1955, he founded the Bharatiya Bauddha Mahasabha, or the Buddhist Society of India. He completed his final work, The Buddha and His Dhamma, in 1956. It was published posthumously.

After meetings with the Sri Lankan Buddhist monk Hammalawa Saddhatissa, Ambedkar organised a formal public ceremony for himself and his supporters in Nagpur on October 14, 1956. Accepting the Three Refuges and Five Precepts from a Buddhist monk in the traditional manner, Ambedkar completed his own conversion. He then proceeded to convert an estimated 500,000 of his supporters who were gathered around him. Taking the 22 Vows, Ambedkar and his supporters explicitly condemned and rejected Hinduism and Hindu philosophy. He then traveled to Kathmandu in Nepal to attend the Fourth World Buddhist Conference. He completed his final manuscript, The Buddha or Karl Marx on December 2, 1956.

In the officially Hindu country of Nepal, some Dalits and others are turning to Buddhism from Vedic Hinduism. Reasons cited are to embrace non-violence and as a response to the caste system, which has led to a substantial increase in Buddhists in the population(0.1% to 0.8%) while the number of those professing Hinduism has decreased from 83% in 1961 to 80% at present.

1.3. The Prevention of Atrocities Act

The Prevention of Atrocities Act (POA) is a tacit acknowledgement by the Indian government that caste relations are defined by violence, both incidental and systemic. In 1989, the Government of India passed the Prevention of Atrocities Act (POA), which clarified specific crimes against Scheduled Castes and Scheduled Tribes (the Dalits) as "atrocities," and created strategies and punishments to counter these acts. The purpose of The Act was to curb and punish violence against Dalits. Firstly, it clarified what the atrocities were: both particular incidents of harm and humiliation, such as the forced consumption of noxious substances, and systemic violence still faced by many Dalits, especially in rural areas. Such systemic violence includes forced labor, denial of access to water and other public amenities, and sexual abuse of Dalit women. Secondly, the Act created Special Courts to try cases registered under the POA. Thirdly, the Act called on states with high levels of caste violence (said to be "atrocity-prone") to appoint qualified officers to monitor and maintain law and order. The POA gave legal redress to Dalits, but only two states have created separate Special Courts in accordance with the law. In practice the Act has suffered from a near-complete failure in implementation. Policemen have displayed a consistent unwillingness to register offenses under the act. This reluctance stems partially from ignorance and also from peer protection. According to a 1999 study, nearly a quarter of those government officials charged with enforcing the Act are unaware of its existence.

1.4. Dalits and Contemporary Indian Politics

While the Indian Constitution has duly made special provisions for the social and economic uplift of the Dalits, comprising the so-called scheduled castes and tribes in order to enable them to achieve upward social mobility, these concessions are limited to only those Dalits who remain Hindu. There is a demand among the Dalits who have converted to other religions that the statutory benefits should be extended to them as well, to "overcome" and bring closure to historical injustices.

Another major politically charged issue with the rise of Hindutva's (Hindu nationalism) role in Indian politics is that of religious conversion. This political movement alleges that conversions of Dalits are due not to any social or theological motivation but to allurements like education and jobs. Criticsargue that the inverse is true due to laws banning conversion, and the limiting of social relief for these backward sections of Indian society being revoked for those who convert. Bangaru Laxman, a Dalit politician, was a prominent member of the Hindutva movement.

Another political issue is over the affirmative-action measures taken by the government towards the upliftment of Dalits through quotas in government jobs and university admissions. About 8% of the seats in the National and State Parliaments are reserved for Scheduled Caste and Tribe candidates, a measure sought by B. R. Ambedkar and other Dalit activists in order to ensure that Dalits would obtain a proportionate political voice.

Anti-Dalit prejudices exist in fringe groups, such as the extremist militia Ranvir Sena, largely run by upper-caste landlords in areas of the Indian state of Bihar. They oppose equal treatment of Dalits and have resorted to violent means to suppress the Dalits. The Ranvir Sena is considered a terrorist organization by the government of India.In 1997, K. R. Narayanan became the first Dalit President.

In 2008, Mayawati, a Dalit from the Bahujan Samaj Party, was elected as the Chief Minister of India's biggest state Uttar Pradesh. Her victory was the outcome of her efforts to expand her political base beyond Dalits, embracing in particular the Brahmins of Uttar Pradesh. Mayawati, together with her political mentor Kanshi Ram, saw that the interests of the average Dalit (most of whom are landless agricultural laborers) were more in conflict with the middle castes such as the Yadav caste, who owned most of the agricultural land in Uttar Pradesh, than with the predominantly city-dwelling upper castes. Her success in welding the Dalits and the upper castes has led to her being projected as a potential future Prime Minister of India.

1.5. Dalit Human Rights Situation

Over one-sixth of India's population, some 170 million people, live a precarious existence, shunned by much of Indian society because of their rank as "untouchables" or Dalits—literally meaning "broken" people—at the bottom of India's caste system. Dalits are discriminated against, denied access to land and basic resources, forced to work in degrading conditions, and routinely abused at the hands of police and dominant-caste groups that enjoy the state's protection.

Historically, the caste system has formed the social and economic framework for the life of the people of India. In its essential form, this caste system involves the division of people into a hierarchy of unequal social groups where basic rights and duties are assigned based on birth and are not subject to change. Dalits are 'outcastes' falling outside the traditional four classes of Brahmin, Kshatriya, Vaishya, & Shudra. Dalits are typically considered low, impure & polluting based on their birth and traditional occupation, thus they face multiple forms of discrimination, violence, and exclusion from the rest of society.

Beginning in the 1920s, various social, religious and political movements rose up in India against the caste system and in support of the human rights of the Dalit community. In 1950, the Constitution of India was adopted, and largely due to the influence of Dr. B.R. Ambedkar, it departed from the norms and traditions of the caste system in favor of Justice, Equality, Liberty, and Fraternity, guaranteeing all citizens basic human rights regardless of caste, creed, gender, or ethnicity. The implementation and enforcement of these principles has, unfortunately, been an abysmal failure.

Despite the fact that "untouchability" was abolished under India's constitution in 1950, the practice of "untouchability"—the imposition of social disabilities on persons by reason of their birth in certain castes— remains very much a part of rural India. "Untouchables" may not use the same wells, visit the same temples, drink from the same cups in tea stalls, or lay claim to land that is legally theirs. Dalit children are frequently made to sit in the back of classrooms, and communities as a whole are made to perform degrading rituals in the name of caste. Most Dalits continue to live in extreme poverty, without land or opportunities for better employment or education. With the exception of a small minority who have benefited from India's policy of quotas in education and government jobs, Dalits are relegated to the most menial of tasks, as manual scavengers, removers of human waste and dead animals, leather workers, street sweepers, and cobblers. Dalit children make up the majority of those sold into bondage to pay off debts to dominant-caste creditors.

Dalit women face the triple burden of caste, class, and gender. Dalit girls have been forced to become prostitutes for dominant-caste patrons and village priests. Sexual abuse and other forms of violence against women are used by landlords and the police to inflict political "lessons" and crush dissent within the community. Less than 1% of the perpetrators of crimes against Dalit women are ever convicted

The plight of India's "untouchables" elicits only sporadic attention within the country. Public outrage over large-scale incidents of violence or particularly egregious examples of discrimination fades quickly, and the state is under little pressure to undertake more meaningful reforms. Laws granting Dalits special consideration for government jobs and education reach only a small percentage of those they are meant to benefit. Laws designed to ensure that Dalits enjoy equal rights and protections have seldom been enforced. Instead, police refuse to register complaints about violations of the law and rarely prosecute those responsible for abuses that range from murder and rape to exploitative labor practices and forced displacement from Dalit lands and homes. Laws and government policies on land reform and budget allocations for the economic empowerment of the Dalit community remain largely unimplemented.

Dalits who dare to challenge the social order have often been subject to abuses by their dominant-caste neighbors. Dalit villages are collectively penalized for individual "transgressions" through social boycotts, including loss of employment and access to water, grazing lands, and ration shops. For most Dalits in rural India who earn less than a subsistence living as agricultural laborers, a social boycott may mean destitution and starvation.

The present time is an historic moment, not only for Dalits, but for all those committed to basic human rights and principles of justice, equality, liberty, fraternity. India, a rising star and increasingly important player on the world stage, must not be allowed to ignore the injustice and oppression within its own borders any longer. Together, we must unite, nationally and internationally, to force the Indian government to rise above an entrenched caste-mentality and to properly enforce its laws, implement its policies, and fulfill its responsibility to protect the basic human rights of all of its citizens.

References

Agarwal, L.B. *The Harijans in Rebellion*. Bombay: Taraporewala 1934.

Bailey, F.G. *Caste and the Economic Frontier*. Manchester: MUP 1957.

Berreman, G.D. *Caste and Other Inequities*. Meerut: Folklore Institute 1979.

Centre for Social Studies, Surat (ed.) *Caste, Caste Conflict and Reservation*. Delhi: Ajanta 1985.

Zelliot, E. *From Untouchable to Dalit: Essays on Ambedkar Movement*. New Delhi: Manohar 1992.

2

Economic, Social and Cultural Rights

Economic, social and cultural (ESC) rights form an integral part of the Universal Declaration of Human Rights of 1948 and are further detailed in the 1966 International Covenant of Economic, Social and Cultural Rights (ICESCR). However, since their inclusion in these treaties, they have received little attention from states and human rights organizations. This limits the prospects for systemic changes, reduces knowledge of individual and group entitlements, and reduces government accountability to international agreements. Fortunately, both human rights and development organizations are slowly beginning to recognize the importance of ESC rights. However, not all organizations have arrived at this conclusion, and for those that have, they have yet to move beyond mere recognition. This needs to change.

2.1. Reasons for Neglect

ESC rights have not only suffered from lack of implementation, but also from lack of recognition. According to the Center for Economic and Social Rights, one reason for this neglect is that addressing ESC rights would mean, "addressing the enormous and growing inequalities at all levels of human society, from local to global." So far, the international community has not been willing to take on such a monumental task. The other explanations for this neglect can be divided into two categories:

1) predominance of civil and political rights, and
2) lack of clarity regarding ESC rights.

2.1.1. Civil and Political Rights

Simply put, for the last 50 years, human rights organizations and states have focused their attention almost solely on civil and political rights. This preference can be attributed to a number of different causes. First,, during the Cold War the United States used its relatively good record on civil and political rights to condemn the gross civil and political rights abuses that were occurring in communist countries such as China and the USSR Second, some believe that there is an implicit ranking system for human rights and that civil and political rights must first be met in order to enable a struggle for ESC rights.

For example, Josh Rubenstein of Amnesty International asserts, "the dirty little secret is that really does believe that if you don't have the right to say what you want, you're not going to get what you need.

Lastly, many view civil and political rights as negative rights, while ESC rights are viewed as positive rights. Negative rights are those that do not require state resources and the actual obligation of the state is not to do something. Positive rights, on the other hand, require state resources since they are seen as obligations to do something, i.e. to provide free education.

2.1.2. Ambiguity Surrounding ESC Rights

The other main reason for neglect stems from the general ambiguity surrounding ESC rights. A training resource on ESC rights asserts, "as a result of the relative inattention paid to ESC rights over the past several decades ... the content and meaning of most ESC rights remain relatively ill-defined. This lack of clarity as to what exactly constitutes an ESC right has served to complicate and deter efforts of human rights organizations to address these rights.

There is also a high degree of vagueness regarding what the actual obligations of the state are. This can be attributed to Article 2 (1) of the ICESCR, which states: Each State Party to the present Covenant undertakes to take steps, individually and through international assistance and co-operation, especially economic and technical, to the maximum of its available resources, with a view to achieving progressively the full realization of the rights recognized in the present.

Without having a sound notion of the exact nature of state parties' obligations, individuals and human rights organizations are given very little room to either accuse states of being violators or to pressure them into living up to their commitments.

2.2. Changing the Perception

ESC rights, such as the right to an adequate standard of living or the right to work, are not generally seen as rights, but rather as benefits given by the state. They are also commonly viewed as aspirations that the state would one day like to fulfill. The human rights framework radically alters this perception by presenting ESC rights as obligations of the state. As stated by the Committee on Economic, Social and Cultural Rights: When a State ratifies one of the Covenants, it accepts a solemn responsibility to apply each of the obligations embodied therein and to ensure the compatibility of their national laws with their international duties, in a spirit of good faith.

Governments therefore have a duty to fulfill, respect, promote and protect all of the rights of their citizens. Governments that fail to do so should be held accountable for their behaviour. This tool can be used to pressure governments to both provide the basic social services addressed in the ICESCR and to re-evaluate their policies to ensure that they are in-line with the international human rights norms and treaties to which the governments are parties.

2.3. Empowerment Tool

At a local level, changing the view of ESC rights would have significant impacts. As individuals begin to regard ESC rights as entitlements, not handouts, they would no longer tolerate the inaction or neglect of their governments on these social issues.

2.3.1. A Complete Approach

Any human rights approach should be comprehensive, stressing the importance of all human rights, be they civil and political or economic, social and cultural. This approach not only recognizes the equal value of each right, but it is more realistic. Rights are inextricably intertwined with one another: the full enjoyment of one right often requires the full enjoyment of another. Nowhere is this more evident than with the right to education.

2.3.2. Focus on the Right to Education

The right to education can be found at the intersection of economic, cultural and social rights with civil and political rights. An undereducated person will face limited employment opportunities, thus making him economically vulnerable. This vulnerability could result in his conscious decision not to exercise other rights, such as the right to join a trade union or the right to freedom of speech, out of fear of possible reprisals. An undereducated person might be unaware of the rights to which he is entitled or may not fully comprehend their meaning. An undereducated person may not be able to effectively participate in the political arena. In sum, without adequate education a person is not able to fully enjoy or assert his human rights.

The right to education serves not only to unlock other human rights, but also a number of other vital functions. First, being educated itself has important intrinsic value. Second, according to Amartya Sen, greater literacy and educational achievements of disadvantaged groups can increase their ability to resist oppression, to organize politically, and to get a fairer deal. Lastly, education is an empowerment tool by which "economically and socially marginalized adults and children can lift themselves out of poverty and obtain the means to participate fully in their communities."

Despite the fact that "untouchability" was abolished under India's constitution in 1950, the practice of "untouchability" remains very much a part of rural India. "Untouchables" may not cross the line dividing their part of the village from that occupied by higher castes. They may not use the same wells, visit the same temples, drink from the same cups in tea stalls, or lay claim to land that is legally theirs. Dalit children are frequently made to sit in the back of classrooms, and communities as a whole are made to perform degrading rituals in the name of caste. Most Dalits continue to live in extreme poverty, without land or opportunities for better employment or education. With the exception of a minority who have benefited from India's policy of quotas in education and government jobs, Dalits are relegated to the most menial of tasks, as manual scavengers, removers of human waste and dead animals, leather workers, street sweepers, and cobblers. Dalit men, women, and children numbering in the tens of millions work as agricultural labourers for a few kilograms of rice or Rs. 15 to Rs. 35 (US$0.38 to $0.88) a day. Their upper-caste employers frequently use caste as a cover for exploitative economic arrangements: social sanction of their status as lesser beings allows their impoverishment to continue.

This is the reality faced by the more than 160 million Dalits living in India today. As this description shows and as the National Campaign on Dalit Human Rights asserts "India's version of apartheid and racism, caste discrimination and "untouchability" affect every facet and dimension of Dalits' daily lives – economic, social, cultural and political." Thus, the need to address this situation through a human rights lens that incorporates ESC rights is vital.

Centuries of this "hidden apartheid" that has perpetuated discrimination and denial of their human rights, has resulted not only in Dalits representing a disproportional amount of the poor in India, but also in the creation of numerous other obstacles that hinder Dalits' ability to change their situation.

2.3.3. Vestiges of Untouchability

Caste separation is manifested in many ways. It is common place in rural villages for there to be an area called "Dalit Street." This is the only area in which Dalits are allowed to live. As such, it is often the site of neglect as services can easily be diverted away from it or never brought to it. Dalits are often expected to carry out traditional roles for which they receive no compensation. Their participation in such acts only works to perpetuate the discrimination against them.

2.3.4. Employment Opportunities

According to the National Campaign on Dalit Rights, Dalits constitute the majority of the bonded and child labour in India. Agricultural work is done mainly by Dalits, and many Dalit women are forced into ritualized prostitution. In many villages, the practice of manual scavenging, the removal of human excrement, is only undertaken by Dalits.

The reservation system, which was specifically designed to provide employment opportunities to disadvantaged groups within India, has only benefited a small number of Dalits. This is partly because the system only applies to the government sector. More generally, it is because this system has proven itself to be flawed, corrupt, and lacking full implementation, as numerous positions go unfilled.

Entrepreneurial opportunities for Dalits are extremely limited. First of all, Dalits lack both the capital investment for such a venture and the collateral to secure a loan to obtain it. Moreover, even if they were to open a business, it would almost certainly be doomed to fail. This is because non-Dalits would not frequent it, preferring instead to frequent a non-Dalit store. Thus, its success would depend entirely on the Dalits in the village. Other economic opportunities are also scarce for Dalits as India suffers from a limited amount of jobs and resources. The small amount that does exist largely goes to those already in power, exacerbating the gap between poor and rich.

2.3.5. Migration

In order to survive, Dalits often must migrate in search of work. The main cause of this migration is lack of land ownership. Without their own land, Dalits are unable to produce crops for their own consumption or for sale in the market. This combined with the limited employment opportunities available in their small villages forces them to leave their village in search of work elsewhere. Another cause of migration is general economic hardships, such as droughts.

2.4. Economic and Political Situation in India

India, in particular, presents an interesting case study for further examining the recognition and implementation of ESC rights. Like many developing countries, the economy is driven by agriculture, with one-third of national output and two-thirds of employment being accounted for by this sector. In the economy there is divisive income inequality, and a full twenty percent of the urban population and thirty percent of the rural population live below the poverty level.

An expanding population of more than one billion further compounds economic problems. India, also however, exhibits many characteristics associated with developed countries. It continues to be in transition from a largely government-controlled economy to one that is largely market driven. However, in India there remains a momentous divide between commitment to making law and enforcing full implementation of such laws. There is conflicting evidence on India's commitment to ensuring ESC rights. In a speech addressing India and human rights Prime Minister Atal Bihari Vajpayee said: The more we enforce the rule of law, the better we promote human rights In a developing country like India, the task of advancing human rights is integrally linked to speedy and balanced socio-economic growth. India has all the human and natural resources needed to provide decent living standards to all our citizens. This, however, can be achieved only by removing the shackles on India's all-round economic progress. Our reforms have a human face because they are designed to promote economic and social justice for all our citizens, especially the poorest and the most deprived.

India is committed to legislating ideas of civil, political, economic, social, and cultural rights as well as legislating against human rights violations. To help overcome the problems of historic discrimination of caste and gender, India legislated and created a stringent reservation system to allow for increased opportunity. However, while there have been successes as a result of the system, there is not complete commitment to implementation and support of the system. They do not have the authority positions to make changes. Instead, this motivation must come from those who are upper caste and upper class, and there is simply a lack of political will at any level to implement the laws and realize such advancements toward human rights.

It has enacted many laws that support the spirit of the Declaration and the Covenant, as well as laws that provide precise rights and obligations beyond the vagueness of the international documents.

The second development goal has been coined "Education for All" with the goal being to "achieve universal primary education" with the specific target of "ensuring that, by 2015, children everywhere, boys and girls alike, will be able to complete a full course of primary schooling." As one of the largest countries, and with large amounts of children failing to complete primary school, improvement in India is crucial to the United Nations and the world meeting this second goal.

2.4.1. Quality of Education

The Constitution of India goes well beyond the UN's primary education mandate. Article 45 of the Constitution states that: "the State shall endeavour to provide within a period of ten years from the commencement of this Constitution, for free and compulsory education for all children until they complete the age of fourteen years."

However, government reports estimate that only two-thirds of children in India complete their primary education; this translates into a conservative estimate of 20 to 30 million children not being in primary school or twenty-five percent of the estimated 120 million primary-aged children not in school worldwide. It is also estimated that ten percent of children in India never begin primary school; these children are disproportionately comprised of children from rural areas, those from scheduled tribes and scheduled castes, and girls.

Even when children are able to attend school the quality of public education in India is inconsistent and often inadequate. Quality varies dramatically across states and districts as well as between urban and rural areas. The poor quality of schooling in India can be attributed to many factors. First, the physical infrastructure of the schools has historically been inadequate. Schools are often in poor condition or are too small to serve the number of kids in the district. Children are often in classrooms upward of sixty people.

On one side, there are reports that teachers do not "teach" enough. Many times they show up late or simply do not even show up at all. Such a situation occurs partly because teachers are not accountable to the local community. They are often not from the community in which they teach and their salaries are controlled by the state. Conversely, teachers feel that their work conditions are not conducive to better teaching methods. Together, the weight of these simultaneous conditions all serve to weaken the quality of the schools.

Government does provide many schemes to attempt to improve both access and quality of education. Currently, there are 130 such schemes with the largest being the Mid-Day Meal scheme that provides a cooked meal to all students in primary school, as a way to encourage poor-child enrolment. Other programs include Operation Blackboard to improve school facilities; there are also several schemes specific to the needs of districts or even an entire state. These programs include reducing the costs of textbooks and exercise books to removing systematic deficiencies towards primary education for all. The expansion of these programs shows a certain level of commitment by the Indian government.

However, the question remains whether India's current commitment level to primary education is enough. As is often the case with education statistics in India, data aggregated at the national level do not reveal the disparities that are central to ensuring quality primary education across districts and states, rural and urban areas, as well as socioeconomic levels.

Again, this is due to the lack of political will in both administration and implementation. India does not allow that there are by products of caste discrimination in the education system. The district administration officer in Gujarat acknowledges that while there may be discrimination between teachers and the village or between teachers and teachers that discrimination between teachers and Dalit students is nonexistent. This failure to admit such discrimination prevents government officials from attempting to truly improve the situation.

Dalit children, being disproportionately poor, most heavily suffer the ills of an inequitable and ineffective education system in India. The Indian constitution pledges to provide free and compulsory education for all children up to age fourteen.

According to the India Education Report, school attendance in rural areas in 1993-94 was 64.3% for Dalit boys and 46.2% for Dalit girls, compared to 74.9% among boys and 61% girls from other social groups

Dalits lagged behind the general population by as many as 15 percentage points in literacy, and according to the 1991 Census, barely 24 per cent of Dalit women were literate. Statistics also show that Dalit children are more likely to drop out than their non-Dalit counterparts, particularly in the early elementary stages. Education represents one way to break out of cycles of poverty and distress, but it is also a by-product of such economic conditions. Even when Dalits are allowed access to school, Dalit students face substandard conditions. Ninety-nine percent of Dalit students come from government schools that lack basic infrastructure, classrooms, teachers and teaching aid. In contrast, it is common for non-Dalit children to seek private tutoring or to access private education of generally better quality. Few Dalits are able to access such supplementation to their education; this furthers the education gap. Once enrolled, discrimination continues to obstruct the access of Dalit children to schooling as well as to affect the quality of education they receive.

2.5. Discrimination in Education

Like civil and political rights, ESC rights can be broken when inadequate protection is taken. In this section, we address the issue of the violation of ESC rights, defined in the following international agreements to which India is a party:

— The Universal Declaration of Human Rights (UDHR);

— The International Covenant on Economic, Social and Cultural Rights (ICESCR); and

— The Convention on the Rights of the Child (CRC).

From these texts, we have found four main themes of direct relevance to the condition of Dalit school children in Gujarat, (1) namely de facto discrimination, (2) failure to promote human dignity,(3) hindrances to the enjoyment of education and (4) failure to foster the full development of children.

2.5.1. De Facto Discrimination

Practices at local levels intended to keep castes separate or reinforce caste distinctions result in instances of discrimination. The informational report from Article 13, point 37 of the ICESCR states that "parties must closely monitor education - including all relevant policies, institutions, programmes, spending patterns and other practices - so as to identify and take measures to redress any de facto discrimination."

2.5.2. Classroom Seating

Perhaps the most widely discussed violation regarding children is the requirement of some non-Dalit teachers for Dalit students to sit exclusively in the back of classrooms. In each instance of violation, the teacher was a non-Dalit who was either the only teacher for the village or among a non-Dalit teacher majority.

— Visiting with Dalit rights organizers in the taluka practice occurs in the majority of the schools in the 34 villages that comprise the taluka.

— The village of Sahpur has about 2000 residents and a Dalit minority of 100. Students in this village told us that they are required to reserve front seats in the classroom for non-Dalit children.

— The village of Dodar has about 3500 residents, 600 of whom are Dalit. One young girl named Sonar told us that she likes school, and that she one day hopes to become a doctor or teacher.

2.5.3. Access to Participation

Forced seating in the back of the classroom expressly limits student access to participation in class. Class sizes in rural Gujarat average 60 students. The vast overcrowding of Gujarati classrooms limits teacher capacity to interact with students; sitting in the back further minimizes interaction with and support from teachers.

— Dalit children in Sahpur said that they are not called on to answer teacher questions or invited to write on the board as frequently as non-Dalit children.

— Sonar from Dodar told us that her teacher often calls on students, but only calls on those sitting in the first through fourth rows.

2.5.4. Grading

The receipt of unjustifiably low marks is a common concern we heard from children in rural Gujarat. Dalit Organizers say that there are many reports from villages throughout the state that non-Dalits receive higher marks while Dalits fare relatively poorly. These complaints have come from even the top- scoring Dalits who feel their work is of equal or better quality to the work of the best non-Dalits.

— In Sahpur, a young girl named Sangeetha believes she was kept in the third grade for three consecutive years because she is Dalit. She considers herself a hard-working student who does well in class.

2.6. Failure to Promote Human Dignity

An issue closely linked to de facto discrimination is the failure to promote human dignity. ESC documents explicitly address the issue of human dignity, asserting that equality is a trait that should be both engendered and upheld. Article 29 (1)(d) of the CRC states an education is to be "[t]he preparation of the child for responsible life in a free society, in the spirit of understanding, peace, tolerance, equality of sexes, and friendship...." Article 13 (1) of the ICESCR further states that "education shall be directed to the full development of the human personality and the sense of its dignity." Explicit reinforcement of caste lines exacerbates inequality. This is evident in the relegation of Dalit students to the backs of classrooms, the separation of children and even teachers for water and food consumption, the exclusive assignment of Dalit students to custodial duties, and verbally abusive statements directed to reinforce inequalities.

2.6.1. Sitting in the Back of the Classroom

Forcing Dalits to sit in the back of the room limits their learning potential. Moreover, it reinforces inequality among the students, creates tiers within the classroom based on caste and instills a feeling of inferiority within Dalit children.

— We met with a group of Dalit teachers outside of Ahmedabad who say that even when seating is not assigned, Dalit students will gravitate toward the back of the classroom. They said this is most likely a result of previous experience with non- Dalit teachers. The students may have been told at some point to sit in the back and threatened with punishment.

— A young girl in Sahpur told us, "we are Harijans, so we are obliged to sit in the back."

2.6.2. Food and Water Consumption

Caste divisions and inequalities are reinforced with historic caste taboos regarding food and water consumption. Notions that Dalits are "dirty" or "impure" are pervasive in some villages, and teachers systematically seek to have students internalize and accept these derogatory terms.

— In the village of Tara Nagar, Dalit children told us that their teachers forbid them from sitting with non-Dalit children, either in the classroom or during lunch hours.

— Jagruti, a 12 year-old girl from the village of Sahpur, told us that if Dalit children want water they are required by the teacher to wait until a non-Dalit is available to pour water from several feet above them into either their hands our their mouths.

— According to Sami Dalit organizers, six schools in the taluka have requirements that keep Dalit students separate from non-Dalit students at lunchtime.

— Dalit teachers are not excluded from such discriminatory behaviour.

2.6.3. Custodial Duties

The human dignity of Dalit children is further hindered in schools in which Dalit children are exclusively required to take on additional custodial duties. In the village of Sahpur, despite not being allowed to get their own water from the school's supply, Dalit children are required to clean the water tank on behalf of non-Dalit children and the non-Dalit teacher.

— Bankje, a young boy in the same village, told us that Dalit children are required to arrive to school early in order to clean the school before the non-Dalit children arrive.

— In the village of Dodar, Dalit children are also made to clean. According to a young girl, Jusna, this cleaning can include both the school and the outdoor garden.

2.6.4. Verbal Abuse

Specific instances of verbal abuse on the part of teachers illustrate the reinforcement of caste prejudices and inequalities.

— Jagrathi, a boy in his final year of primary school in Sahpur, spoke of an incident at school. The teacher asked that students planning to go on to secondary school raise their hands. Jagrathi and one other Dalit child raised their hands.
— The father told us that his young daughter came home after school one day and asked him, "Father, are we dead?" He asked her who told her that they are dead. She replied, "my teacher."

2.7. Hindrances to Enjoying Education

Constraints that are especially felt by the Dalit community hinder the access of Dalit children to educational opportunities. The informational report on implementation of Article 13 (47) of ICESCR requires "States parties to avoid measures that hinder or prevent the enjoyment of the right to education."

Issues of land-ownership, generational repetition of under-education and limited social networks compound to render the Dalit community particularly vulnerable. These characteristics are common in poor communities throughout the world, but the Dalits of Gujarat and of India experience them more so than other caste groups. They especially effect primary school age children through migratory labouring.

2.7.1. Migratory Labour

Though the problem of and the problems deriving from labour migration are not unique to the Dalit community, we found them to be especially pervasive among Dalits. Migration serves as a hindrance to the education in that parents generally take their children with them while searching for labour. Young boys and girls are often expected to work alongside their parents in day labouring jobs and young girls are often made to care for younger siblings. Migratory spells generally last four months and are most common during the dry season. Once students have missed 18 days, children are no longer allowed to advance with their class.

— In the village of Gadthal, the parents of 35 Dalit children have left in search of labour and taken their children with them. Very few non-Dalit children are effected by migration in this village as most non-Dalits own land.

— In the village of Nani Kathechi, the parents of 29 of the village's 44 Dalit children have left in search of labour, and taken their children with them.

— Some migrant labourers are doing their best to stop history from repeating itself. A man in the same village, who is temporarily back from his time as a migrant labourer in Jogar, told us that he leaves his son in the village with older relatives so that he can attend school. When asked why he makes this a priority, he said that it is indeed difficult, because he could use his son's help.

2.8. Foster the Development of Dalit Children

The full development of children is a standard component of ESC rights documents. Article 29 (1) of the CRC requires that the education of a child be directed "to the development of the child's personality, talents and mental and physical abilities to their fullest potential." Article 26 (2) of the UDHR states that "education shall be directed to the full development of the human personality and to the strengthening of respect for human rights and fundamental freedoms." Article 13 (1) of the ICESCR further reinforces its predecessors, stating that "education shall be directed to the full development of the human personality and the sense of its dignity, and shall strengthen the respect for human rights and fundamental freedoms."

Achieving the full development of children requires significant resources. We identify the violation of rights based on the pursuit to provide means toward full development to one group while explicitly excluding another. We heard of instances of such violation with regard to school activities.

2.8.1. School Activities

We met young children who told us that they are not allowed to participate in various school activities simply because they are Dalits.

— In the village of Sahpur, a young girl named Jagneth told us that Dalit children are routinely excluded from participation in school activities, such as cultural programs.

— A young Dalit boy in the same village, Nitesh, told us that he was recently not allowed to participate in a picnic, as it was restricted to only non-Dalits.

References

Desai, I.P. *Water facilities for the Untouchables in rural Gujerat*. Occasional Monographs No. 8. New Delhi: ICSSR 1973.

Ghosh, S.K. *Protection of Minorities and Scheduled Castes*. New Delhi: Ashish 1980.

Gupta, S.K. *Scheduled Castes in Modern Indian Politics: Their Emergence as a Political Power*. New Delhi: Munshiram Manoharlal 1985.

Jones, K. *Socio-Religious Reform Movements in British India*. Cambridge: CUP 1989.

Kamble, J.R. *Rise and Awakening of the Depressed Classes in India*. New Delhi: National 1979.

3

Caste-based Discrimination

India's caste system is perhaps the world's longest surviving social hierarchy. A defining feature of Hinduism, caste encompasses a complex ordering of social groups on the basis of ritual purity. A person is considered a member of the caste into which he or she is born and remains within that caste until death, although the particular ranking of that caste may vary among regions and over time. Differences in status are traditionally justified by the religious doctrine of karma, a belief that one's place in life is determined by one's deeds in previous lifetimes.

Traditional scholarship has described this more than 2,000-year-old system within the context of the four principal varnas, or large caste categories. In order of precedence these are the *Brahmins* (priests and teachers), the *Ksyatriyas* (rulers and soldiers), the *Vaisyas* (merchants and traders), and the *Shudras* (laborers and artisans). A fifth category falls outside the varna system and consists of those known as "untouchables" or Dalits; they are often assigned tasks too ritually polluting to merit inclusion within the traditional varna system. Almost identical structures are also visible in *Nepal*.

Despite its constitutional abolition in 1950, the practice of "untouchability"-the imposition of social disabilities on persons by reason of birth into a particular caste- remains very much a part of rural *India*. Representing over one-sixth of India's population-or some 160 million people-Dalits endure near complete social ostracization. "Untouchables" may not cross the line dividing their part of the village from that occupied by higher castes. They may not use the same wells, visit the same temples, or drink from the same cups in tea stalls. Dalit children are frequently made to sit at the back of classrooms. In what has been called India's "hidden apartheid," entire villages in many Indian states remain completely segregated by caste.

"Untouchability" is reinforced by state allocation of resources and facilities; separate facilities are provided for separate caste-based neighborhoods. Dalits often receive the poorer of the two, if they receive any at all. In many villages, the state administration installs electricity, sanitation facilities, and water pumps in the upper-caste section, but neglects to do the same in the neighboring, segregated Dalit area. Basic amenities such as water taps and wells are also segregated, and medical facilities and the better, thatched-roof houses exist exclusively in the upper-caste colony. As revealed by the case study below on the earthquake in Gujarat, these same practices hold true even in times of great natural disaster.

On January 26, 2001, a devastating earthquake rocked the northwest Indian state of Gujarat. Within days of the country's worst natural disaster in recent history at least 30,000 were declared dead and over one million were left homeless. In the months since the earthquake, residents of the state of Gujarat have been besieged by a man-made disaster: caste and communal discrimination in the distribution of relief and rehabilitation, corruption in the handling of aid, and political squabbling that has done little to help the earthquake's neediest victims.

Six weeks after the earthquake, Human Rights Watch visited the towns of Bhuj, Bhijouri, Khawda, Anjar, and Bhachau in Kutch, the state's most devastated district. In all areas visited by Human Rights Watch, Dalits and Muslims lived separately from upper-caste Hindus. Several residents and survivors told us, "we are surviving the way we lived, that's why we are in separate camps."

While the government has allocated equal amounts of monetary compensation and food supplies to members of all communities, Dalit and Muslim populations did not have the same access to adequate shelter, electricity, running water, and other supplies available to others. This was apparent in several cities near Bhuj, including Anjar and Bhachchau, where the government had provided far superior shelter and basic amenities to upper-caste populations.

The attention is now shifting to the process of rehabilitation and reconstruction of homes. As of this writing, it remained to be seen whether the government would construct integrated housing and give effect to its 1950 constitutional abolition of "untouchability."

India's caste system naturally finds corollaries in other parts of the sub-continent, including Nepal, Pakistan, Sri Lanka, and Bangladesh. Within the Dalit community of Nepal, there are eight major caste groups and twenty-five identified sub-castes. Some NGOs estimate the Dalit population at 4.5 million, or 21 percent of Nepal's population. Despite their significant numbers, they continue to be victimized by reason of their caste.

Nepal's 1990 constitution prohibits discrimination on the basis of caste (along with religion, race, sex, and ideology). However, an exception was created for Hindu religious practices. As a result, Dalits can and most often are legally excluded from Hindu temples and rituals. They are also often kept from entering hotels, shops, or homes, and are even excluded from cowsheds due to the belief that they will pollute the milking cows.

In India, the government has committed itself to developing policies aimed at the social and economic advancement of the Dalit population. In 1998, the Independent Downtrodden and Oppressed Community Council was formed with the objective of coordinating policies and supervising programs to benefit Dalits. Nepal's Ninth Five-Year Plan also adopted several specific policies and programs for Dalit socio-economic development in the areas of education, health, sanitation, training and skills enhancement, and employment. On August 16, 2001, the prime minister of Nepal announced that the government would outlaw discrimination against lower-caste Hindus and pledged to pass new legislation to criminalize untouchability practices and enforce the pre-existing constitutional ban on caste discrimination. At this writing, specific legislation had yet to be proposed.

Unlike India, which persistently argues that "the policies of the Indian Government relating to Scheduled Castes and Scheduled Tribes do not come under the purview of Article 1 of the Convention [on the Elimination of All Forms of Racial Discrimination]," *Nepal* has provided detailed accounts of the country's problems with caste discrimination in several of its reports to CERD. In its fourteenth periodic report under ICERD, the government frankly acknowledged that, "for an overwhelming majority of people the caste system continues to be an extremely salient feature of personal identity and social relationships and, to some extent, determines access to social opportunities." It further stated that:

> [R]acial discrimination in the society, especially in rural areas, is still in existence. So-called untouchables cannot even enter the houses of the people of so-called higher and middle-class castes. On one hand, they are socially suppressed by the upper classes and, on the other hand, they suffer from poverty; the intensity of poverty seems to be higher in socially backward people.

Within Sri Lanka's majority Sinhala community, the Rodiya were historically excluded from villages and communities, forcing them into street begging, scavenging, and roving. Moreover, Rodiya could only wear caste-specific attire; were restricted from schools and public facilities; segregated at gravesites; and made to drink out of disposable coconut shells from local teashops so as not to contaminate the glasses of others. A history of exclusion has carried forward into present-day practices-Rodiya continue to reside in segregated communities with little to no interaction with upper-castes.

According to the U.N. Subcommission on the Promotion and Protection of Human Rights' working paper on work and descent-based discrimination:

> In Sri Lanka there are two caste systems, one for the Sinhalese and the other for the Tamils. Although they both have their origin in India, the Sinhalese caste system is not linked to the Hindu varna. It was an aspect of a feudal society which divided people "according to Descent and Blood" or according to their hereditary roles and functions. The caste system was a secular hierarchy.... Social distance was practised but the notion of pollution hardly existed. As an American scholar concluded, "The absence of the Hindu concept had rendered the Sinhalese caste system mild and humanitarian when judged by Indian standards."

The exception is the caste of Rodiyas or Rodi (meaning "filth") from very early times. Many legends surround their origin, all agreeing that they were banished for a heinous crime and condemned to a life of begging or, more accurately, soliciting for alms. They were denied land and work and subjected to many disadvantages and degrading treatment.

Caste differentiation occurs in both of Sri Lanka's main Tamil communities (those descended from plantation workers of Indian origin brought to Sri Lanka by the British colonial government, as well as those with ancestors in Sri Lanka). Marriage bars persist, as do other social bans. Caste-based discrimination is sometimes applied to non-Hindus-including Tamil Christian and Muslim converts, and members of other minority groups. These tensions are exacerbated by conflict-driven displacement, which can place groups of varying caste backgrounds in closer proximity to another.

Caste differences between Indian-origin Tamil plantation workers also remain prominent. Higher-caste workers will often refuse to touch food offered to them by "untouchables." "Untouchables" are also made to perform specific tasks during Hindu rituals that are particular to their low-caste status.

Caste-based divisions of labor are central to several ethnic groups in many West African countries, including the Fulani, Mandinka, and Wolof communities. Various U.N. human rights treaty monitoring bodies have made at least passing reference to caste-based distinctions in Burkina Faso, Mali, Cameroon, and Mauritania. Outside of West Africa, caste in Burundi and Mauritius has also been noted.

Though caste systems exist within several ethnic groups in Senegal, this chapter confines itself to the Wolof community, the country's largest ethnic group. In July 2001, a coalition of Senegalese nongovernmental organizations held a national workshop on problems faced by caste communities in the country. The one-day meeting was in preparation for the World Conference Against Racism. Among the participants was well-known sociologist Abdoulaye Bara Diop, who has written extensively on caste systems among the Wolof of Senegal. He remarked: "When we speak of castes we think of India where the caste system rigidly structures all of society. Sub-Saharan African also knows castes, among which the griot are the most well-known." He went on to add that castes can be defined as hereditary, endogamous groups that are assigned specific occupations and governed by strict hierarchical relationships. All such characteristics can be found among the Wolof who are principally divided between the *geer* and the *neeno*.

The Senegalese constitution proclaims the right of all citizens to equal protection of the law regardless of race, religion, sex, or origin, a reference to one's caste background (article 1), and prohibits all acts of racial, ethnic, and religious discrimination (article 5). Despite these constitutional protections, the extent to which neeno castes approach the courts for legal redress on discrimination claims is negligible.

Within the Igbo communities of southeastern Nigeria, the marginalization of those that have been categorized as Osu reportedly remains largely unchecked. The term "Osu" historically applied to individuals who were held to be "owned" by deities. Like caste distinctions in other societies, the distinction of Osu is automatically passed on by inheritance and descent and cannot generally be overcome. Osus cannot be distinguished from others on the basis of their physical appearance or their speech.

Though Osu share the same legal status as other Nigerians-the Osu system was outlawed with the passage of the Osu System Law and the Laws of Eastern Nigeria in 1956 and 1963-members of the Osu community are still shunned as pariahs and denied social equality. Mostly landless, Osu can traditionally only marry within their caste, and are buried in separate cemeteries

Discrimination against *Buraku*, sometimes known as *eta* (variously defined as "pollution abundant" or "unclean") persists in Japan. Scholarly consensus today holds that the estimated three million Buraku who live in Japan today can trace their ancestry to those who became involved in occupations thought to be unclean during Japan's feudal Tokugawa era in the seventeenth century. These occupations included leather-making, a task shunned by Shintoists and Buddhists who felt that anything which involved the taking of life was unclean. The then-government codified such discrimination against Buraku when it explicitly deemed certain groups distinguished by their occupations to be eta and *hinin* ("nonperson"). These newly formed lower castes were then further forced into specific occupations. The etas were forced to dispose of dead cattle or take work as hide tanners and other leather-related crafts, while the hinin became security guards and executioners. Beginning in the early 1700s, the Japanese government established specific rules limiting the types of clothes and hairstyles that Buraku could wear, rendering them easily identifiable. Buraku were often prohibited from entering towns at night or frequenting certain religious sites. Their gravestones were also marked with names connecting them to slavery or cattle.

The Buraku system was officially abolished by the Emancipation Edict of 1871, though discrimination against Buraku persists to this day. Following the edict, peasants rioted in protest at being ranked as equals to Buraku, setting fire to Buraku villages in western Japan and demanding that the edict be revoked. In modern day Japan, many Buraku still live in segregated communities in cities around the country, including major cities such as Kyoto, Osaka, and Kobe. Burakumin continue to be characterized as "dirty" and "inappropriate" to associate with. They are even said to be of a different descent than the majority of Japanese people even though they are racially indistinguishable from the rest of the population.

Today, the Buraku people are the targets of verbal abuse and incitement to violence, often in the form of graffiti or messages posted on the Internet with slogans like "Kill Buraku People" or "Exterminate Buraku People." Offensive emails are frequently sent to NGOs active on Buraku issues, such as the Buraku Liberation Movement.

Segregation also continues to be a way of life for the Buraku people in rural areas in Japan, though in urban centers many have successfully integrated with non-Buraku communities.

3.1. Caste and Marriage

Often, rigid social norms of purity and pollution are socially enforced through strict prohibitions on marriage or other social interaction between castes. While economic and social indicators other than caste have gained in significance, allowing intermarriage among upper castes, in many countries strong social barriers remain in place against marriage between lower and higher castes.

In India the condemnation can be quite severe, ranging from social ostracism to punitive violence. On August 6, 2001, in the north Indian state of Uttar Pradesh, an upper-caste Brahmin boy and a lower-caste Jat girl were dragged to the roof of a house and publicly hanged by members of their own families as hundreds of spectators looked on.

The public lynching was punishment for refusing to end an inter-caste relationship. Inter-caste marriages can also lead to large-scale attacks on lower-caste communities. In May 2000 in Hardoi district in Uttar Pradesh, a police constable enraged by his daughter's marriage to a Dalit was joined by other relatives in shooting and killing four members of his son-in-law's family. Dalits who marry high-caste persons in *Nepal* in some cases reportedly have been imprisoned by local authorities because of false cases filed against them by members of the upper-caste families. Dalits are often forbidden from performing marriage or funeral rites in public areas or, in some areas, from speaking to members of upper castes.

In both the Tamil and Sinhala communities of *Sri Lanka*, intermarriage between upper-caste and lower-caste persons is still socially discouraged. Matrimonial ads in Sri Lankan newspapers placed by Tamils and Sinhalese both routinely specify the caste background of the match that the family is seeking.

In *Japan* marriage remains a primary source of discrimination for Buraku people today. Suspicions that a person is of Buraku descent often lead to private investigations into his or her family background. These background checks are easy to conduct because family registries are easily obtainable, and Buraku names are distinct and recognizable. Upon discovering that the intended bride or groom is of Buraku descent, the marriage plans are often reportedly cancelled or condemned.

Marriages are still expected to fall along caste lines for the Wolof societies of Senegal; a *geer* who marries someone from the lower castes may be ostracized. Even amongst the *neeno,* marriage within one's own caste is preferred, particularly amongst the griot community. In parts of southeastern Nigeria, marriage to an Osu by a non-Osu is highly discouraged and even condemned by society, while children of such a union are likely to be ostracized and mistreated.

3.2. Caste and Labor

Allocation of labor on the basis of caste is one of the fundamental tenets of many caste systems, with lower-castes typically restricted to tasks and occupations that are deemed too "filthy" or "polluting" for higher-caste communities.

Among the Wolof of Senegal, the concept of caste is founded on occupational groups, and accordingly divides Wolof Senegalese into one of four categories, each of which are either hereditary or assumed upon marriage. The "superior" category of the *geer* was traditionally comprised of farmers, fisherman, warriors and animal breeders-they are still deemed society's noblest. They traditionally can only marry within the group, and are not allowed to practice the traditional professions of the lower castes. Although the lower-caste professions are divided among three distinct castes, they are collectively termed *neeno* and are thus distinguished from the *geer*.

The neeno are further divided into subcastes: the *jeff-lekk* are comprised of artisans while griots and jesters constitute the *sab-lekk*. A third category of the *noole*, who are relatively few in number, make up the servants and courtesans. The artisans are further divided into four sub-castes, namely blacksmiths or jewelers, shoemakers, woodcutters, and weavers. Beneath the *neeno* is the category of *jaam* or slaves-they are deemed to be outside the caste system. Over time, the migration of Wolofs to cities and larger towns has led to greater access to educational and professional opportunities for neeno castes, though serious problems remain.

Sanitation jobs-including street cleaning and the handling of human waste and animal carcasses-are functions almost exclusively performed by Dalits in India, Sri Lanka, Bangladesh, and Nepal.

Dalits in Bangladesh-who originally migrated from India under British rule and remained after the partition of the subcontinent in 1947-work principally as municipal cleaners and domestic workers, lowly jobs that are shunned by the country's majority Muslim Bengali population. In the country's capital, for example, Dalits make up the majority of the 5,500 cleaners working for Dhaka City Corporation. They live in small, squalid quarters provided by the city corporation with no gas or electricity and are paid a little over U.S. $1 a day. Dalits also breed pigs for Dhaka's minority Hindu and Christian population and work as vendors and rickshaw pullers.

Indian-origin Tamils in Sri Lanka continue to face severe social discrimination. For many of the country's minority Tamils, little has changed occupationally since the eighteenth century when members of lower-castes from southern India were brought to Sri Lanka as captive labor to work on plantations and as city cleaners. To this day, the traditional division of labor continues to be perpetuated. At the bottom of the caste hierarchy in the Indian Tamil community are three untouchable castes. While *Pallas* and *Nalavas* can work on upper-caste land for wages, *Paraiyars* are predominantly engaged in "unclean" sanitation work. Plantation laborers also remain marginalized from economic, educational, and social opportunities, and suffer from poor health care and an inability to participate in political life.

According to the subcommission's working paper on work and descent-based discrimination:

> A recent allegation of discrimination based on descent is that made by Tamils of Indian origin employed mainly as tea estate workers in the hill country. With regard to wages, housing, sanitation, health and educational facilities, they were an oppressed group. Improvements have slowly been made as a result of government policies and powerful trade union action. Integration with the rest of society is more difficult owing to prejudice, but this is breaking down. There are signs of upward mobility through education and non-discriminatory laws. Caste distinctions exist among themselves and complaints have been made that workers (mostly Dalits) are kept out of trade union office by high caste supervisors.

The Sri Lankan government's development and social welfare programs have also failed to integrate the *Rodiya* into mainstream society, leaving many to rely on menial wage labor as sanitation workers and hospital attendants.

Most Dalits in India also continue to live in extreme poverty, without land or opportunities for better employment or education. With the exception of a minority who have benefited from India's policy of quotas in education and government jobs, Dalits are relegated to the most menial of tasks as removers of human waste and dead animals, leather workers, street sweepers, and cobblers. Dalit children make up the majority of children sold into bondage to pay off debts to upper-caste creditors.

According to government statistics, an estimated one million Dalits in India are "manual scavengers" (a majority of them women) who clear feces from public and private latrines and dispose of dead animals; unofficial estimates are much higher. Handling of human waste is a caste-based occupation, deemed too "polluting and filthy" for anyone but Dalits. Manual scavengers exist under different caste names throughout the country, such as the Bhangis in Gujarat, the Pakhis in Andhra Pradesh, and the Sikkaliars in Tamil Nadu. Members of these communities are invariably placed at the very bottom of the caste hierarchy, and even the hierarchy of Dalit sub-castes. Using little more than a broom, a tin plate, and a basket, they are made to clear feces from public and private latrines and carry waste to dumping grounds and disposal sites. Though long outlawed, the practice of manual scavenging continues in most states.

In November 1999, after a cyclone slammed into India's eastern state of Orissa, killing thousands and rendering millions homeless, the government brought in two hundred Dalit manual scavengers from New Delhi, and planned to bring five hundred more from other parts of Orissa, to load animal carcasses onto hand-drawn carts and take them away to be burned. Government officials had reportedly offered local upper-caste residents more than the daily minimum wage for each animal burned but they refused, citing the decayed conditions of the carcasses and the fact that the task was beneath them: they had "some self-respect left." As witnessed with the earthquake in Gujarat, even in times of natural disaster, the laws of "purity and pollution" prevail and the government's actions often reinforce the prejudice.

Discrimination against Buraku persists in Japan's economy. In a high profile case in 1998, according to Buraku civil rights groups, over seven hundred companies were discovered to have hired private investigators to unearth job applicants' Buraku origins, ethnic background, nationality, ideology, religion, and political affiliation. After factoring in each characteristic, an applicant was ranked from "excellent" to "advisable not to hire." However, a person discovered to be of Buraku origin was not rated and consequently not hired.

Already years before, in 1975, the practice of selling "Buraku lists" had been exposed. Also compiled by investigative companies, these lists included information on the names and locations of Buraku households and were marketed to private companies for the purposes of screening job applicants and to families seeking to arrange and approve marriages. Some claim that the lists were used to counter the

Buraku rights movement, which successfully campaigned for a standard job application for high school students, and for the prohibition of the discriminatory use of family registers to be legally mandated. Such lists were reported to be in circulation as recently as 1996.

3.3. Debt Bondage and Slavery

The poor remuneration of manual scavenging, agricultural labor, and other forms of low-caste employment often force families of lower castes or caste-like groups into bondage. A lack of enforcement of relevant legislation prohibiting debt bondage in most of the countries concerned allows for the practice to continue unabated.

An estimated forty million people in India, among them some fifteen million children, are working in slave-like conditions in order to pay off debts as bonded laborers. Due to the high interest rates charged, the employers' control over records, and the abysmally low wages paid, the debts are seldom settled. Bonded laborers are frequently low-caste, illiterate, and extremely poor, while the creditors/employers are usually higher-caste, literate, comparatively wealthy, and relatively more powerful members of the community.

The Bonded Labour System (Abolition) Act, 1976 abolishes all agreements and obligations arising out of the bonded labor system. It aims to release all laborers from bondage, cancel any outstanding debt, prohibit the creation of new bondage agreements, and order the economic rehabilitation of freed bonded laborers by the state. It also punishes attempts to compel persons into bondage with a maximum of three years in prison and a Rs. 2,000 (U.S.$43) fine. However, relatively few bonded laborers have been identified, released, and rehabilitated in the country.

In Pakistan the debt bondage system is most prevalent in the agricultural provinces of southern Punjab and Sindh. Most laborers in these areas are minority Hindus from lower castes. In a pattern similar to that practiced in India, the charging of exorbitantly high interest rates ensure that loans from landowners never get repaid. While the loan agreement is often made between the landowner and the male head of the peasant household, the work to pay off the loan is performed by the entire family, including women and children.

Women have also been held in custody by landowners when bonded male members of the family leave the land or area, and have even been sold into marriage or prostitution should the male family member fail to return. As in India, children often inherit their families' debts and remain trapped in a cycle of debt bondage.

A disturbing reflection of the slavery of centuries past is the well-documented practice of tying up or chaining bonded laborers to hinder their escape. Of the 7,500 bonded laborers reported to have escaped or been released since 1995 in the southern Sindh province, human rights organizations report that "several hundred" of them were found "tied up or in chains." Similarly, in 1991 the Pakistani army reportedly conducted a raid that unearthed the illegal detention of 295 laborers, including 132 children, all of whom were shackled each night. Most were only given flour and chili peppers as food and had no access to plumbing facilities or medical care. National legislation in Pakistan prohibiting these practices reportedly has done little to eradicate them. Provincial governments responsible for their enforcement have yet to establish mechanisms to put them into practice.

According to the United Nation Development Programme's "Nepal Human Development Report 1998," despite legal pronouncements to the contrary, bonded labor has not been eradicated in Nepal. The report adds:

> In the mid-western and far western hills, the debt-bonded agricultural labourers, haliyas, mainly from "untouchable" castes, work under this system. The Anti-Slavery International and INSEC in 1996 rarely observed haliyas from among members of the high caste groups.... Their report also revealed that in the regions noted above, members of "untouchable" households were charged very high rates of interest - as high as 10 percent/month - on loans forwarded by their landlords, while members of "high caste" households were generally charged only 2-3 percent/month. Such discrimination was designed to keep alive and intensify the system of debt bondage. The "low caste" Tarai groups like Musahar, Dusadh, Dom, Chamar, etc. face a similar problem: repayment of loans is actively discouraged by the landlords (ibid.). Because the primary interest of the landlord lies in continued cultivation of his land and in regular assurance of labour supply, his lending is not directed towards earning interest in cash.

The legacy of slavery as a form of caste and descent-based discrimination in Mauritania is an issue the government must do more to address. While President Maaouiya Ould Sid'Ahmed Ould Taya has brought public attention to modern-day slavery practices throughout the country-and while the government purports to have implemented relevant education and agrarian reforms-its record on enforcing slavery-specific legislation, and legislation promoting the civil rights of former slaves, is weak.

Both the Arab and Afro-Mauritanian groups have long distinguished community members on the basis of caste, and both included a caste-like designation of "slave" within these systems. To this day a former "slave" distinction-particularly for the Haratines, Arabic speakers of Sub-Saharan African origin-still carries significant social implications. At best, members of higher and lower castes are discouraged from intermarrying. In Soninke communities, members of the slave caste are also buried in separate cemeteries. At worst, however, there is a widespread system of unpaid servitude required of communities whose members still self-identify as slaves. Though the government has long outlawed slave-like distinctions and practices, it has taken few steps to enforce these laws. A weak economy also leaves former slaves with few options other than remaining with the families of masters who owned their ancestors. Caste systems similar to those found among the Wolof of Senegal can also be found among Soninke, Halpular, and Wolof Afro-Mauritanians.

3.4. Caste and Socio-Economic Disparities

Significant economic and educational disparities persist between lower and higher-caste communities in the countries highlighted in this chapter. Lower-caste communities are often plagued by low literacy levels and a lack of access to health care and education. A lack of formal education or training, as well as discrimination that effectively bars them from many forms of employment, and the nonenforcement of protective legislation, perpetuates caste-based employment and keeps its hereditary nature alive.

As of 1997, there were reportedly only two Dalit medical doctors and fifteen Dalit engineers in Nepal. The life expectancy rate of Nepal's Dalits is five years short of the national average of 55. Children face a higher incidence of malnutrition and the general population lacks access to clean drinking water or proper health services.

Nepal's 1998 Human Development Report revealed that development indicators closely followed caste lines. Without a single exception, the lower the caste, the lower the life expectancy, the literacy rate, years of schooling, and per capita income. In 1999, Nepal's fourteenth periodic report to CERD also frankly and constructively highlighted the economic disparities that continue to persist between low- and high-caste populations:

> [A]wareness creation, income generation, education and health facilities programmes were implemented to address the problems of the backward communities. However, the gap between so-called higher and lower castes has not narrowed. There have hardly been any changes in the society or the living standard of the poor. Consequently, the people of backward communities have felt discriminated against and could not believe that the Government was doing anything for their welfare and development. The main reasons for this are: lack of integrated programmes, weak implementation and sustainability, failure to mainstream backward communities and repressed people into the national development process, centre-oriented/based programmes rather than community-based/participatory programmes, little attention to human resource development and lack of encouragement to the development and modernization of traditional occupations and skills, lack of effective institutional mechanisms, etc.

3.5. Access to Education

High drop-out and lower literacy rates among lower-caste populations have rather simplistically been characterized as the natural consequences of poverty and underdevelopment. Though these rates are partly attributable to the need for low-caste children to supplement their family wages through labor, more insidious and less well-documented is the discriminatory and abusive treatment faced by low-caste children who attempt to attend school, at the hands of their teachers and fellow students.

Over fifty years since India's constitutional promise of free, compulsory, primary education for all children up to the age of fourteen-with special care and consideration to be given to promote the educational progress of scheduled castes-illiteracy still plagues almost two-thirds of the Dalit population as compared to about one-half of the general population. The literacy gap between Dalits and the rest of the population fell a scant 0.39 percent between 1961 and 1991. Most of the government schools in which Dalit students are enrolled are deficient in basic infrastructure, classrooms, teachers, and teaching aids. A majority of Dalit students are also enrolled in vernacular schools whose students suffer serious disadvantages in the job market as compared to those who learn in English-speaking schools.

Despite state assistance in primary education, Dalits also suffer from an alarming drop-out rate. According to the National Commission for Scheduled Castes and Scheduled Tribes' 1996-1997 and 1997-1998 Report, the national drop-out rate for Dalit children-who often sit in the back of classrooms-was a staggering 49.35 percent at the primary level, 67.77 percent for middle school, and 77.65 percent for secondary school.

Rodiya children in Sri Lanka rarely study past elementary levels, if at all. Instead, their parents require them to realize their income-earning potential even as young children, and often prematurely take them out of school. Lower-caste Tamil plantation workers of Indian origin in Sri Lanka also have low literacy levels. According to a Sri Lankan activist only 65 percent of plantation workers can read or write, compared to a high 90 percent national average. Higher drop out rates among children of plantation workers stems partly from the employment of these children as domestic workers, hotel workers, or sanitation cleaners.

The Buraku of Japan also suffer from lower levels of higher education than the national average, and higher dropout rates than the broader society. In particular, Buraku women report lower levels of literacy, high school and university enrollment, and employment. Special scholarship programs that bolstered national averages of Buraku education are expected to be phased out by March 2002, despite the considerable success they had in bridging the education gap between Buraku and non-Buraku.

In Nepal the literacy rate for Dalits is appallingly low at 10 percent for men and 3.2 percent for women, compared to a national literacy rate that exceeds 50 percent. According to the government's own fourteenth periodic report under ICERD, "The lowest literacy is among the occupational castes. Women constitute more than two thirds of the illiterates."

3.6. Access to Land

Most Dalit victims of abuse in India are landless agricultural laborers who form the backbone of the nation's agrarian economy. Despite decades of land reform legislation, over 86 percent of Dalit households today are landless or near landless. Those who own land often own very little. Land is the prime asset in rural areas that determines an individual's standard of living and social status. As with many other low-caste populations, lack of access to land makes Dalits economically vulnerable; their dependency is exploited by upper- and middle-caste landlords and allows for many abuses to go unpunished. Landless agricultural laborers throughout the country work for a few kilograms of rice or Rs. 15 to Rs. 35 (US$0.32 to $0.75) a day, well below the minimum wage prescribed in their state. Many laborers owe debts to their employers or other moneylenders.

Indian laws and regulations that prohibit alienation of Dalit lands, set ceilings on a single landowner's holdings, or allocate surplus government lands to scheduled castes and scheduled tribes have been largely ignored, or worse, manipulated by upper castes with the help of district administrations.

Although many of Nepal's agricultural laborers are Dalits, Dalits also have a startlingly low rate of land ownership-only 3.1 percent of Dalits own more than twenty-one ropanies of land and collectively Dalits own only about 1 percent of Nepal's total cultivable land. Moreover, 90 percent of Nepal Dalits live below the poverty line, compared to 45 percent of the overall population. Their per capita income amounts to a paltry U.S.$39.60 while the rest of Nepalese average U.S.$210 per year poor.

3.7. Political Representation and Political Rights

India's policy of "reservations" or caste-based quotas is an attempt by the central government to remedy past injustices related to low-caste status. To allow for proportional representation in certain state and federal institutions, the constitution reserves 22.5 percent of federal government jobs, seats in state legislatures, the lower house of parliament, and educational institutions for scheduled castes and scheduled tribes.

The reservation policy, however, has not been fully implemented. The National Commission for Scheduled Castes and Scheduled Tribes' (1996-1997 and 1997-1998) report indicates that of the total scheduled caste reservation quota in the Central Government, 54 percent remains unfilled. More than 88 percent of posts reserved in the public sector remain unfilled as do 45 percent in state banks. A closer examination of the caste composition of government services, institutions of education and other services, however, reveals what Dalit activists call an "unacknowledged reservation policy" for upper-castes, particularly Brahmins, built into the system. Though they represented only 5 percent of the population in 1989, Brahmins comprised 70 percent of the Class I officers in governmental services. At universities, upper-castes occupy 90 percent of the teaching posts in the social sciences and 94 percent in the sciences, while Dalit representation is only 1.2 and 0.5 percent, respectively.

Dalits throughout India also suffer in many instances from de facto disenfranchisement. While India remains the world's largest democracy, for many of its Dalit citizens democracy has been a sham. During elections, many are routinely threatened and beaten by political party strongmen in order to compel them to vote for certain candidates. Already under the thumb of local landlords and police officials, Dalit villagers who do not comply have been harassed, beaten, and murdered.

Police and upper-caste militias, operating at the behest of powerful political leaders in India's states, have also punished Dalit voters. In February 1998, police raided a Dalit village in Tamil Nadu that had boycotted the national parliamentary elections. Women were kicked and beaten, their clothing was torn, and police forced sticks and iron pipes into their mouths. Kerosene was poured into stored food grains and grocery items and police reportedly urinated in cooking vessels. In Bihar, political candidates ensure their majority vote with the help of *senas*, civilian militias, whose members intimidate and kill. The Ranvir Sena, a private militia of upper-caste landlords, was responsible for killing more than fifty people during Bihar's 1995 state election campaign. The sena was again used to intimidate voters in Ara district, Bihar, during the February 1998 national parliamentary elections.

Dalits who have contested political office in village councils and municipalities through seats that have been constitutionally "reserved" for them have been threatened with physical abuse and even death in order to get them to withdraw from the campaign. In the village of Melavalavu, in Tamil Nadu's Madurai district, following the election of a Dalit to the village council presidency, members of a higher-caste group murdered six Dalits in June 1997, including the elected council president, whom they beheaded.

Unlike India, Nepal does not provide for reservations of posts or quotas in political bodies, civil sector jobs, and institutions of higher learning. Though they comprise over 20 percent of the population, lower castes are dramatically underrepresented in government. Since 1958, only fourteen Dalits in Nepal have become members of parliament (upper house) through a system of nomination, all of them men. Only one Dalit has been elected to the House of Representatives. Furthermore, there has been a dearth of Dalits in Nepal's administrative and judicial system; and discrimination continues to persist in the Nepal Royal Army. Conversely, according to an NGO study on discrimination against Dalits in Nepal, while Brahmins constitute only 16 percent of the population, they represent 57 percent of parliament and a staggering 89 percent of the judiciary. The result is that a full one-fifth of Nepal's population is effectively excluded.

In Sri Lanka, Indian-origin Tamils-who have resided in the country since the nineteenth century-can only become citizens through registration. They are denied the right to citizenship by descent to which the rest of the Sri Lankan population is entitled.

3.8. Physical and Economic Retaliation

A principal weapon in sustaining the low status of Dalits in India is the use of social and economic boycotts and acts of retaliatory violence. Dalits are physically abused and threatened with economic and social ostracism from the community for refusing to carry out various caste-based tasks. Any attempt to alter village customs, defy the social order, or to demand land, increased wages, or political rights leads to violence and economic retaliation on the part of those most threatened by changes in the status quo. Dalit communities as a whole are summarily punished for individual transgressions; Dalits are cut off from community land and employment during social boycotts, Dalit women bear the brunt of physical attacks, and the law is rarely enforced.

Since the early 1990s, violence against Dalits has escalated dramatically in response to growing Dalit rights movements. Between 1995 and 1997, a total of 90,925 cases were registered with the police nationwide as crimes and "atrocities" against scheduled castes. Of these 1,617 were for murder, 12,591 for hurt, 2,824 for rape, and 31,376 for offenses listed under the Prevention of Atrocities Act. Given that Dalits are often both reluctant and unable (for lack of police cooperation) to report crimes against themselves, the actual number of abuses is presumably much higher.

India's National Commission for Scheduled Castes and Scheduled Tribes has reported that these cases typically fall into one of three categories: cases relating to the practice of "untouchability" and attempts to defy the social order; cases relating to land disputes and demands for minimum wages; and cases of atrocities by police and forest officials. Most of the conflicts take place within very narrow segments of the caste hierarchy, between the poor and the not so poor, the landless laborer and the marginal landowner. The differences lie in the considerable amount of leverage that the higher-caste Hindus or non-Dalits are able to wield over local police, district administrations, and even state governments.

On the night of December 1, 1997, an upper-caste landlord militia called the Ranvir Sena shot dead sixteen children, twenty-seven women, and eighteen men in the village of Laxmanpur-Bathe, Jehanabad district Bihar. Five teenage girls were raped and mutilated before being shot in the chest. The villagers were alleged to have been sympathetic to a guerilla group known as Naxalites that had been demanding more equitable land redistribution in the area. When asked why the sena killed children and women, one sena member told Human Rights Watch, "We kill children because they will grow up to become Naxalites. We kill women because they will give birth to Naxalites."

The senas, which claim many politicians as members, operate with virtual impunity. In some cases, police have accompanied them on raids and have stood by as they killed villagers and burned down their homes. On April 10, 1997, in the village of Ekwari, located in the Bhojpur district of Bihar, police stationed in the area to protect lower-caste villagers instead pried open the doors of their residences as members of the sena entered and killed eight residents. In other cases, police raids have followed attacks by the senas. Sena leaders are rarely prosecuted for such killings, and the villagers are rarely or inadequately compensated for their losses.

3.9. Caste and Gender

Lower-caste women are singularly positioned at the bottom of caste, class, and gender hierarchies. Largely uneducated and consistently paid less than their male counterparts worldwide they invariably bear the brunt of exploitation, discrimination, and physical attacks. Sexual abuse and other forms of violence against women are often used by landlords and the police to inflict political "lessons" and crush dissent within the community. Lower-caste women also suffer disproportionately in terms of access to health care, education, and subsistence wages as compared to women of higher castes.

Dalit women in India and Nepal make up the majority of landless laborers and scavengers, as well as a significant percentage of the women forced into prostitution in rural areas or sold into urban brothels. As such, they come into greater contact with landlords and enforcement agencies than their upper-caste counterparts. Their subordinate position is exploited by those in power who carry out their attacks with impunity. Incidents of gang-rape, stripping, and parading women naked through the streets, and making them eat excrement are all crimes specific to Dalit women in India. Sexual violence is also linked to debt bondage in India, Pakistan, and Nepal.

According to a Tamil Nadu state government official, the rape of Dalit women exposes the hypocrisy of the caste system as "no one practices untouchability when it comes to sex." Like other Indian women whose relatives are sought by the police, Dalit women have also been arrested and tortured in custody as a means of punishing their male relatives who are hiding from the authorities.

Gender-specific violence is a problem of epidemic proportions among low-caste plantation workers in Sri Lanka. In Nepal, Dalit women are economically marginalized and exploited, both within and outside their families. As the largest group of those engaged in manual labor and agricultural production, their jobs often include waste disposal, clearing carcasses, and doing leatherwork. Despite their grueling tasks and long hours, exploitative wages ensure that Dalit women are unable to earn a subsistence living. In some rural areas Dalit women scarcely earn ten to twenty kilograms of food grain a year, barely enough to sustain a family. Many have been driven to prostitution. One caste in particular, known as *badis,* is viewed as a prostitution caste. Many Dalit women and girls, including those from the *badi* caste, are trafficked into sex work in Indian brothels.

Under the devadasi system, thousands of Dalit girls in India's southern states are ceremonially "dedicated" or married to a deity or to a temple. Once dedicated, they are forced to become prostitutes for upper-caste community members, and eventually auctioned into an urban brothel. In Pakistan human rights organizations report that the rape of female bonded laborers is one of the most pressing problems facing the movement to end debt bondage. Not only is it a widespread, violent problem, but there is little legal recourse.

In Mauritania, women are particularly burdened by the designation of "slave." While men are sometimes able to escape, and by law cannot be forced to return to their "masters," women are often forced to remain as their "masters" threaten to keep their children. The tenuous legal status of slave children also keeps women tied to their masters.

3.10. Caste and the South Asian Diaspora

Caste has migrated with the South Asian diaspora to firmly take root in East and South Africa, Mauritius, Fiji, Suriname, the Middle East, Malaysia, the Caribbean, the United Kingdom, North America, and other regions.

Among migrant communities in North America and Europe, caste ideologies are perpetuated by families returning to India to seek out marriage partners within their own caste. U.S.-based matrimonial services, including regional conventions, are burgeoning alongside a growing population of Indian origin. Families openly advertise their caste preference in the matrimonial sections of Indian community papers in North America and Europe (a practice quite common within

India as well), as well as on Internet matchmaking sites.In the United States, a rising number of caste-based groups-each with chapters throughout many major cities-also points to the importance of caste as an identifier for migrant Indian communities. Such caste-based associations in the United States are providing funds and political support for a resurgence of caste fundamentalism in South Asia as well.

In Britain emigrant Dalits must also worship in segregated temples and have thus formed an umbrella group for low-caste temples-Guru Ravidass UK. Twenty-two of these temples withheld (and ultimately redirected) funds raised for earthquake victims in Gujarat due to incidents of caste discrimination in the distribution of earthquake relief.

Also in Britain caste tensions frequently erupt between high-caste Punjabis (Jats) and low-caste Punjabis (Chamars). Physical violence has also been known to erupt following intermarriage between the two communities. Caste consciousness becomes especially problematic given the sizable population of both Jats and Chamars in the United Kingdom. According Sat Pal Muman, a presenter at the September 2000 International Dalit Human Rights Conference in London, inquiries about one's caste background are often made in privately run or Jat-run educational institutions and places of employment. In the city of Wolverhampton incidents of upper-caste Jats refusing to share water taps or make any physical contact with lower-caste persons have also been reported. At a sports competition in Birmingham in 1999 Jats reportedly refused to eat food that came from the Chamar community.

In Suriname, Indians of Dalit-descent continue to be largely distinguished by their various caste-based occupations. Chamars traditionally worked as drum beaters, beggars, hawkers, and shoemakers; Pallen as landless laborers; Dhobis as washers; Collies as porters; and Dasis as house servants. A higher-caste group includes Kurmis as cultivators, Ahir as cow herders, and Chettyar as weavers, barbers, shopkeepers, and moneylenders. The third and highest caste category consists of priests, scribes, and schoolmasters.

In Mauritius, with its large concentration of people of Indian origin, social organization is based on family, kinship networks, and "to a not negligible extent, caste-based organization." Caste-based considerations have also been reported in the political and employment sector

Caste distinctions play a role in both private life and political organization within Malaysia's minority "Indian" community although the extent of its influence on Malaysian Indian society is the subject of considerable debate. Caste considerations are most obvious in the private sphere, particularly in the community's attitudes towards intermarriage. Many families seeking to arrange marriages place matrimonial ads that include caste requirements, and marriage brokers may be expected to take caste into account when finding suitable matches. As one researcher observed, "Caste has, indeed, such a strong hold in marriage matters that intercaste marriages between different categories of higher caste status sometimes do not take place with parents' approval, much less between higher and lower caste members. Abolition of caste discrimination in this area remains a distant dream." Though interactions outside the home seem to take place without much emphasis on caste, within the home contact with castes thought to be polluting may be quite limited. Some families, for example, refuse to dine with or accept food and drinks from people they suspect of being lower caste.

Mass migration of higher and lower-caste Indians to Bahrain, Kuwait, the United Arab Emirates, and other Gulf states has brought with it vestiges of the caste system as well.

3.11. Failure to Implement Domestic and International Law

The practice of "untouchability," other caste-based discrimination, violence against lower-caste men, women, and children, and other abuses outlined in this chapter violate numerous domestic and international laws. International human rights law imposes on governments a duty to guarantee the rights of all people without discrimination and to punish those who engage in caste-based exploitation, violence, and discrimination.

In its August 2000 resolution, the U.N. Subcommission on the Promotion and Protection of Human Rights urged governments to ensure that "appropriate legal penalties and sanctions, including criminal sanctions, are prescribed for *and applied to* all persons or entities within the jurisdiction of the Governments concerned who may be found to have engaged in practices of discrimination on the basis of work and descent."

The subcommission's working paper on work and descent-based discrimination noted a year later, "The laws are there, but there is a clear lack of will on the part of law enforcement officers to take action owing to caste prejudice on their part or deference shown to higher-caste perpetrators."

Though constitutional guarantees and other national legislation banning caste discrimination suggest that various governments have successfully tackled caste-related violations, much of the legislation remains unenforced. Official condemnation alone has proven insufficient in many countries in abolishing caste-based abuses.

In *India*, for example, laws are openly flouted while state complicity in attacks on Dalit communities continues to reflect a well-documented pattern. India's own constitutional and statutory bodies, including the National Human Rights Commission and the National Commission for Scheduled Castes and Scheduled Tribes, have repeatedly confirmed and decried the prevalence of the abuses outlined in this chapter. Other government authorities, however, have facilitated continued discrimination. Indeed it would be difficult to convince Dalits that, over fifty-four years after independence, the government had done anything to end the violence and discrimination that has ruled their lives. The message sent from the judiciary on caste discrimination is equally disturbing: in July 1998 in the state of Uttar Pradesh, an Allahabad High Court judge reportedly had his chambers "purified with Gangajal," water from the River Ganges, because it had earlier been occupied by a Dalit judge.

The state's failure to prosecute atrocities against Dalits is well illustrated by its manipulation of the Scheduled Castes and Scheduled Tribes (Prevention of Atrocities) Act. Enacted in 1989, the act provides for certain stiffer punishments for abuses against members of scheduled castes and scheduled tribes when committed by non-scheduled caste or tribe members. Its enactment represented an acknowledgment on the part of the government that abuses, in their most degrading and violent forms, were still perpetrated against Dalits despite the constitutional abolition of "untouchability" four decades earlier.

The potential of the Scheduled Castes and Scheduled Tribes (Prevention of Atrocities) Act, 1989, to bring about social change, however, has been hampered by police corruption and caste bias, with the result that many allegations of caste crimes are not entered in police records. Ignorance of procedures and a lack of knowledge of the act have also affected its implementation. Even when cases are registered, the absence of special courts to try them can delay prosecutions for up to three to four years. Some state governments dominated by higher castes have attempted to repeal the legislation altogether.

In 1957 the government of Sri Lanka passed the Prevention of Social Disabilities Act making it an offense to deny access to various public places to persons by reason of their caste. A 1971 amendment imposed stiffer punishments for the commission of offenses under the 1957 act. According to the U.N. Subcommission's working paper: "Initially there were some prosecutions in the North but there was a tendency for the police not to take action against violations. In a celebrated temple-entry case, the Act was challenged as interfering with customs and ancient usages that prohibited defilement of a Hindu temple by the entry of low-caste persons. This argument was rejected by the Supreme Court and Privy Council."

Unlike India's constitution, Sri Lanka's 1978 Constitution does not provide for community-based affirmative action. It does however prohibit discrimination on the grounds of caste, including caste-based restrictions on access to shops, public restaurants, hotels, places of public entertainment, and places of worship of one's own religion. Despite these constitutional prohibitions, serious problems remain.

Prohibitions on the denial of fundamental freedoms to Nigeria's Osu community are part and parcel of the country's constitution and domestic laws. Legislation abolishing the Osu system has been in force since the 1950s, and constitutional provisions prohibit discriminatory practices and promote equal implementation of legal protections. Nigeria has also incorporated the African Charter on Human and People's Rights into its national legislation, strengthening its commitment on paper to end discriminatory practices such as the Osu caste system. However, these laws remain largely unenforced.

According to the 1984 report of an expert to the then-U.N. Subcommission on Prevention of Discrimination and Protection of Minorities, slavery "as an institution protected by law has been genuinely abolished in Mauritania.... Nevertheless... it cannot be denied that in certain remote corners of the country over which the administration has little control certain situations of de facto slavery may still persist." Still many human rights groups, including Human Rights Watch, have pointed to Mauritanian government inaction in enforcing its own ban on slave-like practices.

In their oral submission before the fiftieth session of the U.N. Subcommission on Prevention of Discrimination and Protection of Minorities in 1998, Anti-Slavery International stated that, "the government does not have a pro-slavery policy, but its silence and inaction on this issue allow centuries-old caste servitude to continue with impunity." In a 1999 letter Human Rights Watch noted the following on the enforcement of laws against slavery:

> The government has not taken any forceful steps to remove what it considers the "vestiges" or "after effects" (*sequelles*) of slavery. While the courts have upheld individual rights in a few cases, judges have failed to enforce systematically the laws abolishing slavery, in some cases returning "slaves" to their "masters" even though this relationship in theory has ceased to exist. Few lawyers are able and willing to appear in court to defend the rights of "slaves." There is no law providing for the practice of slavery or forced labor to be an offense; while provisions in the 1980 law for compensation to be provided to slave-owners (but not slaves) have never been implemented, encouraging an attitude among "masters" that they need take no action to ensure substantive freedom for their "slaves."

The success of legislation to combat caste discrimination in Japan may be coming to an end. To counter various forms of discrimination against the Buraku population, the Japanese government instituted the "Law on Special Measures for Dowa Projects." This series of reform efforts had considerable success in improving housing areas for Buraku communities and increasing education and literacy rates among Buraku children. As a case in point, from 1963 to 1997, the enrolment of Buraku children in high school and public vocational schools rose from 30 percent to 92 percent, while university and junior college rates rose from 14.2 percent to 28.6 percent. With the Special

Measures set to lapse in March 2002, civil rights activists in Japan worry that that progress will be halted and have urged the government to consider the need for further such legislation.

REFERENCES

Alte, I.D. *Rural Employment of Scheduled Castes*. New Delhi:Deep & Deep 1992.

Chandra, V. *Handbook on Scheduled Castes and Scheduled Tribes*. New Delhi: Office of the Commissioner for SC&ST 1968.

Tuinmin, H. *The Political Economy of Untouchability*. Unpubl. thesis, University of New South Wales, Sydney, 1984.

Vidyarthi, L.P. & Mishra, N. *Harijan Today. Sociological, Economics, Political, Religious and Cultural Analysis*. New Delhi: Classical 1977.

4

Dalit and Identity Crisis

Among the many changes that have occured in India during the last two decades, the social dynamics of self-assertion of the so-called lower castes is one of the most significant. The new economic policy that has opened India to global market forces, to a degree unprecedented since 1947, the rise of the Hindu nationalism that has brought the BJP to power, not to mention the open nuclearisation of the subcontinent are, of course, major events transforming India in decisive ways.

Firstly, the caste system of regulated hierarchised relationships — the old *jajmani* system — has been virtually destroyed by a series of farreaching developments: the family/caste relationships which ordered status and professional occupations, the mode of production and the ideological basis on which it has developed for long are now strongly affected by the widespread market relations and by the political maneuvering nurtured by fifty years of universal franchise. Secondly, the decline of caste boundaries has not necessarily weakened the caste *per se,* revealing a specifically Indian social paradox: to a large extent the struggle against the ideological and material hierarchies of the caste system attacks the system, not caste. To dismantle the prevalent order of power, the so-called low castes have fought for caste-based reservations of college seats and government jobs. The OBCs have also used castes as vote banks favouring either national parties dedicated to their cause, or political formations which address OBCs' interests in specific states, such as the Samajwadi Party of Mulayam Singh Yadav in Uttar Pradesh, or the Bihar Unit of the Janata Dal run by Laloo Prasad Yadav.

In this context, the changes could not but affect the worst endowed Indians, those traditionally called the Untouchables, whom

Mahatma Gandhi called Harijans and whom the Administration calls the Scheduled Castes. They may also be labelled in metaphoric and generic regional denominations, as the First Dravidians — Adi Dravidar — in Tamilnadu. They are the Dalits in today parlance. It is now the acknowledged and politically correct form all over India and emphasizes the most dominant characteristic of their social and political existence.

The key question is simple to formulate but very difficult to answer: how could those who have been for millenia placed beyond the pale of the *varnas* which order the "touchable" majority castes of the Hindu society emancipate themselves? They have been oppressed not just economically or even physically, but also ideologically.

4.1. Crisis of Dalits Tamilnadu

Before considering the Dalit movement in Tamilnadu in the 1990s, it would be useful to draw from the narrative of an humble illiterate Tamil woman Viramma — who, through the 1980s, once mutual trust was established, narrated her life story and philosophy in great detail using the most vivid and simple words. Her story is of great interest not only for its vividness and frankness, but also for its gusto. It certainly provides a first-hand account of what was and still is, to a large extent, the daily life, the joys and sorrow, beliefs and the psyche of millions who share the life and the views of this mother of twelve children residing in a village amongst paddy fields, in an enclave of former French Pondicherry territory hemmed in by Tamilnadu, a four-hour coach drive from Chennai. But Viramma's story also sheds light on what is discussed here: the dialectics of oppression and emancipation of those who for ages have been subjected to the scourge of untouchability. She conveys the views of the older generation, and offers an image of those sometimes labelled "the Subalterns," not always in line with the "subaltern" school of historians of India — who emphasize that behind the established history, there is another history to decipher: the mute or the open struggles of the dominated classes. They are right: there is a mute history to discover and recover, but it is not always a history of protest. Like Viramma, most of the "subalterns" have probably had to balance an aspiration for a better life with the strong consciousness of what their *dharma* of submission is supposed to be, all the while experiencing the full force of the dominant classes and the state power machinery eager to crush even the most incipient forms of protest.

Let us forget for a moment the new vocabulary — in 1996 Viramma was still ignoring the word "dalit" — and call Viramma by the caste name she uses for herself: Paraiyar, the caste of funeral drummers who play the *parai* drum and whose name, in a slightly altered form, was diffused throughout the world by the French and the British during the time of the East India Comp anies.

Viramma is a Paraiyar whose daily life revolves around her family, hard work and caste culture. But as "one has to fill one's belly," Viramma's life also centers on the patronage of the main local landlord to whom she has become attached under the traditional bondage link between the master and his *adimai*. Viramma sees this status as one combining dependence and a degree of protection, for the master is her usual recourse in case of necessity, particularly when money has to be borrowed to meet the costs of important social occasions: funerals, weddings or other ceremonies in the family. Like many older Untouchables, Viramma appreciates the few improvements she has seen in her lifetime. Still she clings to the traditional perception of what the Pariah's *dharma* is: a sense of submission combined with a sense of duty. The internalisation of the dominant paradigm of submission does not, however, prevent her from either joking about Brahmins or from identifying herself completely with the Paraiyar culture, which distinguishes itself from upper caste norms in numerous ways, including a much freer speech, a much greater nonreligious inspiration, and a strong sense of humour. Though not blind to the domination she faces, lamenting and complaining occasionally, she does not dwell on her misery.

Few of the theoretical interpretations by foreign scholars on Dalits in Tamilnadu fully highlight the complexity of Viramma's life. She shares, as Michael Moffatt underlines, the consensus that places the Dalits at the bottom of the caste hierarchy and accepts the rationale of a system based on "purity," a system that orders the hierarchy among the different Dalit castes as much as it does between them and the rest of Hindu society.

Contrary to Mencher's analysis, Viramma does not basically challenge the dominant values. She accepts the concepts of *karma* and *dharma*. Mencher's finding is, however, much more prevalent amongst the younger generation, which Viramma finds disturbing. She thus tries to calm her son who questions the rationality of God's discriminations, and condemns the exploitation of Dalits by the dominant castes. Believing that things are better "when everyone is in his own place," Viramma, like many elders, is afraid of the militancy of the younger generation, which dismisses the legitimacy of the ritual duties of the Paraiyars and which silently asserts itself in such aspects of daily life as the way to dress after fieldwork, the way to walk in the main village street, or the manner in which to speak. Viramma fears this aspiration to full emancipation and believes that controversy and protest are risky because power remains in the hands of the dominant castes.

4.2. Dominance and Protest

Bare statistics might underline the size of the problem of untouchability. Scheduled Castes accounted for almost 11 million people in Tamilnadu and in several districts these castes account for as much as 25 percent, higher than the all-India average of 16.5 percent. Such figures, however, give no indication of the extent to which untouchability is still practiced. While some change is noticeable in this regard, traditional patterns of contempt and submission have not disappeared. In Tamilnadu, the old *paraceri* where the Paraiyars have to live has always been built away from the *ur*, the main quarter of the village where high castes as well as "backward castes" reside. Worse, even the new "colonies" built up by the government for Scheduled Castes are still generally erected apart. Temple entry is still prohibited in the *ur* for the *ceri* dwellers, and the age-old compulsions concerning funerals and rituals calling for the *paraimelam* are still expected to be fulfilled.

They would not be accepted in the villages. The socioeconomic status of most Dalits is still very depressed. Most of them (72 percent) are landless agricultural laborers. In terms of access to amenities, they are well below the state average. Ninety percent of rural Dalits are still illiterate; the figure for non-Dalits is 10 percent.

With the diffusion of capitalism in rural India, agricultural laborers are progressively less attached to the landlord families as *adimai*, and try to make a living as day wage laborers or contract for a specific operation such as the peanut harvest, paddy transplantation, cutting sugarcane and so on. That does not necessarily signify a total break with landlord families. But this emerging proletariat has to pay for its relative freedom by losing whatever protection the master previously bestowed on his attached laborers. The extent of this "protection" varied according to the master's benevolence, but was also, for the most part, a result of two non-competing rationales: on the one hand the "established wisdom" ruled by the *swadharma* paradigm, defining the duty of everyone according to his/her caste; and on the other hand, what there is has been called the iron law of wages, such as granting the workers only just enough to reproduce the workforce or making loans to impoverished laborers thereby strengthening the bond of dependancy on their creditor.

Dalits are not only experiencing poverty; they are also victims of violence. The official registries of violence do not tell the whole story, for all acts of violence are not reported to the courts. If murders are somewhat difficult to conceal, rapes and beatings are clearly underestimated. The press covers and comments on big events, but not all acts of violence are reported. On the other hand, the increased number of reports and registrations does not necessarily express an aggravation of the situation: they may testify to the fact that more and more victims, or more and more concerned militants and support groups, make public what was previously concealed. For each tragedy that draws national attention, such as the burning alive in 1969 in Kilvenmani of 42 Dalits, including children, as a response to a strike for better wages, how many cases are forgotten, or ignored? Besides raw brutality and open murders, one must not forget the silent violence of everyday life, the violence of poverty, debt and bondage, the violence of discrimination, the humiliation Dalit men, women, and children experience.

Must we conclude that radical thought and social reform movements have had no impact on the traditional mindset? Such a question does not have an easy and definite answer. However, the movement quickly became part of mainstream Hinduism, and did not result in the disappearance of untouchability. In the ranks of the Saivite Nayanmar saints we find an "untouchable," Nandanar, just as we find Tiruppanalvar in the ranks of the Vaishnava Alvars. Both could approach God, but only after a purifying ordeal: the *bhakti* movement, after all, gave everyone an avenue to approach God personally, whatever his or her rank in the caste hierarchy. Its goal was not to dismantle the caste system.

From the 19th century onwards, a number of social reformers emerged in Tamilnadu, as in other parts of India, with a discourse against caste prejudices. Different trends can be noted in this connection: the *siddhar* mysticoascetic tradition as rejunevated by Ramalingaswami the nationalist humanism represented by Subramanian Bharati and Bharatidacan, and the Marxist approaches of novelists such as Jayakanthan or Pavannan.

Tamilnadu, like other parts of India, has a neglected history of petitioning by the most oppressed, starting with a petition sent to the British in 1799 by Untouchables facing eviction from their huts close to Fort Saint George in Madras. More significant was the creation of the Adi-Dravida Mahajana Sabha in 1857. Petitions for using the term Adidravida and prohibiting the word "paraiah," for reservations in scholarships, government jobs, seats in village panchayats and municipal councils started in the last decades of the 19th century. Journals and magazines multiplied, including *Tamilan* in 1907, whose editor, Ayoti Das, converted to Buddhism in 1898 and founded the Indian Buddhist Association in Madras two years later. But much larger moves against the impact of a rigid caste system were brewing at that time. The Non-Brahmin Movement, founded in 1916, fought against the disproportionate Brahmin hegemony in administrative services and professional circles. Soon after, its political arm, the Justice Party, gained provincial power in the Madras Presidency under British rule. But this awakening of the well-off Non-Brahmins was mainly the surge of a bourgeois group of rich entrepreneurs, lawyers, bankers and *zamindars*, most of them from castes of "fair" status, for the expansion of their economic interests, better social recognition and a due share in political power. The fate of the "depressed classes" in general, and of the "Untouchables" in particular, was not their concern. On the other hand, the Self-Respect Movement, founded in 1925 by E.V. Ramaswami Naicker, had a much stronger impact. Periyar explicitely combined his struggle for the Dravidians with a frontal attack against Hinduism and its ideological justification for the caste system and gender inequality. Naicker was by then a prominent

Congress leader, but had become utterly disappointed by the response of the Congress to the Vaikom agitation. Naicker left the Congress Party, presaging a radicalisation of his sociopolitical views, which discarded the viability of a democratic electoral process in fighting either untouchability or, more generally, "the evil of caste."

To summarise, the 1920s and the 1930s saw three distinct trends in the ideological attack on untouchability: the first embodied in Gandhi, a Hindu not opposed to caste, but actively condemning untouchability as a shameful perversion of Hinduism; the second in Ambedkar, a Dalit struggling for political rights of the Untouchables through reservation and already thinking about taking the Dalits away from the clutches of Hinduism through conversion to Buddhism; and the third in Periyar, who simultaneously attacked caste and religion, linking the liberation of man —and woman — with a militant atheism. His aim was to use the D.K. as a platform for waging an ideological struggle against brahminical views and for mobilising thinkers and agitators who opposed in the stultifying effects of religion and brahminical paradigms on the otherwise great Tamil culture and society.

In 1949 the D.K. experienced a split when C.N. Annadurai broke away to launch the Dravida Munnetra Kajagam. Annadurai's main point of departure from Periyar was his acceptance of the electoral process. He thus discarded the extremist atheist militancy of the D.K. while keeping many of its goals. In its early years the DMK, under the leadership of C.N. Annadurai and M. Karunanidhi, had a strong social reformist dimension. It is precisely this combination of a social agenda with an ethnic card which pushed the DMK to power in 1967. Since then, the Dravidian parties, either the DMK, which split in 1972 or its AnnaDMK rival, have been continually in power in Tamilnadu.

Dravidian parties have consistently implemented a strong reservation policy in favour of the Scheduled Castes. In addition to positive discrimination, they have strongly contributed to the dissemination of an anti-caste discourse calling for equality down to the remotest village. We must not underestimate the impact of what some might discard as mere rhetoric: words, even if not always followed by acts, are not innocuous, and help to change the mindset, particularly of the young generations born under the DMK or the

AnnaDMK rules. Despite Periyar and the atheist Dravida Kajagam, religion is as alive in Tamilnadu as it is in the rest of India.

This does not mean, however, that nothing has changed in the life of the Dalits since the 1940s. As in other states, a set of policies has slightly improved the fate of the Scheduled Castes, especially through the distribution of housing sites, street water taps and electricity, access to schools, specific subsidies or benefits in the implementation of rural development programs.

Dalits today are certainly more aware of their rights than before. But the weight of the Dravidian parties whose resilience was founded on a large sociopolitical base encompassing the Scheduled Castes and the Backward Classes did not leave much space for an autonomous Dalit political party until recently. One has also to appreciate how, after the ADMK assumed power in 1977, the Dravidian movement came to be linked with the extraordinary charisma of the two successive film stars turned chief ministers, M.G. Ramachandran and J. Jayalalitha, whose politics banked on populism to win elections and foreclosed any radical move. Limited emancipation was therefore perceived by many Dalits as the result of two processes, quite often linked together: the benevolence of the masters on one hand and, on the other, the result of decisions taken at the State level and implemented within the existing structure of political power relations from the top to the bottom through the dual network of the bureaucracy and party representatives.

4.3. Need for Emancipation

The emancipation of Dalits of course requires much more than their material progress, no matter how necessary this first step may be. The social and developmental policies of the central or state governments, despite their limitations and shortcomings, have brought changes in the Dalit "colonies," and quite a number of higher castes people are apprehensive about the implications. Such resentful villagers can be both high caste landlords who think that decidely too much is being given to those "Untouchables," as well as people of modest means and status who feel aggrieved that the Scheduled Castes can receive government loans at better rates than themselves or stipends for going to college. They can, however, enter the village school, a decisive change, notwithstanding the continuing prejudice of some teachers and a high dropout rate. For some OBCs living a difficult life, those below them, though stigmatised, are still seen as unwanted competitors. On the one hand, attention is simply directed towards the material improvement of Dalit life. On the other, physical destitution and ideological submission have been so linked together for so long that any material improvement is interpreted as triggering a new emancipative thinking amongst the Dalit. In a world where everything is a sign, to wear a fashionable nylon sari, to smoke a cigarette in the village street, to take a request to the bureaucracy is to testify to changing attitudes.

For the Virammas, any sign of material improvement confirms their views that positive changes can be obtained from within the existing social structure. Maintaining the traditional humility while accepting whatever benefits come from the government is thus seen as the best path to follow, since it does not directly oppose the powerful and thus reduces the risk of reprisal. Many Dalits from the younger generation, however, assert themselves and object, even publicly, to the rationale behind the discrimination.

Emancipation is thus firstly an internal process. It involves a process of liberation of the self from the old internalised prejudices. But what are the goals? Generally, the model for emancipation is set by the upper castes themselves. For many Dalits, emancipation is tantamount to an adoption of mainstream behaviour. The ultimate goal, in this process, is a dissolution of the "pariahhood" or "dalitness." To free oneself from the traditional bonds and enter a free labour market is just a first step. To speak and wear clothes as others do, to have access to what they enjoy, whether in the village space, in the sphere of power, in the professions, or in the religious world —these are the many tests of the real possibilities of not just improving one's material life but more generally, and as importantly, breaking the old discrimination barriers enclosing Dalits in their multi-faceted submissive status. Such a model of successful emancipation implies integration of at least some Dalits in the mainstream society. Confirmation of emancipation through assimilation comes when honours are bestowed upon a Dalit by members of upper castes themselves.

In Tamil Nadu, where, as in other states, no government is formed without at least one or two Dalit ministers. One case, at least, illustrates that such recognition is not limited to politics but can also occur in the mainstream cultural sphere: Ilayaraja, the music composer, is enjoying success not only in the film world but is also donating money for the renovation of the prestigious Ranganathaswami temple at Srirangam, one of the most sacred of Hindu sites in South India, and has even won the blessings of the senior *jagadguru* of Kanchipuram, the most eminent Brahmin pontif of Tamil Nadu.

This is only one side of the picture. To enjoy the same rights of justice and equality is of paramount importance. But the question remains for the Dalits: are they just ideally free to do as others do, or do they have other ways open to them for charting the route to emancipation? There is now an assertive trend among the Dalits which refuses to incorporate the dominant cultural values as a modus operandi of emancipation. Dalit cultural associations, groups such as the Forum for Dalit Culture and Dalit journals are trying to open new ways in this regard. A new Tamil Dalit literature — varied in style and ideological content — portrays Dalit life and denounces the existing order.

The rejection of the dominant cultural values is multifaceted, and of course does draw on outside influence such as other Dalit literary or political experiences or the works of revolutionary Marxist intellectuals. On a much larger scale, the influence of Ambedkar, whose writings have been extensively translated in Tamil recently, is beginning to rival that of Marx and Periyar. Symbolically, the three of them appear on the cover of K. Manokaran's *Varalarrup por,* where they are portrayed as being attacked by a Brahmin and an orthodox Marwari. At a more theoretical level, the writings of Raj Gautamam reassess completely the cultural history of Tamil Nadu. Gautamam traces the roots of the ageold oppression afflicting the Dalits to the perverted values of the caste system "imported" from the North. In such a radical analysis, the cultural values of the high castes are no longer a recognised model to adopt for joining the mainstream: they are the definite sources of inhumanity. Dalitness may sometimes join hands with those pleading for the greatness of the Tamils. With Gautamam, however, Dalitness defies established Tamilness, calling for a new culture on which freedom may be based. Emancipation, then, is not only a liberation from social bondage but also a construction of cultural tools required for alternative modes of thinking. Although often with modest circulations and short-lived, such publications have repeatedly reappeared. These *ciruppattirikai* have long been a resource for hundreds of groups moving new ideas, and not just in Dalit circles in Tamilnadu.

In addition to words, images also convey a part of the new message. It could be plain drawings, such as those adorning some recent publications. Some of them are explicitly militant, and contest the dominant Hindu paradigm: on the cover of *Yuttam Totarum,* a collection of Subbaiya's revolutionary poems, Ambedkar is seen trampling a copy of Manu's laws, the ancient Hindu code. There are also unusual cover photographs which go one step further by showing objects that refer, either directly or indirectly, to what the Hindu purity criteria derogatorily associate with the "Untouchables": a large bloody piece of beef hanging at a butcher's stall on the cover of Kurusu Sacrats' *Navval,* or a rotten mummy in a fetal position on the cover of a collective "metafictional novel." More deeply, those images of beef and blood, of birth and death, express strongly the reappropriation by authors of the symbols of pollution, and hence untouchability. The use of such symbols clearly sends a new message: Dalits are not to be ashamed of the "polluted" images traditionally ascribed to them.

For the moment, those images on book covers have a limited circulation, even amongst literate Dalits. There is, however, a much more prevalent symbol around which Dalit identity is expressing itself: the portraits and the statues of Ambedkar. The Ambedkarite Republican Party and the Ambedkar People Movement are still not very widespread, but they are now much more visible than before. Ambedkar's statues are to be seen in large numbers, blue flags flutter in towns and villages. Ambedkar is very much present these days in intellectual debates, bookshops, newspaper columns, academic conferences and so on. Skeptics might contend that sheer opportunism drives all sorts of orators and politicians to pay tribute to the new hero as a means of cornering the Dalit vote. Yet empty though it might be, the rhetoric is itself both a testimony to and an instrument of change among those without voice. It shows that, like other groups, they have a figure revered by the establishment, a highly educated Dalit, a key redactor of the Indian Constitution who rejected Hindu domination and converted to Buddhism, a modern-day Dalit saint complete with his suit and tie. An attack on a statue of Ambedkar, a not uncommon occurrence, is seen as a desecration. The Republican Party he founded has not met with his expectations, but his example and his motto, "Educate, organise and agitate," is still the guideline for many NGOs who believe that dignity and justice are not just bestowed from above but have to be gained through struggle.

4.4. Paths of Militancy

Dalit liberation movement today pursues three main lines of action. The first seems to equip the Dalits with confidence; the second resorts to militant action; and the third raises the issue of the appropriate political tools. The first two lines of action can be combined to a certain extent. As the name suggests, this Madras NGO, run by Christian Dalits, identifies education as a powerful tool for social change, though without denying the need for action. It helps to rethink the conditions for liberation and, like other NGOs, tries to place the traditional oppression and the quest for justice in a broader framework with large implications in the field of civil and human rights. To equip Dalits with a better knowledge of their rights helps to bridge the gap between theory and practice.

A second line of struggle resorts to spectacular militant action. Sometimes the goal is symbolic and the figure of Ambedkar as an icon of Dalit emancipation is often privileged in such actions. The best known has been the long struggle by Dalit groups from Maharashtra to have the Marathwada University renamed Dr. Babasaheb Ambedkar University. Protest or revendicative marches, or celebrations of Ambedkar's anniversary, not to mention the collective reaction to attacks on Ambedkar statues, offer opportunities for public expressions of Dalit identity and aspirations which are sometimes serious enough to attract national attention.

But action can also have economic goals, taking the protest beyond identity symbols, as the agitation for *panchami* lands shows. *Panchama* is a very old term for those beyond the pale of the four varnas. In 1890 the British regime in the then Madras Presidency passed a law assigning land to the Dalits. It took more than 50 years for 650 acres of uncultivated land to be distributed to about 500 Dalits families in seven villages of Chingleput district, south of Madras.

Despite the law prohibiting the sale of such lands to non-Dalits, other castes were able to gain control of them in the 1950s. It expanded in 1994, when village police fired on a crowd in Karanai protesting the forcible removal of a statue of Ambedkar installed just hours earlier on claimed lands. The incident, in which two Dalits died, had a profound impact in the state, and resulted in the consolidation of the Panchami Land Committee.

The emergence of such large movements raises two distinct issues. The first relates to the structure of the Dalit movement itself, which is riven by internal divisions. The more radical groups are close to the Communist Party of India, which is marginal politically but plays an important ideological role. Other radical Dalit groups combine an ultra-left ideology with a concern for Tamilness as articulated by the Liberation Panthers, a Southern Dalit group supporting the Tamil Tigers in nearby Sri Lanka. Christian Dalits are much more important in struggle than their small numbers might suggest, and include Protestants like Rt. Rev. M. Azariah, Bishop of Madras, Church of South India, and Catholics. The most militant follow Liberation theology, which finds in Dalit emancipation an obvious field of action and theorisation. Militant groups can sometimes bridge religious and philosophical differences.

The second issue is political. Before independence, Gandhi persuaded Ambedkar to renounce the separate Dalit electorate the British were ready to concede. After 1947, for decades the Dalit vote was not autonomous. Most rural Dalits have, for long, "voted for the master." But Dalits were not seen as a special entity needing more than specific reservations and development programs offered to the Scheduled Castes. Like the Congress Party at the national level, the DMK saw itself as an umbrella organisation, able to mu ster votes from everybody from the Dalit agricultural labourer to his landlord. The Communist parties have certainly had an impact in some areas, particularly with labour movements among agricultural laborers. But the established communists of the CPI and CPI-M, faithful to the doctrine, could not emphasize caste differences in their organising. The Marxist-Leninists of the CPI-ML are certainly much more engaged in the Dalit struggle for land, and may even believe in the revolutionary potential of a Dalit mass movement, but they are a very small minority. The major parties in the state — the DMK and

AnnaDMK — are now perceived by many Dalit groups and NGOs as mainstream structures, paying mere lip service to the Dalits without offering them sufficient room in the leadership or adequate support to make a real difference.

The caste movement reappeared in Tamilnadu with a bang in 1987 when the Vanniyars launched an agitation in the northern districts to highlight their problems, at the cost of numerous lives. Shortly thereafter, their organisation, the Vanniyar Sangam, set up a political party, the Pattali Makkal Katchi (PMK), the Workers Party, which failed in successive elections to attract sufficient Vanniyar votes to elect representatives who could air their grievances in the Legislature. Subsequently the PMK, under its Vanniar founder leader C. Ramadoss, developed a new and inclusive strategy, presenting itself as the party of the OBCs, Muslims and Dalits, and adopting the North Indian concept of *bahujan* which extends the definition of the oppressed far beyond the Scheduled Castes. This strategy seeks to overcome the fact that, in the field, OBCs have been as violent adversaries of the Dalits as the high castes, exemplified by the history of clashes between the Vanniyars and the Paraiyars in Northern Tamilnadu and even more so by the violent confrontations between Pallars, a Dalit caste renamed Devendra Kular Velalar and Thevars. Alliance building and the arithmetic of electoral politics may help Dalits and OBCs gain access to power, through coalition if necessary. This is the story of the Bahujan Samaj Party in Uttar Pradesh, the most populous Indian state, where Mayawati had the distinction of being, albeit briefly, the first Dalit Chief Minister in India, first with the support of the Samajwadi Party, backed largely by OBCs, and then paradoxically with the support of the Bharatiya Janata Party, which, whatever its present policy of wooing Dalit voters and offering party seats to Dalits and Tribals, still has a high caste image. Having learned from the tactics of the Bahujan Samaj Party, the PMK leader, not without some debate in the party, decided to back the apparently disgraced leader of the AnnaDMK, Jayalalitha, who had allied herself with the BJP during the 1998 general election. The AnnaDMK made an unexpected comeback and for the first time the PMK won four seats to the Indian Parliament. In the fluid political situation prevailing in an uncertain coalition, the PMK even got one ministerial appointment in the BJP-led Vajpayee Government. The happy nominee, it must be noted, was not a Vanniyar, but a Dalit, publicising his identity in his very name: Dalit Ezhilmalai. Neither in Tamilnadu nor in Uttar Pradesh is the alliance between Dalits and the BJP fortuitous. It may sound strange that Dalits should ally with the political arm of the hard core Rashtriya Swayamsevak Sangh, whose religious sister organisation, the Vishva Hindu Parishad, pretends to embody the eternal values of Hinduism. Despite a high caste leadership, the strategy of the Sangh Parivar, the coalition of organisations that propagate Hindutva, is to try to accommodate all Hindus in its fold, including Dalits and Tribals. In the very fluid situation that has followed the decline of the Congress Party, political risks, including odd and unstable alliances, are sometimes the necessary precondition for political power. Dalit political parties are caught in this general predicament.

Caught between this drift and the bane of division which has so weakened the Ambedkarite Republican Party, the road is not an easy one. Clearly enough, new formations will emerge, the last one in Tamilnadu being the "New Tamil Country" founded in 1998 by a noted Dalit militant, K. Krishnasami, Chairman of the Devendra Kula Velalar Federation, the association of the main Dalit caste of South Tamilnadu. Whether such Dalit parties succeed or fail is not the issue; their very appearance is significant.

As a matter of fact, the Pudiya Tamilagam appears in a context marked by deep conflicts. In 1997 the relationship between the OBC Thevar caste and the Devendra Kula Velalars (DKV) took a turn for the worse. With the higher castes migrating to urban areas, the Thevars have become landowners, and rely upon the DKV for agricultural labour. But the social equation has changed, and the Dalits aspire to more than mere survival. They are not satisfied with whatever little land the state has given them. While elders like Viramma point out that their situation has improved in the last fifty years, the younger generation expects a lot more, including jobs and respect. As V.S. Sambadan has observed, the sparks of violence which disturbed the southern districts in 1997 have been symbolic: desecrations of Ambedkar statues, changes in the names of districts or public transport corporations. But behind the sparks basic issues continue to divide "backward caste" like the Thevars from the Dalit Pallars: based on economic competition, social assertion and political access to power.

Politics and symbols met unfortunately in the gruesome murder of six Dalits from Melavalavu village, in Madurai district, on June 30, 1997. In a number of reserved constituencies, no Dalit had dared to contest. Murugesan was convinced to do so, despite severe obstruction by the local dominant castes to "reversed" constituencies. He was elected, but prevented from taking office, and finally mu rdered, and even beheaded.

The divergent fates of the two Presidents is not just paradoxical. It emphasizes that much is still to change, and that what is possible and even celebrated at the national level is not necessarily accepted at the ground level of the village. George Matthew, Director of the Institute of Social Sciences, has rightly pointed out that the Melavalavu mu rders are not just "one more instance of caste tension. It was a serious attack on the institution of the *panchayati raj* which has the potential of changing the powerful rural groups." Since the recent administrative reforms, the *panchayat* is not just an honourable body of elected villagers, without much say on real issues. It now has control of local resources, and its president enjoys both status and power. Hence the reluctance of many established castes to accept a Dalit leadership, which offends them on both accounts, status and power. The necessary change of mind is not just a matter of Dalit consciousness. Change is needed as well among those high castes or OBCs who believe they are born leaders.

The PMK and the new Dalit party would therefore compete on the same field. Once a party chooses to contest elections, this must sooner or later result in dialogue with other groups and parties. The very names of the two formations open perspectives larger than caste: workers, in the case of the PMK, and a renovated Tamilness in the case of the Pudiya Tamilagam. The key question remains: Is the concept of *bahujan* a myth, or a hopeful anticipation? Or does such a hope result from a simplistic reading of the power distribution in Indian society, separating the "high caste oppressors" from all the other groups? This brings us to the basic question of caste. Faced with "broken promises," Dalits have to consider conducting their struggle in a specific caste frame to implement specific actions linked with reservation and human and civil rights. But how to reconcile such a choice with the Ambedkarite concept of the annihilation of caste? What is needed is not just the political tool of a caste party, and even the hypothetical all-

India confederation of Dalit regional parties, however necessary that might be at this moment. The need of the times is also to carry on a cultural revolution.

4.5. Culture, Identity and Empowerment

Whatever interpretation is given to the interaction between castes of different status in the old *jajmani* relationship, caste culture is hierarchical and divisive. With the weakening of the caste *system*, the interplay of unequal but regulated relations between castes is bound to collapse, except on the new level of political alliances. But neither political tools nor the new National Human Rights Commission and its state counterparts that help to implement the existing legislation are enough. In most cases, the goal is to free the Dalits from the dominant Hindu paradigm.

Conversion has sometimes been seen as the best opportunity, be it to Buddhism, Christianity or Islam. But conversion does not solve all problems on the ground or in the larger social context: converts may also be discriminated against, in or/and outside their new community. Furthermore many Dalits are not ready to convert, and conversion can hardly be a precondition for change. The program for action published in Madras by Katti Padma Rao, a Dalit leader from Andhra Pradesh, is an attempt to address the challenge of emancipation in all fields. A mix of strong anti-Hinduism, socialism and radical opposition to the caste logic, it is certainly not crédible and practical on all points. But it illustrates the difficulties faced by militants who believe that the overarching reality of untouchability calls for an equally overarching emancipation strategy, one that is attentive not only to socioeconomic contexts and political tools but also emphasizes a radical rethinking of attitudes, ideas, daily practices.

Padma Rao's first point is certainly too radical to be implemented. Impracticable and as much of a restraint on freedom as the old system, though in different ways, it goes to the core of the caste problem, that is, endogamy: "intracaste marriage must be banned. Inter-caste marriage must become mandatory." A second line of action recommends alternatives to the dominant culture in terms of names and celebrating festivals honoring Dalit leaders instead of Hindu gods. A third line of action addresses the "reconstruction of rural culture," banning caste titles from villages names or village streets, stopping construction of specific Dalit "colonies" in favour of mixed settlements, in addition to eliminating illiteracy, establishing health centers and rural libraries and opening community halls for meetings. The fifth proposal addresses the spread of education and calls for the multiplication of village schools, educational institutions and research centers, not to mention the revision of curriculum and text books. The sixth recommendation focuses on the necessity to spread alternative culture among women in order "to encourage them to resist the pressure of patriarcal domination" brought by Hindu culture. Padma Rao also calls for economic reorganisation and political reorganisation.

The radicalism of such a program limits its practicability, but the attempt to build up a detailed line of action at least identifies clearly the fields where change is needed and defines one line of thinking. The resolute denunciation of the dominant Hindu culture supposes profound changes in the daily life and in the "empire of signs" which governs its semiology. Politically and socially, Padma Rao suggests a blue and red perspective where the blue emancipation calls for a class (red) alliance with "backward and minority classes" against the upper castes Hindu ruling classes.

The question remains whether an alternative Dalit culture and Dalit activism is enough, or does Dalit emancipation also require a change in the mainstream culture? S.K. Thorat, in a paper on "Dalit and Human Rights" has seen the Dalits today as "a part of the whole, but a part apart." One can hardly find a better formulation of the present dilemma facing Dalit militants and all those struggling for Dalit emancipation. A part apart" could also convey the mixed feelings of a large part of the 80 percent non-Dalit Indians who do not see themselves as oppressors but still believe that the former "Untouchables" are not really fit for integration into the mainstream.

Let us consider the thoughts of a noted fellow-traveller of the Dalit movement, D.N. Nagaraj, on the dialectics of Dalit oppression and emancipation in a small but very dense book: *The Flaming Feet.* His experience is largely drawn from the Dalit movement in Karnataka, and combines themes in cultural politics with motifs and metaphors in literature. But Nagaraj offers clues and raises issues which are of much larger value, in space as well as in content. What history shows in this regard is that what is needed is not the Gandhian emphasis on Dalit quest for self-purification as a precondition for the eradication of untouchability. Against Gandhi's self-purification need, Ambedkar posits a quest for Dalit self-respect, which raises immediately the question of identity and the need for the emergence of an alternative culture which could eliminate the stigma of untouchability and stand in opposition to the established logic and psychology of the caste system. But while his neo-Buddhists followers and a number of intellectuals would define themselves today as non-Hindus, it is still doubtful that the Dalit masses would follow suit.

Is Indian democracy able to help Dalit emancipation, not just through reservation by law but also through the diffusion of new perceptions among Dalits and non-Dalits alike? The question centers partly on the place given to the individual, and partly on accepted norms. Nagaraj, addressing the problem of violence against Dalits, notes rightly that the village, as Ambedkar saw it, cannot be the basic unit for justice, for traditionally "the structure of justice rests on the consensus of the entire village, which could also mean the unchallenged rule of the upper castes." Here again, the caste ethos has to be rightly assessed: as Nagaraj notes, if an upper caste Hindu misbehaves in the village, this will be considered as an individual act, involving individual responsibility. But if a Dalit break the norms, he will be perceived first as a member of his group, and the entire Dalit community could suffer retaliation. A narrow path is thus open to Dalit militants who seek a way to attack oppression by combining ideology and material domination but also by trying to respect the "code of conduct," in the process gaining greater legitimacy in the "traditional" society, which is vital for the success of the Movement. In the meantime, the Dalit activist, "in a paradoxical position," has to recognise that "on him or her is the larger responsibility of creating a new sense of ethics for both the conflicting communities."

Looking at the bleak picture of untouchability in rural India, must we believe, as some Dalit militants do, that emancipation in the villages will be impossible against so many odds, however resolute the struggles, and that migration to town is the only way to free oneself? True, the rule of caste is not so rigid in large cities. But are Indian towns really such an attractive promised land? Urban India might also bring up much more acutely the problem of cultural memory, a memory already challenged either because it is lost in a silent history or because of the contempt it raises not just among non-Dalits but also sometimes among Dalits as well.

Last but not least stands the Dalits' "rights to cultural space." In Dalit writing in the Kannada language, Nagaraj finds two schools. The "school of social rage" "concentrates basically on the experiences of anger, agony and revolutionary hope." The "school of spiritual quest" transmutes the social rage "into a spiritual vision of equality." Why "spiritual quest?" Not necessarily because of an attachment to a defined religious line, but because this school "tries to understand the world of poverty and untouchability in terms of metaphysical dismay over the nature of human relationship. The ethos of the portrayal of life is not informed by anger and agony, but by a celebration of the joys of life and its possibilities, which also includes the will to change."

Beyond the sphere of literature, these two schools can also suggest a model, a metaphor for the choices offered to the Dalit society at large, or for the types of action open to militants. Those animated by an intimate or spectacular social rage might feel that no middle ground exist between nihilist or desparate intellectual marginality and strident revolutionary advocacy and militancy. There is an unavoidable contradiction between activist groupings and larger party politics, the former being generally prone to isolation and/or repression, the latter bringing quickly enough, after the first electoral successes, the need for compromise. On the other hand, the spiritual quest is more prone to being coopted by the system. The real challenge for the second path is to resist this cooptation while transforming the system. Nagaraj pleads "for a radical reconstruction of villages from a critical-modernist perspective which can also mean a radical revision of existing values along the lines of Indian religious reformers." Some Dalit militants or leftist radicals would call for a complete break with religion, reformed or not. Others would follow Nagaraj in opting for a middle-of-the-road line. A third group might find that this complex goal offers a path of change more acceptable to Indian society, because it is less disconnected from the legacy of a past not entirely encapsulated in upper caste orthodoxy. It will involve Dalits and non-Dalits, the past and the present, the community as a whole and its fragments, and the self. It is a total enterprise, with innumerable implications. But it is clearly a process in which Indian Dalits are engaged today.

4.6. CHANGE

Castes are very much a part of the political game, but the caste system as such is condemned. The OBCs are asserting themselves everywhere, including in the decisive circles of power. One finds more and more Dalits in positions of responsibility and power, largely through the reservation system, while most of the community is still subject to various sorts of overt or covert discrimination. Promises have neither been fulfilled or forgotten. But the Dalit aspiration for change has become too strong in the minds of millions for backing down. Myriads of daily struggles, spectacular or not, sustain this aspiration, which has now gained access to the media and the political field. But Dalit emancipation remains a challenge for it raises formidable issues pertaining not just to the fate of the Dalits but also to Hinduism and to the Indian society as a whole. Seven points might call for answers, that only the future will provide:

— The first addresses Dalit identity itself: must the Dalits place themselves behind the blue standard and, faithful to Ambedkar, find a place in the larger society without abandoning their sense of belonging? But how to reconcile the legitimate revendications of a caste so oppressed for centuries with the goal of "annihilation of caste?" This goal supposes that members of other castes, both the oppressed and oppressor will let castes be annihilated. Could it be the historical mission of the Dalits to constantly harass the dominant paradigm and shake the old oppressive order?

— The second point is a correlate of the first one: how to preserve Dalit memories? Can the experiences, the history of millions of Dalits simply be abandoned for the sake of joining the mainstream? This could be a temptation for urban intellectuals. But how can the past and the present of more than 150 million people be ignored for long? The urban-rural divide between Dalits becomes an additional challenge. Will the political and the NGOs activists bridge a potential gap between a growing corps of urban Dalit intellectuals and the mass of rural illiterates? The answer varies.

— A third point relates to the nature and the real extent of the "mainstream" Hindu identity. Is there only one Hindu ideality set by the *shastras* of the brahminical tradition? Is there not also a legacy of other traditions on which to build the future, a large and diverse cultural space which encompasses not just the Dalits but also the Tribals, the reformist movements formulating a new Hinduism where the individual has a place, the secular democratic ideal, not to mention eventually other faiths not based officially on caste? Where do the OBCs stand in this landscape? The fourth varna, the Shudras, were also excluded from knowledge and power by the dominant classical paradigm.

— The fourth point takes us to the impact of regional parameters. In the Tamil case, the legacy of the Dravidian movement is decisive. Even if the fragmentation of the Dravidian parties' vote banks opens the field to more autonomous formations, the question of competing identities remains, unavoidably perhaps, a challenge. Dalit or Tamil? It is not by chance that the new Dalit party calls itself "New Tamilnadu." The Dravidian ideology offers a way out of the dilemma of Dalitness/ Tamilness, for it offers a seducive interpretation of history: by putting the blame for the scourge of caste and untouchability upon "the Brahmins who came from the North," one may link the future Dalit emancipation to the more egalitarian and secular values attributed to the old Tamil civilisation.

— The fifth point queries the possibility of the union of the Red and the Blue. The established Left has always tried to circumscribe the challenge of caste, without really addressing it, and simply denounced caste as a mask for class. With the Dalit issue gaining momentum, it will be more and more difficult for the Left to ignore this challenge for long, partly because Dalit sensibilities on this issue can no longer be ignored and the concept of "oppressed" requires urgent theorising.

— The sixth point is about alliances between the Dalit and other social movements. The alliance between Dalits and OBCs is not simply a matter of political convenience and electoral arithmetic. Politics is not just a matter of power: it is more basically a question of goals, policy and change. What are the forces that are bringing changes to the daily life of millions of Dalits? Will they transform the socioeconomic fundamentals of Dalit life and, indeed, affect the entire social balance? Dalit emancipation requires the imperative need for fresh thinking amongst non-Dalits about untouchability. On a wider level, how to connect the Dalit movement with the women's movement?

— The seventh point brings us back to the difficulty to forge a stronger relationship with OBCs if Dalit emancipation calls for, as many militants contend, a rupture with Hinduism? Or put differently and abstractly: how must Hinduism itself change in relation to Dalit emancipation? If the duality/dichotomy between "the brahmin" and "the untouchable" was a foundation of the caste system, what will happen with the latter rejecting his/her status?

In this context, one cannot underestimate the strategy of Hindutva, which tends, despite the weight of its high caste leadership, to weaken caste differences in order to forge a pan-Indian Hindu identity. Dalits and Hindu tribals are clearly being invited to hitch their wagons to the communal project, and to let them assert an overarching Hindu identity rather than a primordial affiliation. Will the saffron hypothesis of the Sangh Parivar offer a major temptation to Dalits to join a new communal mainstream, which would also subvert more radical Dalit leanings?

All these issues, and many more, pose uncertain and difficult questions to which the answers are, as yet, inchoate. But the Dalit movement is definitely here to stay and will probably, as today, continue along diverse paths, tempted sometimes by isolation and at others opening itself to other forces. Blue, red and saffron are the predominant colours of change. In the end a rainbow might emerge from the synthesis of now-divergent paths. At minimum it will have to be a secular, democratic synthesis consistent with the Dalit movement's call for justice, respect and progress. This challenge is not just a matter of intellectual analysis or social theory. In thousands of Indian towns, in hundreds of thousands of Indian villages, the fate of the Dalits will largely fashion India's future, and this is not irrelevant to India's ambition for the next century.

References

Ambedkar, B.R. *What Congress and Gandhi Have Done to the Untouchables*. Bombay: Thacker 1945.

Berreman, G. *Hindus of the Himalayas: Ethnography and Change*. Berkeley: University of California Press 1963.

Beteille, A. *The Backward Classes in Contemporary India*. Delhi: OUP 1992.

Bhave, S. *Pan on Fire: Eight Dalit Women Tell Their Story*. New Delhi: 1988.

Tripathi, R.S. & Tiwari, P.D. (eds) *Dimensions of Scheduled Caste Development in India*. New Delhi: Uppal 1991.

5

Rights of Dalit Women

Even as we are in the 21st millennium, caste discrimination, an age-old practice that dehumanizes and perpetuates a cruel form of discrimination continues to be practiced. India where the practice is rampant despite the existence of a legislation to stop this, 160 million Dalits of which 49.96% are women continue to suffer discrimination. The discrimination that Dalit women are subjected to is similar to racial discrimination, where the former is discriminated and treated as untouchable due to descent, for being born into a particular community, while, the latter face discrimination due to colour. This is a complete negation and violation of women's human rights. We urge this august body to pay special attention to this issue and come up with recommendations to eradicate the caste system.

Dalit women are thrice discriminated, treated as untouchables and as outcastes, due to their caste, face gender discrimination being women and finally economic impoverishment due to unequal wage disparity, with low or underpaid labour. According to the Hindu caste hierarchy, there are four castes namely the Brahmins, the Kshatriya the Vaishyas. Below this four tier caste ladder is another rung, who are called the untouchables. Among the untouchables, the status of women is further eroded and closely linked to the concept of purity. This is what the rigid, fundamentalist Hindu promotes through continuation of caste system, imposing the Brahminical values to maintain the caste system' The creation of a number of Hindu religious books including the *Manusmriti, Atharva Vedas, Vishnu smriti*, and many others like these and their strict compliance by the Brahmans led to a society in which equality between men and women was far from existent. Dr. B.R. Ambedkar, an architect of the Indian constitution, also makes it very clear in his article titled "The rise and fall of Hindu woman" that the root cause of suffering for women in India are these so called Hindu religious books. Books like the Manusmriti divide people into a stratified caste system and promotes inequality between men and women.

According to the *Manusmriti*, women have no right to education, independence, or wealth. It not only justifies the treatment of dalit women as a sex object and promotes child marriage, but also justifies a number of violent atrocities on women as can be seen in the following verses. Even the killing of a dalit woman is explicitly justified as a minor offence for the Brahmins: equal to the killing of an animal. If the killing of an untouchable was justified as a minor offence, you can imagine the treatment they received throughout their lives.

In a male dominated society, Dalit women suffered unimaginable oppression, not only through caste, but gender too, from which there was no escape. The laws in the *Manusmriti* and other Vedic scriptures close all economic, political, social, educational, and personal channels through which Dalit women could be uplifted. The horrendous Laws in the *Manusmriti* were incorporated into Hinduism because they were favourable only to the Upper castes, which form the majority of India.

The caste discrimination inherited by birth results in Dalit women facing multiple oppression that violates their economic, political, social and cultural rights. The women face not just caste violence inflicted on them by the dominant castes, but also state violence.

Dalit women in India are targeted for violence and discrimination not just because of their gender, but also on the basis of their caste, community, religious affiliation and other factors. The rape is a major means for isolating her and her husband within the community because of the stigma attached to this crime in India. Other common forms of violence perpetrated against Indian women include: female feticide (selective abortion based on the fetus' gender); domestic violence; dowry death; mental and physical torture; sexual trafficking; and public humiliation.

Many dalits are not aware of their rights under special legislation designed to protect them, and it is rare that police voluntarily inform them of those rights. Police are also accused of withholding and destroying evidence in many cases, usually at the behest of the accused, with whom they may have caste or other links. Witnesses often withdraw testimony after taking bribes or being threatened by the accused; medical evidence is lost because simple procedures are not followed. The discouraging length of time required to pursue torture cases through the courts often causes victims to make compromises or to withdraw their cases entirely.

There are seven major areas of discrimination against women belong to poor section in India. They are:

i) *Malnutrition*: India has exceptionally high rates of child malnutrition, because tradition in India requires that women eat last and least throughout their lives, even when pregnant and lactating. Malnourished women give birth to malnourished children, perpetuating the cycle.

ii) *Poor health*: Females receive less health care than males. Many women die in childbirth of easily prevented complications. Working conditions and environmental pollution further impairs women's health.

iii) *Lack of education*: Families are far less likely to educate girls than boys, and far more likely to pull them out of school, either to help out at home or from fear of violence.

iv) *Overwork*: Women work longer hours and their work is more arduous than men's, yet their work is unrecognised. Men report that "women, like children, eat and do nothing." Technological progress in agriculture has had a negative impact on women.

v) *Unskilled*: In women's primary employment sector - agriculture - extension services overlook women.

vi) *Mistreatment:* In recent years, there has been an alarming rise in atrocities against women in India, in terms of rapes, assaults and dowry-related murders. Fear of violence suppresses the aspirations of all women. Female infanticide and sex-selective abortions are additional forms of violence that reflect the devaluing of females in Indian society.

vii) *Powerlessness*: While women are guaranteed equality under the constitution, legal protection has little effect in the face of prevailing patriarchal traditions. Women lack power to decide who they will marry, and are often married off as children. Legal loopholes are used to deny women inheritance rights.

5.1. Economic Status

Of the total population, Dalit women constitute 16.3% of which 18% women live in rural areas. The women perform hard domestic labour which is unpaid and as agricultural labourers or casual labourers they continue to toil under the burning sun, with no protection or benefits that labour laws should provide, since majority of these women are in the unorganized sector. Dalit women undertake manual, low paying, tedious, time consuming work. They earn less than one U.S. Dollar.

The women have to walk miles to fetch drinking water and often the water is not safe and potable. Dalit hamlets are usually at the end of the main village or in the village outskirts. They live in small huts and even the few who may have slightly better housing are devoid of basic amenities such as sanitation, light and safe and clean drinking water. The women work on construction sites, carrying heavy loads of construction material. The women have to walk miles not just for collecting water but also fuel and fodder for their domestic chores. Dalit women are victims of bonded labour, they are abused, sexually exploited by other caste, humiliated and are easy targets of insult.

A study conducted come up with some shocking facts about the work of dalit women. What is horrifying is that Dalit women work more than bullocks and men. Bullocks and men work in a hectare in a year for 1064 hours and 1202, respectively, while women work for more than 3485 hours. She has to work to survive. She is powerless and has neither access nor control over resources.

Manual scavenging continues as an occupation in India and most of the manual scavengers are Dalit women. The women are subjected to do this humiliating and degrading work, which further results in discrimination and social exclusion.

The process of globalisation has affected Dalit women considerably. With the introduction of new farming techniques such as, mechanization for harvesting and transplanting, women have lost their traditional work in the agricultural sector. Food crops have been replaced by Cash crops. Horticulture has been introduced by, big agrobusiness corporations for export purposes. This has deprived Dalit women of their land and the common resources in the village. Formerly women used to collect greens, fish, and shells from fields free for their food requirements. The Globalisation process has increased the feminisation of poverty and this has affected Dalit women in every sphere of their lives. There is also large scale migration from rural areas to the urban centres in search of better livelihood options. Women are left behind to bear the responsibility of the family. This further adds to the existing burden that Dalit women are trying to cope with. Such situations push the women into further situations of impoverishment, making them more and more vulnerable to all forms of discriminations and violations.

5.2. Health Status

The health condition of Dalit women is alarming with high incidence of maternal mortality and infant mortality. This is due to the fact that Dalit women are unable to access health care services. Due to denial and sub standard healthcare services the life expectancy of Dalit women is as low as 50 years. The infant mortality rate is 90 / 1.000. The sex ratio of Dalit women is 922 / 1000 compared to 927 / 1000 for rest of the population in India. Due to poverty, Dalit women are malnourished and anemic. Early marriage and multiple child births causes the women to suffer from prolapsed uterus. They also develop skin irritation and allergy due to excessive use of pesticides. As they work barefoot and the soil is damp and wet, the women develop soars between their toes.

Dalit women are easy target for the Government Birth Control Schemes. Women face forced sterilization, are tested for the use of new invasive hormonal contraception like guinea pigs. They are forced to use long-acting, hormonally dangerous contraceptives.

5.2.1. Malnutrition and Poor Health

Traditionally, women bear primary responsibility for the well-being of their families. Yet they are systematically denied access to the resources they need to fulfil their responsibility, which includes education, health care services, job training, and access and freedom to use family planning services. In short, the poor care that is afforded to girls and women by their husbands and by elders is the first major reason for levels of child malnutrition that are markedly higher in South Asia than anywhere else in the world.

India, is the world's second most populous country. Of that number, 120 million are women who live in poverty. India has 16 per cent of the world's population, but only 2.4 per cent of its land, resulting in great pressures on its natural resources. Over 70 per cent of India's population currently derive their livelihood from land resources, which includes 84 per cent of the economically-active women.

The Indian constitution grants women equal rights with men, but strong patriarchal traditions persist, with women's lives shaped by customs that are centuries old. In most Indian families, a daughter is viewed as a liability, and she is conditioned to believe that she is inferior and subordinate to men. Sons are idolised and celebrated. May you be the mother of a hundred sons is a common Hindu wedding blessing.

The exceptionally high rates of malnutrition in South Asia are rooted deeply in the soil of inequality between men and women. Gender has been the most statistically significant determinant of malnutrition among young children and malnutrition is a frequent direct or underlying cause of death among girls below age 5. Girls are breast-fed less frequently and for shorter durations in infancy; in childhood and adulthood, males are fed first and better. One study found anaemia in over 95 per cent of girls ages 6-14 in Calcutta, around 67 per cent in the Hyderabad area, 73 per cent in the New Delhi area, and about 18 per cent in the Madras area. Besides posing risks during pregnancy, anaemia increases women's susceptibility to diseases such as tuberculosis and reduces the energy women have available for daily activities such as household chores, child care, and agricultural labour. Any severely anaemic individual is taxed by most physical activities, including walking at an ordinary pace.

The practice of breast-feeding female children for shorter periods of time reflects the strong desire for sons. If women are particularly anxious to have a male child, they may deliberately try to become pregnant again as soon as possible after a female is born. Conversely, women may consciously seek to avoid another pregnancy after the birth of a male child in order to give maximum attention to the new son. A primary way that parents discriminate against their girl children is through neglect during illness. When sick, little girls are not taken to the doctor as frequently as are their brothers.

Studies on attendance at rural primary health centres reveal that more males than females are treated in almost all parts of the country, with differences greater in northern hospitals than southern ones, pointing to regional differences in the value placed on women. Women's socialisation to tolerate suffering and their reluctance to be examined by male personnel are additional constraints in their getting adequate health care. India's maternal mortality rates in rural areas are among the highest in the world. A factor that contributes to India's high maternal mortality rate is the reluctance to seek medical care for pregnancy — it is viewed as a temporary condition that will disappear.

The estimates nationwide are that only 40-50 per cent of women receive any antenatal care. Evidence from the states of Bihar, Rajasthan, Orissa, Uttar Pradesh, Maharashtra and Gujarat find registration for maternal and child health services to be as low as 5-22 per cent in rural areas and 21-51 per cent in urban areas. Even a woman who has had difficulties with previous pregnancies is usually treated with home remedies only for three reasons: the decision that a pregnant woman seek help rests with the mother-in-law and husband; financial considerations; and fear that the treatment may be more harmful than the malady. It is estimated that pregnancy-related deaths account for one-quarter of all fatalities among women aged 15 to 29, with well over two-thirds of them considered preventable.

Women's health is harmed by lack of access to and the poor quality of reproductive services. About 24.6 million couples, representing roughly 18 per cent of all married women, want no more children but are not using contraception. The causes of this unmet need remain poorly understood, but a qualitative study in Tamil Nadu suggests that women's lack of decision-making power in the family, opportunity costs involved in seeking contraception, fear of child death, and poor quality of contraceptive service all play an important role.

Some 5 million abortions are performed annually in India, with the large majority being illegal. As a result, abortion-related mortality is high. Although abortion has been legal since 1972 in India, studies suggest that although official policy seeks to make pregnancy-termination services widely available, in practice guidelines on abortion limit access to services, particularly in rural areas. In 1981, of the 6,200 physicians trained to perform abortions, only 1,600 were working in rural areas. The tasks performed by women are usually those that require them to be in one position for long periods of time, which can adversely affect their reproductive health.

Women's health is further harmed by air and water pollution and lack of sanitation. The impact of pollution and industrial wastes on health is considerable. The smoke from household biomass (made up of wood, dung and crop residues) stoves within a three-hour period is equivalent to smoking 20 packs of cigarettes. For women who spend at least three hours per day cooking, often in a poorly ventilated area, the impact includes eye problems, respiratory problems, chronic bronchitis and lung cancer. One study quoted by WHO in 1991 found that pregnant women cooking over open biomass stoves had almost a 50 per cent higher chance of stillbirth.

Anaemia makes a person more susceptible to carbon monoxide toxicity, which is one of the main pollutants in the biomass smoke. Given the number of Indian women who are anaemic — 25 to 30 per cent in the reproductive age group and almost 50 per cent in the third trimester — this adds to their vulnerability to carbon monoxide toxicity. Additionally, with an increasing population, diseases caused by waste disposal, such as hookworm, are rampant. People who work barefooted are particularly susceptible, and it has been found that hookworm is directly responsible for the high percentage of anaemia among rural women.

5.3. Educational Status

A large majority of the illiterate population comprise of Dalit women with 76.24% of Dalit women being illiterate. The girl drop out rate among Dalit families is increasing with girl-children are forced to work as child laborers, More and more girl children from Dalit communities are school drop-outs and working as child labourers. Dalit women are illiterate because they have less access to education which is an inherent part of the caste system. Dalit girl children are involved mostly in hazardous work like Beedi making, working in match factories and in the fire-works industry.

Traditionally dowry, which is not a practice of the Dalits has now became a bane. Due to Sanskritisation by the caste Hindus, the Dalits have begun to emulate the customs and rituals of the hindus. Dowry is one such custom. The Dalit families have succumbed to the societal pressures, added to this the fear of sending the girls to schools which are usually located in distant places deprive them of education. They do not get uniforms, school books, special fees, and have to walk long distances to reach their school. This is a limiting factor for dalit children.

India's constitution guarantees free primary school education for both boys and girls up to age 14. This goal has been repeatedly reconfirmed, but primary education in India is not universal. Overall, the literacy rate for women is 39 per cent versus 64 per cent for men. The rate for women in the four large northern states — Bihar, Uttar Pradesh, Rajasthan and Madhya Pradesh — is lower than the national average: it was 25 per cent in 1991. Attendance rates from the 1981 census suggest that no more than 1/3 of all girls (and a lower proportion of rural girls) aged 5-14 are attending school.

Although substantial progress has been achieved since India won its independence in 1947, when less than 8 per cent of females were literate, the gains have not been rapid enough to keep pace with population growth: there were 16 million more illiterate females in 1991 than in 1981. Parents have several incentives for not educating their daughters. Foremost is the view that education of girls brings no returns to parents and that their future roles, being mainly reproductive and perhaps including agricultural labour, require no formal education. As more and more boys are engaged in education, there is a growing reliance on the labour of girls. Girls are increasingly replacing their brothers on the farm while carrying on their usual responsibilities in housework. A large proportion of the roughly 40 million "nonworking" girls who are not in school are kept at home because of responsibilities in housework.

The role of parents is to deliver a chaste daughter to her husband's family. When schools are located at a distance, when teachers are male, and when girls are expected to study along with boys, parents are often unwilling to expose their daughters to the potential assault on their virginity. There is little response to counter these obstacles: school hours remain inflexible to the labour demands of girls; many villages do not have a school; and fewer than 1/3 of India's primary and middle-school teachers are women.

Budgetary provisions for non-formal education have been cut by 17 percent, leading to closure of many night schools and adult education programs in which working-class women participate. Reduction in government expenditures on higher education and encouragement to private colleges will reduce women's opportunities for higher education since privatisation in education promotes only male-dominated professional and technical courses, as they are lucrative.

Dalit females have one of the lowest levels of literacy of all groups in India. Their low level of literacy is due to three interrelated factors:

(a) continued monopolization of state, economic, cultural and other resources by middle and upper class groups;

(b) the stronger influence of casteism in rural areas on dalit females; and

(c) the control of dalit males over dalit women and girls.

About ninety percent of dalit women are rural; most are landless or marginal farmers who live in abject poverty with grinding labor. Many work as coolies, or day-to-day manual workers, at less wages than men. Their economic situation has worsened due to the overall deteriorating rural economic conditions over the last five years as a result of the New Economic Policy. So too, the deterioration and privatization of common forest resources on which many rural dalit women depend for survival. Water and fuel scarcity have a direct influence on dalit girls's access to education.

Dalit women are the target of government population programs, and female literacy is viewed as part of this strategy. In other government programs and schemes for rural and urban women, it is Other Backward Castes (OBCs), middle and upper hindu caste women who derive most of the benefit; dalit women are left out, with few exceptions.

In all cases of caste conflict, dalit women are the first victims. They are raped and gang-raped in order to terrorize a whole caste and community. Even though these incidents of violence against women are extreme, nevertheless, some of these caste biases exist in schools among caste hindu teachers. In addition, dalit females are invisible in school curricula and text books.

Poverty compels most rural dalit parents to send their children to work rather than to school. Many dalit parents view education for girls as a luxury, pointing out that it is expensive and there is a lack of gainful employment opportunities after graduation. For example, dalit women's participation in the organized sector is negligible. However, many parents also feel that education beyond the primary level for girls will affect their household management.

Controls by men over women starts as a girl child where infant mortality due to neglect and malnutrition is very high. Many dalit girls and women are used and abused by drunken male relatives. The sexual division of labor, child marriage, and restricted mobility also limit dalit females' access to education.

These factors contribute to a high dropout rate among dalit female children, especially at the secondary school level and higher. Dropout and non-enrollment is also due to several other factors, including the lack of childcare facilities in villages; cooking, cleaning and other domestic chores; employment as child laborers to help support the family, education and marriage of siblings; and the attitudes of parents and the dalit community.

5.3.1. Problems of Educated Dalit Women

Educated dalit women encounter discrimination as well, for example in employment and wages, appointments and promotions, in political representation, demands made for dowry, and in personal relations. The major beneficiaries of education and employment reservations for Scheduled Castes (SCs) and Scheduled Tribes (STs) are men from the 'forward' castes among the dalits. This fact reveals at least two issues:

(a) that not all dalits have equal access to reservations, and

(b) that dalit women, especially do not have equal access as men to benefits reserved for SC/ST.

Further, as a result of persistent casteism and corruption, many seats in college and positions in government reserved for Scheduled Castes and Scheduled Tribes go unfilled, though qualified dalit candidates do apply. Thus, if a qualified dalit woman applies for a job or college seat reserved for an SC/ST, she is told to apply as a woman; if she applies for a job or college seat reserved for women, she is told to apply as an SC/ST.

Given these trends, it is doubtful whether the recent debate over granting reservation for women in parliament would have much benefit for dalit women in general. Even though 25 per cent of the seats in local assemblies, like the panchayat raj, are reserved for women in Karnataka, the reservation for dalit women only amounts to twenty percent of the women's quota. Those dalit women who are elected are restricted by their lack of education and ownership of land. Even if educated, their power as landless, female representatives in a body comprised of powerful landed, caste hindu groups is still limited.

With diminished marriage prospects due to lack of dowry, many educated dalit women become educated unemployed and underemployed single women. In marriage, educated dalit women are still subordinated within the family; educated dalit males are refuters of Manuism, but followers in regards to women.

Due to triple oppression of class, caste and gender, dalit females have the least access to education and other opportunities for social and economic mobility. Their liberation does not lie purely in economic or political terms, but social and cultural liberation must also be taken into account.

Education of dalit girls and women is necessary for their full participation in all aspects of society. Despite multiple obstacles and oppression, many dalit females are struggling daily to gain access to educational opportunities. Their resistance and determination to obtain access to information is but one aspect of their agency and power.

The results of such actions are the independent anti-alcohol movements in several states spawned in part by the government's Total Literacy Campaign. These results were not what literacy planners expected, but serves to show the power of dalit and other women's learning and cooperation.

Literacy can be empowering, however, it must be done at a pace and level determined by women themselves. And most importantly, it must address issues important to dalit women and be accompanied by other social and economic reforms such as the following: sanitation, health, childcare; credit and loans, land reform; water and fuel supply and conservation; and reservation and scholarships for dalit women.

5.3.2. Employment Issues

Women's contribution to agriculture — whether it be subsistence farming or commercial agriculture — when measured in terms of the number of tasks performed and time spent, is greater than men. The extent of women's contribution is aptly highlighted by a micro study conducted in the Indian Himalayas which found that on a one-hectare farm, a pair of bullocks works 1,064 hours, a man 1,212 hours and a woman 3,485 hours in a year.In Andhra Pradesh, found that the work day of an woman agricultural labourer during the agricultural season lasts for 15 hours, from 4 am to 8 pm, with an hour's rest in between. Her male counterpart works for seven to eight hours, from 5 am to 10 am or 11 am and from 3 pm to 5 pm. Another study on time and energy spent by men and women on agricultural work found that 53 per cent of the total human hours per household are contributed by women as compared to 31 per cent by men. The remaining contribution comes from children.

Rice transplantations, the most arduous and labour intensive task in rice cultivation, is carried out entirely by women without the help of any tools. "Girls learn to assist their mothers in almost all tasks, and from the age of 10 years participate fully in the agricultural work done by women. Mies cites the case of Laxmi, a three-year-old infant who, along with her mother, pulled seedlings for transplanting. Boys on the other hand were seldom seen transplanting or weeding though they did help out in ploughing or watering the fields." Not only do women perform more tasks, their work is also more arduous than that undertaken by men. Both transplantation and weeding require women to spend the whole day and work in muddy soil with their hands. Moreover, they work the entire day under the intensely hot sun while men's work, such as ploughing and watering the fields, is invariably carried out early in the morning before the sun gets too hot. Mies argues that because women's work, unlike men's, does not involve implements and is based largely on human energy, it is considered unskilled and hence less productive. On this basis, women are invariably paid lower wages, despite the fact that they work harder and for longer hours than do men.

Women's employment in family farms or businesses is rarely recognised as economically productive, either by men or women. And, any income generated from this work is generally controlled by the men. Such work is unlikely to increase women's participation in allocating family finances. In a 1992 study of family-based textile workers, male children who helped in a home-based handloom mill were given pocket money, but the adult women and girls were not. Technology has been introduced in areas where women worked, women labourers have often been displaced by men. Threshing of grain was almost exclusively a female task, and with the introduction of automatic grain threshers—which are only operated by men—women have lost an important source of income.

The male dominated extension system tends to overlook women's role in agriculture and proves ineffective in providing technical information to women farmers. Mapping Progress, states, in the farm sector, the process of mechanisation of agricultural activities has brought in tendencies for gender discrimination by replacing men for a number of activities performed by women and also by displacing the labour of women from subsistence and marginal households. Women are employed only when there is absolute shortage of labour and for specific operations like cotton-picking.

A number of factors perpetuate women's limited job skills: if training women for economic activities requires them to leave their village, this is usually a problem for them. Unequal access to education restricts women's abilities to learn skills that require even functional levels of literacy. In terms of skill development, women are impeded by their lack of mobility, low literacy levels and prejudiced attitudes toward women. When women negotiate with banks and government officials, they are often ostracised by other men and women in their community for being 'too forward.' Government and bank officials have preconceived ideas of what women are capable of, and stereotypes of what is considered women's work.

5.4. Political Power

Dalit women are excluded from decision making. They are not in a position to exercise their power. Wherever dalit women have contested, they have faced stiff opposition and even been brutally attacked. Ranganayaki was deposed for solemnising an inter-caste marriage. Banwari was gang raped when she objected and reported to the authorities against child marriage in her village. Gowri was made to parade naked for hoisting a flag on Independence Day. Dalit women are militant and powerful. They are now fighting for political power within this caste system.

There are instances where Dalit women have been elected into local governance and through the reservation policy nominated as the President of the local governing unit called Panchayat. But when these women have endeavoured to exercise their role, it has met with resistance even to the extend of physical violence. She is forced to be a mere figure head, while the functioning of the Panchayat is taken over by other upper caste members.

There are several traditional practices and customs that violate human rights. The practice of dedicating girl-children to become Devadasis, Basavis and Mathammas. This practice is a violation of Dalit Women's Rights. Dalit women are discriminated and treated as untouchables.

Superstition coupled with poverty and illiteracy is responsible for such practices. It is also using religion to sanction prostitution through the interpretation of mythology by the upper caste so that they can both economically and sexually exploit dalit women. It also is a form of upper caste manipulation to control the lives of Dalits. There is a strong belief that the goddess has healing powers. So when a Dalit girl is sick. As already mentioned the economic situation is another reason that Dalits are unable to spend money to buy good health service. Once the child is cured, the child is named after Mathamma and married to the goddess with the "Pottu Thali". After she becomes a dancer she belongs to the temple. During temple festivals she dances and earns her livelihood. She is not treated with respect and publicly humiliated by men who harass her sexually.

The team which plays music with her exploits her by having a share in what she earns.

Once the girl is dedicated to Mathamma, she cannot marry and lead a family life, as she is wedded to the Goddess. Therefore, she is sexually exploited by her partner who leaves her, to fend for herself and her child. Other men also tend to sexually exploit these Dalit women.

Dalit women who are dedicated to Mathammas end up in the sex trade and become vulnerable to sexually transmitted diseases including HIV/AIDS. Dalits facing Human Rights violations is a legion. A random sampling of headlines in mainstream Indian newspapers tells their story: "Dalit boy beaten to death for plucking flowers"; "Dalit tortured by cops for three days"; "Dalit 'witch' paraded naked in Bihar"; "Dalit killed in lock-up at Kurnool"; "7 Dalits burnt alive in caste clash"; "5 Dalits lynched in Haryana"; "Dalit woman gang-raped, paraded naked"; "Police egged on mob to lynch Dalits".

India's Untouchables are relegated to the lowest jobs, and live in constant fear of being publicly humiliated, paraded naked, beaten, and raped with impunity by upper-caste Hindus seeking to keep them in their place. Merely walking through an upper-caste neighborhood is a life-threatening offense.

5.4.1. Powerlessness

Traditional Hindu society in northern rural areas is hierarchical and dominated by men, as evidenced by marriage customs. North Indian Hindus are expected to marry within prescribed boundaries: the bride and groom must not be related, they have no say in the matter, and the man must live outside the woman's natal village. "Wife givers" are socially and ritually inferior to "wife takers", thus necessitating the provision of a dowry. After marriage, the bride moves in with her husband's family. Such a bride is "a stranger in a strange place." They are controlled by the older females in the household, and their behaviour reflects on the honour of their husbands. Because emotional ties between spouses are considered a potential threat to the solidarity of the patrilineal group, the northern system tends to segregate the sexes and limit communication between spouses — a circumstance that has direct consequences for family planning and similar "modern" behaviours that affect health.

The primary duty of a newly married young woman, and virtually her only means of improving her position in the hierarchy of her husband's household, is to bear sons. The perception that sons are the major source of economic security in old age is so strong in the north that many parents, while visiting their married daughters, do not accept food or other hospitality from them. However, given women's low independent incomes and lack of control over their earnings, few can provide economic support to their parents even if parents were willing to accept it.

In southern India, men are likely to marry women to whom they are related, so that the strict distinction found in the north between patrilineal and marital relatives is absent. Women are likely to be married into family households near their natal homes, and are more likely to retain close relationships with their natal kin. In the early decades, however, marriage patterns have changed markedly. Social, economic, and demographic developments have made marriages between close relatives less common, and the bride price has given way to a dowry system akin to that in the north. Nevertheless, as long as the underlying ethic of marriage in the south remains the reinforcement of existing kinship ties, the relatively favourable situation of southern Indian women is unlikely to be threatened.

A 1976 amendment to the Child Marriage Restraint Act raised the minimum legal age for marriage from 15 to 18 for young women and from 18 to 21 for young men. However, in many rural communities, illegal child marriages are still common. In some rural areas, nearly half the girls between 10 and 14 are married. Because there is pressure on women to prove their fertility by conceiving as soon as possible after marriage, adolescent marriage is synonymous with adolescent child-bearing: roughly 10-15 per cent of all births take place to women in their teens.

Although both Hindu and Muslim law recognise the rights of women and children to maintenance, in practice, maintenance is rarely set at a sufficient amount and is frequently violated. Both Hindu and Muslim personal laws fail to recognise matrimonial property. Upon divorce, women have no rights to their home or to other property accumulated during marriage; in effect, their contributions to the maintenance of the family and accumulation of family assets go unrecognised and unrewarded. Women's rights to inheritance are limited and frequently violated. In the mid-1950s the Hindu personal laws, which apply to all Hindus, Buddhists, Sikhs and Jains, were overhauled, banning polygamy and giving women rights to inheritance, adoption and divorce. The Muslim personal laws differ considerably from that of the Hindus, and permit polygamy. Despite various laws protecting women's rights, traditional patriarchal attitudes still prevail and are strengthened and perpetuated in the home. Under Hindu law, sons have an independent share in the ancestral property. However, daughters' shares are based on the share received by their father. Hence, a father can effectively disinherit a daughter by renouncing his share of the ancestral property, but the son will continue to have a share in his own right. Additionally, married daughters, even those facing marital harassment, have no residential rights in the ancestral home. Even the weak laws protecting women have not been adequately enforced. As a result, in practice, women continue to have little access to land and property, a major source of income and long-term economic security. Under the pretext of preventing fragmentation of agricultural holdings, several states have successfully excluded widows and daughters from inheriting agricultural land. The highest national priority must be the unleashing of woman power in governance. Through the experience of the Indian Panchayat Raj Institutions (PRI) 1 million women have actively entered political life in India.

The 73rd and 74th Constitutional Amendment Acts, which guarantee that all local elected bodies reserve one-third of their seats for women, have spearheaded an unprecedented social experiment which is playing itself out in more than 500,000 villages that are home to more than 600 million people. Since the creation of the quota system, local women–the vast majority of them illiterate and poor–have come to occupy as much as 43 per cent of the seats, spurring the election of increasing numbers of women at the district, provincial and national levels. Since the onset of PRI, the percentages of women in various levels of political activity have risen from 4-5 per cent to 25-40 per cent. Women leaders in the Panchayati Raj are transforming local governance by sensitising the State to issues of poverty, inequality and gender injustice. Through the PRI, they are tackling issues that had previously gone virtually unacknowledged, including water, alcohol abuse, education, health and domestic violence.

5.5. Non-implementation of Existing Safeguards

Despite the existence of constitutional, administrative and legal provisions to protect women from all communities, and specific provisions for women in the Scheduled Caste and Scheduled Tribes Act women of disadvantaged groups are vulnerable to gender-specific abuses such as rape, stripping and being paraded naked. AI found non-implementation of the provisions set up to protect these very women against such abuses and to enable them to take advantage of the criminal justice system.

5.5.1. The Appeal

Caste, class and gender discrimination prevents Dalit women from enjoying their basic human rights, particularly to dignity, equality and development. Atrocities and violence against Dalit women are both a means of sustaining systemic discrimination, as well as a reaction when particularly untouchability practices and caste norms are challenged or not adhered to. Before Dalit women can enjoy their human rights, and before the Millennium Development Goals can be achieved, discrimination, violence and impunity must stop.

5.6. Violation of Human Rights of Dalit Women

All human beings have the right to live as human beings. Human rights are not conferred or given. They already exist in society. The concept of human rights aims at protection of rights like right to life, liberty and property. These rights are attributed to human beings irrespective of class, caste, gender, colour and religion. The preamble of Indian constitution adequately empowers the central and state government to eliminate human rights violation in the country.

Inspite of these international and national declarations and resolutions, human rights are violated in different countries all over the world. In Indian society, due to the social barriers such as castetism, untouchability, patriarchy, disparity, superstition, religious exploitation and class variations, specific groups are becoming weaker and marginalised. These groups are facing the problems of identity crisis, deprivation, discrimination and atrocities. These marginalised groups are also identified and recognised as dalits, SC ST, OBC NT DT religious and linguistic minorities.

Violence on human beings in any form results in violation of human rights. Human rights of dalits and women in general are normally violated by high castes and powerful communities to practice and exhibit patriarchy and castetism. But human rights of dalit women are violated extremely and in peculiar form.

It is easy for the historically dominating caste and gender to violate human rights of dalit women who are at the lowest rung of the hierarchical ladder. The type of violence inflicted on dalits is in the form of severest violation of human rights.

The recent incident of Khairlanji Massacare is not something new. A dalit family had refused to let upper caste villagers built a road through their fields. Hence on September, 29th, 2006, Bhaiyalal Bhotmange's family, – wife Surekha, daughter Prinyanka and two sons were killed by the villagers of Khairlangi in Bhandra district of Maharashtra. Surekha and Priyanka were paraded naked and raped, and later, their bodies were mutilated and thrown into a pond.

This shows that dalit women are easy targets for any perpetrator Upper caste considers them to be sexually available. Hence they are largely unprotected by the state machinery. Further, there is prevalence of violence, making dalit women eat human excreta, parading them naked, gang- rape, murder, dacoity, robbery and burning of their huts or communities. These are the types of crime, which violate their human rights.

The main complaints of the poorer dalit women are that they have no good houses. In urban areas most of them stay in unhygienic slums and in rural areas their houses are away from main stream society. Under conditions of grinding poverty and severe exploitation at work place, dalit women also suffer caste specific ban on water access from upper castes and may be beaten up in their own houses as well.

At the outset, prevailing caste and secondary status of women in the society is largely responsible for violation of human rights of dalit women. To understand the root cause of the situation it is essential to examine basic factors responsible for their vulnerability.

First and foremost dalit women are victims of social, religious and cultural practices like Devdasis and Jogins. In the name of these practices, village girls are married to God by their helpless parents. These girls are then sexually exploited by the upper caste landlords and rich men and directed in to trafficking and prostitution. In his autobiography, Kale has described a ritual called 'chira'. The literal meaning of the word 'chira', is to cut or break. In this ritual when a girl from the lower caste community reaches the age of puberty, an elderly prestigious man from the higher caste breaks the hymen of the girl child by sexual act. The 28th report of SC/ST commission reported that in February 1986 there were about ten thousand Jogins belonging to SC in Nizamabad district of Andhra Pradesh. The survey submitted by the district collector to Schedule Caste Finance Corporation revealed prevalence of 15,850 cases. This data is just an example of one district of the country. Practices such as Chira, Jogins, Devdasi which are prevalent even today are harmful and threaten the dignity of dalit women and violate their human rights.

Low level of education is a problem in itself and in turn gives rise to many other problems. In 1991, literacy among the dalit women was indeed quite low. In rural areas only 19.46 percentage women were literate. A report published by Ministry of Welfare, Government of India in 1998 showed that there is much difference in the literacy rate of dalits and non-dalits in general, and gender specific. There is a large disparity in the literacy rate due to wide spread prejudice based on castetism and patriarchy against dalits and women in general and dalit women in particular.

A careful look at the economic situation of dalit women reveals that their work force structure is such that they rarely own any land. A large majority of them are agricultural labourers. About 90% of women working in unorganized sector are mainly from lower castes. In 1991, about 71% of dalit women workers in rural area were agricultural labourers. Only 19% of them owned land.

A prominent researcher and sociologist while sharing her experience from a research on gender and land issue, informed that, when she enquired with dalit women about land owned by them in their names, they wondered about permissibility of owning land in their name. This indicates that neither do they own any land nor are they aware of their rights on land. When enquiries were made with Stri-mukti sanghatana and Prerana, Mumbai based organizations working on the issue of rag picking and prostitution respectively, to ascertain the proportion of dalit women in these occupations, it was learnt that NGOs usually do not keep record of caste. These women have to face steep discrimination in the matters of social relation and employment due to their engagement in these occupations.

5.6.1. Crime against Dalit Women

Violence against women and girls is the most pervasive human rights violation in the world today. Opening the door on the subject of violence against the world's females is like standing at the threshold of an immense dark chamber vibrating with collective anguish, but with the sounds of protest throttled back to a murmur. Where there should be outrage aimed at an intolerable *status quo* there is instead denial, and the largely passive acceptance of 'the way things are.' Male violence against women is a worldwide phenomenon. Although not every woman has experienced it, and many expect not to, fear of violence is an important factor in the lives of most women. It determines what they do, when they do it, where they do it, and with whom.

Fear of violence is a cause of women's lack of participation in activities beyond the home, as well as inside it. Within the home, women and girls may be subjected to physical and sexual abuse as punishment or as culturally justified assaults. These acts shape their attitude to life, and their expectations of themselves. The insecurity outside the household is today the greatest obstacle in the path of women. Conscious that, compared to the atrocities outside the house, atrocities within the house are endurable, women not only continued to accept their inferiority in the house and society, but even called it sweet.

In recent years, there has been an alarming rise in atrocities against women in India. Every 26 minutes a woman is molested. Every 34 minutes a rape takes place. Every 42 minutes a sexual harassment incident occurs. Every 43 minutes a woman is kidnapped. And every 93 minutes a woman is burnt to death over dowry. One-quarter of the reported rapes involve girls under the age of 16 but the vast majority are never reported. Although the penalty is severe, convictions are rare. The most extreme expression of the preference for sons is female infanticide and sex-selective abortion. A study of amniocentesis in a Bombay hospital found that 96 per cent of female fetuses were aborted, compared with only a small percentage of male fetuses.

Government officials event suspect that the dispro-portionate abortion of female fetuses may be a major underlying cause of the recent decline in the nation's sex ratio. In 1971 there were 930 females for every 1,000 males. A decade later this figure had increased to 934, but by 1991, instead of continuing to rise, the ratio dropped to 927, lower than the 1971 figure. This sex ratio is one of the lowest in the world. Government has passed legislation to curb the misuse of amniocentesis for sex selection and abortion of female fetuses. Women activists have been critical of this act because of its provision that calls for punishing the women who seek the procedure. These women may be under pressure to bear a male child. Legal protection of women's rights have little effect in the face of prevailing patriarchal traditions. Exposure to and interactions with the outside world are instrumental in determining the possibilities available to women in their daily lives. The situation of women is affected by the degree of their autonomy or capacity to make decisions both inside and outside their own household.

Violence against women remains one of the most intractable violations of women's human rights. In various forms it persisted in times of peace as well as in times of conflict. The perpetrators were as likely to be private actors as public officials. Women were beaten in their homes by intimate partners; raped and otherwise sexually assaulted during times of internal conflict by soldiers; sexually assaulted by law enforcement personnel while in their custody; raped in refugee camps by other refugees, local police, or the military; and targeted for sexual violence based on their low social status.

De jure discrimination, as well as customary practices, often kept women in a subordinate status in their communities. This unequal status made them targets for sexual and domestic violence. The failure of judicial systems to investigate thoroughly and condemn acts of domestic and sexual violence against women further diminished and entrenched women's second-class status through impunity.

Women's complaints of domestic and sexual violence were often met with legal indifference and procedural and attitudinal obstacles. More often than not, it was government agents, in the form of local police, who were the first and most persistent obstacle tojustice for rape and domestic violence complaints. Police exercised undue and arbitrary authority regarding the types of complaints they accepted, and actively discouraged women from filing complaints—a pattern reported by women's advocates in other countries.

The pattern of bias against domestic violence victims extended to the judiciary. Women victims of domestic violence who were able to persuade the police to accept their cases for investigation were later hampered by judicial systems that valued family unity over the safety of women victims of domestic violence. For example, in Peru judges often referred married domestic violence victims and their batterers to counseling before charges could be laid against the accused, with the alleged batterer remaining in the home.

Rape victims in these countries fared just as poorly. They faced many of the same obstacles as victims of domestic violence. Police acted as gatekeepers and allowed their own stereotypes and biases about women's behavior or dress to jeopardize the investigation of cases. Often, women's complaints were met by disbelief and disregard for their privacy and security. Police skepticism toward rape cases compromised official investigations, effectively denying women's equality under the law.

Women's second-class status rendered them vulnerable to rape by intimate partners at home and by strangers on the street. In many countries, sexual violence against women carried no real probability of punishment or penalty, sending the message that these types of crimes were of no importance to the state. This acceptance of sexual violence against women was reflected and magnified elsewhere in times of national or regional unrest or civil strife, when women were targeted for rape as a continuation of the impunity for rape and sexual violence during times of peace. Sexual violence was perpetrated against women in times of conflict as a deliberate political policy of warring factions.

Whether civil unrest was directed at those groups believed to be financially better off or not a trusted part of the social fabric or at those perceived as vastly inferior and challenging the social hierarchy—as was the case of violence directed at lower castes in India—the women of these distinct groups suffered the same fate: sexual assault.

In some instances, socially determined characteristics such as caste affiliation rendered women more vulnerable to rape. In India, despite protective legislation, attacks against members of the lower castes continued to go unpunished. Sexual abuse and otherforms of violence by high-caste men against lower-caste women have historically been a means of maintaining socio-economic divisions in India.

Upper-caste men, landlords, and the police have physically and sexually abused Dalit ("untouchable") women to suppress movements to demand payment of minimum wages, settle sharecropping disputes, or reclaim lost land. Cases of such abuse were documented by Human Rights Watch in 1998. Dalit women were targeted on the basis of both their sex and their caste. They are thought to be available for sexual abuse, and their occupations in agriculture or as prostitutes put them in frequent contact with men who can rape them with impunity. While women all over India found the criminal justice system unsympathetic to sexual assault, Dalit women also confronted officials who were hostile to their low caste status.

Women who suffered sexual and other physical abuse in custody at the hands of government agents were perhaps the most invisible and the most vulnerable, as their abusers held positions of authority and public trust. Governments as diverse as the United States and India repeatedly turned a blind eye to the abuses that those acting under cover of authority were committing. In India, attacks on Dalit women during massacres, police raids, and caste clashes were on the rise in 1998.

As untouchables, Dalit women constituted the majority of prostitutes and landless workers and thus came into frequent contact with law enforcement officials. In Tamil Nadu, for example, women were the primary targets during a February 26 police raid on Dalit villages in the aftermath of clashes between Dalit and middle-caste communities. Police also engaged in instances of "hostage-taking" wherein women were arrested and tortured as a means of punishing their absconding male relatives and forcing them to surrender.

5.6.1.1. Case of Rajastan

Rajasthan has a feudal and patriarchal society where caste divisions are still very strong. The dominant land owning castes continue to wield significant power in all walks of life. The incidents of atrocities and caste-based discriminations on Dalits are increasing day by day in

Rajasthan because of growing awareness and assertiveness of the Dalits.

In Rajasthan, despite existence of very stringent acts and constitutional provisions it is very rare that the culprits are punished under the law of the land. Most of the incidents of the crime against the Dalits go unreported because of the fear of reprisal and the refusal to register the cases of the Dalit atrocities.

Violence against Dalits is normally treated as a very minor and marginal issue, even by the law-enforcement machinery, whether be it police, the prosecution, or the medicolegal fraternity or often even the judiciary.

Non-registration of crimes against Dalits is general problem especially in Rajasthan. Political influence over the police, and caste, class, religion and gender biases are rampant. It is extremely difficult for helpless Dalits to file complaints, particularly against the powerful individuals and or perpetrators. Dalits are so aligned and dependant economically on upper castes that they are afraid even to think of lodging a complaint under the SC/ST (Prevention of Atrocity) Act 1989, because of the adverse consequences, which they anticipate.

In a rape case of Dalit woman, in Dovsa district of Rajasthan, the Medical Officer refused to medically examine the rape victim and suggested her to take bath and come for medical examination. This was intentionally done by the Medical officer to dilute and deviate the evidence and to favour the perpetrators.

In another rape case in Jaipur district of Rajasthan, the local police deliberately omitted the correct version of the complainant in the FIR. On the basis of this manipulated FIR, all the culprits and the perpetrators got released on bail. The case was made very weak and could not stand any scrutiny.

The state government totally failed to provide legally entitled monetary relief to the rape victims belonging to the SC and ST communities even after lodging the FIR and medical examination.

In another incident of Chakwada village, only 50 kms away from the capital Jaipur, there even today dalits are not allowed to take bath in public water tank at the place reserved for privileged classes. On 14 Dec 2001 a Dalit youth named Babu Lal Bairwa asserted his legal right and dared to take bath on the berths (ghats) meant for upper caste people. Branding the act of the Babu Lal Bairwa as revolt at the whole village local body (Panchayat) consisting of upper caste, imposed a fine of Rs. 51,000 on the whole Dalit community to whom Babu Lal Bairwa belongs. Moreover, a mob of privileged classes, surrounded Babu Lal's house shouted abuses and called for a blood bath.

Dalit community ultimately lodged a FIR with the local police and refused to pay the fine imposed on them by the local upper caste families. The Dalits thereafter submitted a petition before the State Human /rights Commission and the Chief Minister and the district administration for ensuring their safety and justice. But till date no justice has been ensured to the Dalits on the contrary the entire Dalit community have been socially and economically boycotted.

Even the State Human Rights Commission has closed the case without fully exhausting all the possible remedies and therefore failed in their duty to not only protect but promote the rights of the dalits to life and security.

The Dalits of Chakwada village are still facing social boycott, harassment and are insecure due to constant threat on their life and security. The state administration, police as well as the district administration have turned a blind eye to these continuing violations. At the root of most of these cases of torture and humiliation, is the refusal of the so called upper castes to grant them access to land, water, housing, decent or minimum wage and the dalits demand of leading life of human dignity.

In Rajasthan, millions of acres of cultivable government land have been encroached upon and usurped by the upper castes who had earlier been feudal landlord. From another side, the newly powerful, that is the bureaucrats, politicians and their family members have occupied another large chunk of government land. Caught between these two elements, Dalits are fast loosing even a few cents of land they have acquired over the years to these two sets of groups and are forced to migrate to cities and other states.

Rajasthan has also openly flouted the affirmative action in the matter of reservation and promotion of SC and ST employees and the government/ public undertaking and particularly in teaching professions.

These are not just isolated incidents in Rajasthan but are indicative of the nature and frequency of the insecurity and torture. Dalit women and men face as they try to lead a humane life. The Dalits are beginning to lead a life of dignity refusing to do unclean occupations and have their own access to livelihood without undue dependency on upper caste landed gentry. This discrimination by the state is aggressively fuelled by the attitudes within the civil society, which are doing their best to block all efforts of Dalits to lead a life of dignity and self-esteem.

5.6.1.2. Case of Tamil Nadu

In Tamil Nadu, due to the Hindu hierarchical caste system which practices the concept of purity and impurity considers Dalit women as impure. The fundamentalists trying to promote Hindutuva are imposing the Brahminical values through rituals to maintain the caste system. Caste discrimination is a form of discrimination based on descent. Dalit women discriminated, are facing multiple oppression on the basis of work and descent. The discriminations determined by birth, violates the Economic, Political, Social and Cultural Civic rights of Dalit Women. Dalit Women are deprived section and the lowest level of Economic and Educational Structures. They are poor, illiterate, Sexually harassed, faces state, caste violences and exploited.

Dalit women constitute 16.3% in the total population. 18% of Dalit Women live in rural areas. After the unpaid hard Domestic work, they continue to toil in the hot sun as a wage earner. Dalit Women undertake manual, low paid tedious, time consuming work. They get low pay, less than an U.S. Dollar. They walk miles to fetch drinking water. They live in huts, denied of basic amenities such as sanitation, light, water. They work in building construction, carry heavy loads, work in brick kiln from early morning till evening. They are employed as casual labourers in laying roads with hot thar in the burning sun without sandals and without any protection. They carry heavy loads, heavily burdened to collect fodder, fuel, water for everyday consumption. They do all kinds of inferior and menial jobs. Dalit women are bonded, they are abused, sexually exploited by other caste humiliated and are easy target of insult. They work more than the bullocks and men. Bullocks and men work in a hectare in a year for

1064 hours and 1202, but women work for more than 3485 hours. The caste and the patriarchal norms legitimises the poor Economic conditions of Dalit women. She had to work to survive. She is resourceless / powerless and has no access to resources.Dalit Women are working in manual scavenging, removing excreta, cleaning sewage, sweeping which are humiliating, degrading and discriminatory.

The process globalisation also affected Dalit Women. Dalit Women are unemployed due to introductions mechanization for harvesting and transplanting. Cash crops, Horticulture has been introduced by big Agro business corporations for export and Dalit Women lost the land the common resources in the village even small things like green, fish, shells from fields which are collected freely are not available any more. Dalit Women are forced into sex trade to earn for their families. The globalisation process has affected Dalit Women in every sphere of their lives.

Dalit Women are deprived of health services. The health services are denied and the life expectancy of Dalit Women are only 50 years. The infant mortality rate is 90 / 100.000. The sex ratio of Dalit Women is 922 / 1000 as against 927 / 1000 in India. Dalit women suffer with prolapsed uteruses. They are malnourished and anemic. They work in Agriculture, bending throug - out creates back pain, skin irritation due to excessive use of pesticides. They suffer with soars in the toes. Most of them have infectious diseases, especially cervical cancer with white discharges. The government Birth Control Schemes targets Dalit Women. They are forced to sterilize and tested on new contraceptives - like guinea pigs. They are forced to use long acting harmonal dangerous contraceptives. They do not get basic medical facilities. The pregnant Dalit women are turned away from Government hospitals for Doctors refuse to conduct delivery on Dalit Women.

More and more girl children from Dalit cômmunities are school drop-outs and working as child labourers. Dalit Women illiterate because they have less access to education which is inherent part of the caste system. There are not enough facilities to educate, insecurity, taking care of small children, joining the adults to add to the income of the family. Dalit girl children are involved mostly in hazardous work like Beedi making, match factories and in making crackers. The fear of paying dowry and the fear of sending the girls to schools which are usually in distant places deprives them of education. Ex. Nirma Rani a Dalit girl student was slapped for saying Namaste to a Brahmin teacher and her father was beaten up later for questioning such act. Caste is practised in schools where Dalit children occupy separate seats given to them. Dhanam lost her eye, she was beaten up by her teacher for taking drinking water by herself without waiting for the other caste follow to serve her from the pot. Due to lack of uniform, school books, special fees, walking miles everyday, limits Dalit girl children to avail education.

Dalit Women are excluded from decision making. They are not in a position to exercise their power. They are brutally attacked. The 73rd amendment allow Dalit Women to be elected to local Government. They are elected but not able to exercise their power. Menaka (a Dalit Women a village Panjayet President) was killed in Day light. Ranganayaki was de throned for solemnising an inter - caste marriage. Banwari was gang raped when she objected and reported to the authorities against child marriage in her village. Gowri was made to parade nakedly for hoisting flag on independence day. Dalit women are militant and powerful. They are fighting for political power within this caste system.

There is an 8% of sharp increase in the crime against women especially on Dalit Women says the report from SC /ST commission.In 1991 more than 2 million women are raped and majority are from Dalits and Tribal community. Dalit women are murdered, gang raped, molested, sexually harassed and auctioned for sex trade. Three Dalit women are raped every day and are victims of caste riots. They are continuously facing violence and atrocities

The provision of civil Rights Act and prevention of untouchability Act have not been implemented to control the atrocities and violence against Dalit Women. Dalit Women were brutally attacked, genitals mutilated and caused miscarriages by police forces whenever Dalit Women approach the police for help.

1st December 1998, police batallion numbering 300 entered Dalit colony in 18 vehicles, mercilesly beaten up the women, men with iron rods lathies and butts of guns. Women were assaulted abused with filthy unsavory words. A Dalit Woman lost her feotus the one she conceived after 15 years.

Mathamma practice, a violation of Dalit Women's Rights. Dalit women are discriminated and treated untouchables. The shoemakers Arunthathiar practice Mathamma, dedicating Dalit girl children to their goddess Mathamma. Due to medical services, people go to Mathamma temples believing that the goddess has healing power when the Dalit girl is sick. she is taken to the temple and left their till her sickness is cured. Economic situation is also a reason that Dalits are not able to spend money to buy good health service. Once the child is cured, the child is named after mathamma and married to goddess with the 'Pottu Thali' (wedlock). After she becomes a dancer she belongs to the temple. During temple festivals she dances and earns her livelihood. She is not treated with respect but in public humiliated by men who harass her sexually. The team which plays music with her exploit her by having a sharing in what she earns. Once the girl is married to mathamma she cannot marry others to lead a family life. Men take her as partner, exploit her and leave her with a child. Mathammas has no family, no security, left all alone with a child to struggle for life long to maintain herself. Mathammas end up into sex trade and most of them suffer with infectious diseases like HIV/AIDS.

5.7. Protection of Dalit Women's Rights

With the realization that violence is one of the potent threats to the peaceful existence of human beings, whole hearted and all round efforts are made at international, national and local level. The preamble to the Universal Declaration of Human Rights (UDHR) serves as a foundation and philosophy of Human rights.

The World Conference Against Racism (WCAR) related to racial discrimination, xenophobia and intolerance held in Durban, South Africa in 2001, brought the issue of caste and untouchability based discrimination on the agenda of UN Conference in Durban. Among the several organisations, the National Campaign on Dalit Human Rights (NCDHR) – a collective of dalit NGOs, other NGOs, academicians', activists and large number of supporters spearheaded the national campaign in India for inclusion of the issue of caste and untouchability based discrimination in the Durban Conference. Based on this article Protection of Civil Rights Act' (PCR), was passed in 1955. However, there was no conviction/ under this Act hence, Thirtyfour years after the introduction of PCR Act, the Scheduled

Caste and Schedule Tribes Act 1989 was enacted to bring various forms of atrocities to an end. In this Act the complainant is given more weightage. There are stringent provisions against the police for negligence.

5.7.1. Formation of Dalit Women's Organisations

The focus on education of low caste women is one of the important factors responsible for the emerging identity of Dalit women. Reformist intervention by Savitribai and Mahatma Phule of opening school for untouchable girls way back in 1848 was a turning point for changing status of dalit women. His movement and especially his organisations encouraged many dalit women to become educated to be active in public life and to gain leadership, self respect in the contemporary period encouraged women to participate in organisation for dalit women at regional, state and national level.

After independence in 1960's and 70's, the dalit movement and women's movement emerged to demand their rights against caste and gender respectively. However, specific problems of dalit women were not acknowledged by these movements. Hence in 1990's there were several special, independent and autonomous assertions of dalit women's identity; a case in point is the formation of National Federation for Dalit Women (NFDW) and All India Dalit Women's Forum (AIDWF) at the state level. The Maharashtra Dalit Mahila Sanghatana (MDMS) was formed in 1995. A year earlier, the women's wing of Bhartiya Republican Party (BRP) and the Bahujan Mahila Sangha (BMS) was set up the Bahujan Mahila Parishad. In December 1996, at Chandrapur, a Vikas Vanchit Dalit Mahila Parishad (VVDMP) was organised and a proposal to commemorate 25th December as Bhartiya Smriti Divas was advanced. The Christi Mahila Sanghatana, an organisation of Dalit Christian Women was established in 1997.

Several efforts have been made since independence to secure human rights of women in general and dalit women in particular. Despite this, human rights of dalit women are seen to be violated in different forms. Such infringement of human rights echoes the need of evolving suitable mechanism to empower dalit women to assert for equal rights and justice in order to live a dignified life.

5.7.2. Strengthening The Capacity Of Dalit Women

To be human is to respond to human sufferings and pain with compassion and effective concern. It is not enough to feel with the dalit women in their pain, There is more need for effective action, otherwise it would be just sentimentalism' says Sequeira in his article 'Human Response to Dalit Women. The needs and the problems of dalit women differ with city, village, area and caste. Therefore to recognise the system and to prohibit violation, first and foremost proper perspectives about the issues has to be developed among all by considering following suggestions:

5.7.2.1. Awareness for assertion

Extensive reading of available literature can be done by young generation to understand the profile and problems of dalit women. Factual incidents & success stories of dalit women namely, 'We made History Too' by Meenakshi Moon & Urmila Pawar can be included in the educational texts.

5.7.2.2. Access and exposure visits

Special exposure visits to dalit localities can be organised for school and college students to assess basic amenities accessible to dalit women namely, water, electricity, health and hygiene. Similarly dalit women's visit to urban structured colonies can be arranged to impress upon the importance of standard of living of non-dalits.

5.7.2.3. Academic activities

Academic institutions need to be encouraged to undertake studies to assess the problems of violence and atrocities against dalit women as also the reasons therefore and to work out ways to overcome them.

5.7.2.4. Campaigns and sessions

Campaigns for equal and rational distribution of natural resources among weaker sections can be organised to secure their rightful means of livelihood.

5.7.2.5. Inclusion of dalit women in various system

More dalit women in their population proportion (16.5% SC, 7.5% ST) should be given chance to enter in the system like police, judiciary, education, health and politics. Sessions can be organised for dalit activist and women activists to sensitize them about the magnitude of torture and oppression faced by the dalit women.

References

Bhai, N. *Harijan Women in Independent India*. Delhi: BR Publishing 1986.

Jain, P.C., Jain Shashi & Bhatnagar, Sudha *Scheduled Caste Women* [Muzaffarnagar District, UP]. Jaipur: Rawat 1997.

Jeffery, P. *et al*. Contaminating states: midwifery, childbearing and the state in rural North India. In H. Afshar (ed.) *Women, State and Ideology*. Basingstoke: Macmillan 1987.

Karlekar, M. *Poverty and Women's Work: a Study of Sweeper Women in Delhi*. Delhi: Vikas 1982.

6

Economic Exclusion of Dalits

In much of South Asia and India in particular, caste has become coterminous with race in the definition and exclusion of distinct population groups because of their descent. For one hundred and sixty million Dalits or 'untouchables' at the bottom of India's caste system – a population on par with that of Russia or Brazil – the exclusion extends to the economic realms of wages, jobs, education, and land.

Dalits are denied access to land, forced to work in degrading conditions, and routinely abused at the hands of the police and of higher-caste groups that enjoy the state's protection. In what has been called India's "hidden apartheid," entire villages in many Indian states remain completely segregated by caste. Untouchability endures as a cover for exploitative economic relationships and the caste system survives a cruel and efficient economic order. Under constitutional provisions and various laws, the state grants Dalits a certain number of privileges, including reservations in education, government jobs, and government bodies.

The government has also attempted to increase the self-sufficiency of the scheduled-castepopulation through financial assistance for self-employment activities and through development programs designed to increase education and skills. Development measures for the educational, social, and economic uplifting of scheduled castes are administered by the Department of Welfare.

Despite this large body of legislation and administrative agency mandates assigned exclusively to deal with the plight of scheduled castes, the laws have benefited few and, due to a lack of political will, development programs and welfare projects designed to improve economic conditions for Dalits have generally had little effect. Upper-caste threats of physical abuse and social boycotts for refusing to perform demeaning tasks also ensure preservation of the economic status quo.

Any strategy to combat racial discrimination against Dalits must begin with a meaningful understanding of the economics of exclusion. This chapter sets out to describe the links between racial and economic discrimination against Dalits in India, and the violent and degrading mechanisms by which each is sustained and institutionalised. It argues that the government's longstanding failure to enforce its own protective legislation or implement strategies to narrow the socio-economic gap between Dalits and the rest of the population has only been exacerbated by India's economic reforms.

6.1. Caste and Employment Discrimination

Allocation of labour on the basis of caste is one of the fundamental tenets of the caste system. In traditional Indian society, Hinduism's fourfold *varna* theory describes a broad functional division of labour. For those within the four principal caste categories, caste has not proved to be a completely rigid system.

For Dalits, however, who occupy the fifth and lowest caste category, caste remains a determinative factor for the attainment of social, political, civil, and economic rights. A lack of training and education, as well as discrimination in seeking other forms of employment, have kept these traditions and their hereditary nature alive.

Many 'untouchable' community members, for example, continue to work as leather workers, disposers of dead animals, and manual scavengers. As part of village custom, Dalits are made to render free services in times of death, marriage, or any village function. The cleaning of the whole village, the digging of graves, the carrying of firewood, and the disposal of dead animals are also tasks that Dalits are made to perform. Those in urban areas, work mostly in the unorganised sector. India's much touted system of affirmative action or reservations for scheduled castes assists less than 1 percent of the Dalit population. In all forms of labour, women are consistently paid less than men, compounding the dual discrimination of caste and gender.

6.2. Manual Scavenging

According to government statistics, an estimated one million Dalits are manual scavengers who clear faeces from public and private latrines and dispose of dead animals; unofficial estimates are much higher. Manual scavenging is a caste-based occupation, deemed too polluting and filthy for anyone but Dalits. Manual scavengers exist under different caste names throughout the country, such as the Bhangis in Gujarat, the Pakhis in Andhra Pradesh, and the Sikkaliars in Tamil Nadu. Using little more than a broom, a tin plate, and a basket, they are made to clear faeces from public and private latrines and carry them to dumping grounds and disposal sites. Though long outlawed, the practice of manual scavenging continues in most states.

Poverty among Bhangis is so acute, that some have even been known to separate nondigested wheat from buffalo dung to make chappatis. When interviewed in early 1998, thirty-year-old Parsotambhai, a mother of three in Ahmedabad district, Gujarat, earned Rs.10 a month for each house she cleaned. She also received small amounts of food once a day and complained that there was too much work.

The Employment of Manual Scavengers and Construction of Dry Latrines Act, 1993 prohibits the employment of scavengers or the construction of dry latrines with imprisonment for up to one year and/ or a fine as high as Rs.2,000. Offenders are also liable for prosecution under the Scheduled Castes and Scheduled Tribes Act, 1989.

In 1992, the government launched a national scheme that called for the identification, training, and rehabilitation of safai karamcharis throughout the country. Yet when confronted with the existence of manual scavenging and dry latrines within their jurisdiction, state governments often deny their existence altogether or claim that a lack of water supply prevents states from constructing flush latrines. This despite the fact that a sum of Rs.4,640,000,000 was allocated to the scheme under the government's Eighth Five-Year Plan.

6.3. Landless Agricultural Labourers

Most Dalit victims of abuse are landless agricultural labourers who form the backbone of India's agrarian economy. Despite a host of land reform legislation, today over eighty-six per cent of Dalit households are landless or near landless.

Lack of access to land makes Dalits economically vulnerable; their dependency is exploited by upper- and middle-caste landlords and allows for many abuses to go unpunished. Landless agricultural labourers throughout the country work for a few kilograms of rice or Rs.15 to Rs.35 a day, well below the minimum wage prescribed in their state. Many labourers owe debts to their employers or other moneylenders. Land reform and increased wages for rural labourers are the central demands of most leftist guerrilla organisations active in West Bengal, Bihar, and Andhra Pradesh. Private landlord militias and state security forces have targeted civilians thought to be guerrilla sympathisers. In Bihar in particular, guerrillas enjoy Dalit support, as most of the Dalit community lives on the edge of starvation. Laws and regulations that prohibit alienation of Dalit lands, set ceilings on a single landowner's holdings, or allocate surplus government lands to scheduled castes and scheduled tribes have been largely ignored, or worse, manipulated by upper castes with the help of district administrations.

In 1996, a door-to-door survey of two hundred and fifty villages in the state of Gujarat found that in almost all villages those who had title to land had no possession, and those who had possession had not had their land measured or faced illegal encroachments from upper castes. Many had no record of their holdings at all. Efforts by Dalits to acquire land through the land reforms are met with social boycotts ostracising them from buying or selling anything in the village. These boycotts and other retaliatory acts are described further below.

6.4. Bonded Labour

Given the insignificant amounts of remuneration in manual scavenging, agricultural labour, and other fields of Dalit employment, it comes as little surprise that many families borrow money from their upper-caste neighbours and consequently go into bondage.

An estimated forty million people in India, among them fifteen million children, are bonded labourers working in slave-like conditions in order to pay off a debt. Bonded labour refers to work in slave-like conditions in order to pay off a debt. Bonded labourers are frequently low-caste, illiterate, and extremely poor, while the creditors/employers are usually higher-caste, literate, comparatively wealthy, and relatively more powerful members of the community.

The Bonded Labour System Act, 1976 abolishes all agreements and obligations arising out of the bonded labour system. It aims to release all labourers from bondage, cancel any outstanding debt, prohibit the creation of new bondage agreements, and order the economic rehabilitation of freed bonded labourers by the state. It also punishes attempts to compel persons into bondage with a maximum of three years in prison and a Rs.2,000 fine. A lack of political will, and outright abuse of the law has also sabotaged any meaningful implementation of protective criminal legislation, affirmative action quotas, or the constitutional promise of universal primary education.

6.5. Education and Reservations

The Indian Constitution mandates the state to provide free, compulsory and universal education for all children up to fourteen years, with special care and consideration given to promote the educational progress of scheduled castes. India's policy of reservations is an attempt by the central government to remedy past injustices related to low-caste status. To allow for proportional representation in certain state and federal institutions, the constitution reserves 22.5 per cent of seats in federal government jobs, state legislatures, the lower house of parliament, and educational institutions for scheduled castes and scheduled tribes. The literacy gap between Dalits and the rest of the population fell a scant.39 percent between 1961 and 1991. Ninety-nine per cent of Dalit students are enrolled in government schools that lack basic infrastructure, classrooms, teachers and teaching aids.

Despite state assistance in primary education, Dalits also face an alarming dropout rate. According to the National Commission for Scheduled Castes and Scheduled Tribes' 1996-97 and 1997-98 Report, the national dropout rate for Dalit children was a staggering 49.35 per cent at the primary level, 67.77 per cent for middle school, and 77.65 per cent for secondary school. Though these rates are partly attributable to the need for Dalit children to supplement their family wages through labour, more insidious and less well-documented are the loss of faith in education as an instrument for socio-economic change, and the discriminatory and abusive treatment faced by Dalit children, who often sit in the back of classrooms, at the hands of their teachers and fellow students.

The National Commission for Scheduled Castes and Scheduled Tribes' report also indicates that of the total scheduled caste reservation quota in the Central Government, fifty-four per cent remains unfilled. More than eighty-eight per cent remains unfilled in the public sector and forty-five per cent in state banks. Though they represented only five per cent of the population in 1989, Brahmins comprised seventy per cent of the Class I officers in governmental services. At universities, upper-castes occupy ninety per cent of the teaching posts in the social sciences and ninety-four per cent in the sciences, while Dalit representation is a lowly 1.2 and 0.5 percent, respectively.

6.6. Physical and Economic Retaliation

A principal weapon in sustaining economic and racial discrimination against Dalits is the use of social and economic boycotts and acts of retaliatory violence. Dalits are physically abused and threatened with economic and social ostracism from the community for refusing to carry out various caste-based tasks. Dalit communities as a whole are summarily punished for individual transgressions; Dalits are cut off from community land and employment during social boycotts, women bear the brunt of physical attacks, and the letter of the law is rarely enforced.

Large-scale clashes between caste communities in Tamil Nadu's southern districts in recent years, for example, have often been triggered by Dalits' efforts to draw water from a "forbidden" well or by their refusal to perform a delegated task. The boycott is reinforced when the village council levies fines against caste Hindus who refuse to participate in it. In villages in Karnataka state, for example, upper castes have been known to fine Rs.501 for giving employment to Dalits during a social boycott.

Despite their appalling work conditions, even manual scavengers are unable to demand higher wages or sanitary instruments for use in the collection of human excreta. Since the early 1990s, violence against Dalits has escalated dramatically in response to growing Dalit rights movements. Between 1995 and 1997, a total of 90,925 cases were registered with the police nation-wide as crimes and atrocities against scheduled castes. Of these 1,617 were for murder, 12,591 for hurt, 2,824 for rape, and 31,376 for offences listed under the Prevention of Atrocities Act. Given that Dalits are both reluctant and unable to report crimes against the ı selves, the actual number of abuses is presumably much higher.

India's National Commission for Scheduled Castes and Scheduled Tribes has reported that these cases typically fall into one of three categories: cases relating to the practice of 'untouchability' and attempts to defy the social order; cases relating to land disputes and demands for minimum wages; and cases of atrocities by police and forest officials. The differences lie in the considerable amount of leverage that the higher-caste Hindus or non-Dalits are able to wield over local police, district administrations, and even the state government.

The state's failure to prosecute atrocities against Dalits is well illustrated by its manipulation of the Scheduled Castes and Scheduled Tribes Act. Enacted in 1989, the Act provides for stiffer punishments for abuses against members of scheduled castes and scheduled tribes. Its enactment represented an acknowledgement on the part of the government that abuses, in their most degrading and violent forms, were still perpetrated against Dalits decades after independence.

The potential of the Scheduled Castes and Scheduled Tribes Act, 1989, to bring about social change, however, has been hampered by police corruption and caste bias, with the result that many allegations are not entered in police books. Ignorance of procedures and a lack of knowledge of the act have also affected its implementation. Some state governments dominated by higher castes have even attempted to repeal the legislation altogether.

6.7. The Impact of Economic Reforms

The impact of India's aggressive shift from a state regulated economy to a market economy with the privatisation of industries and the liquidation of policies and controls in economic planning and regulation has been most acutely felt by Dalits.

Since 1991, the start of India's New Economic Policy, the country has made astounding progress in the areas of technology, infrastructure, machinery, science, space and even nuclear research. Much of this progress has meant little to Dalits; most continue to live without the very basic amenities of electricity, sanitation, and safe drinking water.

According to the Madras Institute for Development Studies, only thirty-one per cent of Dalit households are equipped with electricity, as compared to sixty-one per cent on non-Dalit households. Only ten per cent of Dalit households have sanitation facilities as compared to twenty-seven per cent of non-Dalit ones. Disparities in distribution are not accidental. 'Untouchability' is reinforced by state allocation of facilities; separate facilities are provided for separate colonies. Dalits often receive the poorer of the two, if they receive any at all. In many villages, the state administration installs electricity, sanitation facilities, and water pumps in the upper-caste section, but neglects to do the same in the neighbouring, segregated Dalit colony. Available statistics reveal that between 1987 and 1993, the percentage of Dalits living below the poverty line actually increased by five percent, reversing a declining trend of the previous fifteen years. Half of the Dalit population lived below the poverty line in 1993 compared to a third of the general population.

As liberalisation leads to a capital-intensive mode of production requiring a greater proportion of highly skilled workers to manage automated production processes, a large migration of unskilled labour to the agricultural sector has led to lower wages for agricultural workers as a whole. Eighty-five percent of India's Dalit population lives in rural areas and is directly associated with agriculture and cultivation. In addition to a reduction in agricultural subsidies, Dalits are also affected by the increased acquisition of coastal lands by multinationals for aquaculture projects. Dalits are the main labourers and tenants of coastal land areas and are increasingly being forced to leave these areas as foreign investment rises.

A reduction in the budget and fiscal deficit, devaluation, privatisation, the elimination or reduction in subsidies, and export promotion have also all contributed to inflation. As is true the world over, inflation hits the poorest the hardest. With most of their earnings spent on food, shelter, and clothing, any rise in prices has had a direct negative effect on Dalits' level of consumption. A lack of purchasing power is compounded by the devaluation of currency. The devaluation, aimed at increasing exports and creating more markets for domestic industries, has also led to a rise in prices for general essential imports.

With the underlying economic philosophy of increased reliance on market forces, a dismantling of controls, and a drastically reduced role of the state, the public sector is shrinking. The reservations model is therefore affecting fewer people, inasmuch as government-related jobs are being drastically reduced. Reservations in educational institutions and scholarships for Dalit students represent a critical component in Dalit socio-economic development. Economic reforms have also led to a freezing in grants to many institutions. The privatisation of social services is also turning education and health services into commodities only affordable to the rich.

6.8. Strategies to Combat Discrimination

The exploitation of agricultural labourers and the rigid assignment of demeaning occupations on the basis of caste keep Dalits in a position of economic and physical vulnerability. The triple burden of caste, class, and gender effectively ensures that Dalit women are the furthest removed from legal protections.

Dalits' status as an excluded caste of landless labourers has also made them particularly vulnerable to the global economic forces unleashed by India's economic reforms.

New steps are also required at the national and international level to give effect to international standards on racism in the areas of criminal justice and public administration. The International Convention on the Elimination of All Forms of Racial Discrimination requires remedial action whenever there is a racist effect from public policy, but many states interpret their obligations to combat racism as limited to addressing racist intent.

In India's case, the government must make available to the public government studies on issues affecting Dalits. Specifically, the government should release the white paper on reservations and the white paper on land reform. In particular, attention should be given to implementation of reservations in all ministries, in the secretariats of the Prime Minister and President, and in the police and judiciary. The second outlines the extent to which tenancy acts and acts that establish ceilings on single landowners' holdings have been implemented in all states.

In upholding constitutional guarantees of equality, freedom, justice and human dignity, it must then commit to: land and wage reform and the realisation of primary education for all children; implement measures designed to ensure that states abolish the practice of 'untouchability,' in compliance with Article 17 of the Constitution; prevent further violence and prosecute both state and private actors responsible for caste-motivated attacks on Dalit communities; enforce the Scheduled Castes and Scheduled Tribes Act, 1989 and other relevant legislation; and educate state agents and the Indian population on the rights and constitutional freedoms of all citizens.

The government must also fill all vacant scheduled-caste reservation posts with Dalit candidates, and as recommended by the National Commission for Scheduled Castes and Scheduled Tribes, provide for reservations in the judiciary as well as the private sector, which continues to enjoy government patronage in terms of concessional land, financing, and excise and sales tax relief.

At the global level, a first and essential step is the recognition that caste-based discrimination bars hundreds of millions from the exercise of their civil and political, and their economic, social, and cultural rights – a precondition for international programs to support the abolition of caste discrimination and to remedy abuses.

The World Bank and other international lending institutions operational in India should ensure that anti-discrimination measures are built into World Bank and Asian Development Bank-funded projects in areas where the problems of caste violence and caste discrimination are severe. Of paramount importance is for the World Bank to ensure that its funds are not being routed by the government for the illegal employment of manual scavengers in their sanitation programs. Lending geared toward the promotion of privatisation must first evaluate and then counter the damage to social services resulting from an erosion of the public sector.

India's donors and trading partners must encourage India to implement its own laws and must use every opportunity to raise the problem of caste violence both publicly and privately, at Consultative Group meetings and in meetings with relevant officials. They must also work to develop programs and strategies for bilateral and multilateral aid programs to India that would make funds available to promote legal literacy and economic rehabilitation programs.

United Nations agencies active in India must also pay particular attention to the issue of caste violence and caste discrimination and develop programs and strategies designed to curb abuse and encourage accountability.

References

Bharti, I. Bihar's most wretched, *Economic & Political Weekly* Sept 22, 1990: 2124-25.

Chalam, K.S. Caste and economic reform, *Seminar* 471, Nov. 1998: 33-37.

D'Souza, V. An operational definition of backward groups in India, *Indian Journal of Agricultural Economics* 13, 1958; 33-45.

Galanter, M. Pursuing equality. An assessment of India's policy of compensatory discrimination for disadvantaged groups. In D.K. Basu & R. Sisson (eds) *Social and Economic Development in India*. New Delhi: Sage 1986.

7

Dalits and Social Security

Dalits constitute 16.2% of the total population of the country. Eighty one per cent of the Dalits live in rural areas and mostly depend on work in the primary sector, agriculture, forestry, animal husbandry, and fishing. Many of the customary practices like drum beating, washing, hair cutting, load carrying, weaving, basket making, manual scavenging, traditional birth attendant, sweeping, messengers, domestic servants, cleaning and sweeping, cleaning dead animals, cow rearing, forest produce collection and processing, bamboo and cane work, rope making, stone works, farming, trolley and rickshaw pulling, brick making, etc. are also done by Dalits in rural areas.

Dalit workers are doubly discriminated against: first, as a worker of the unorganized sector and secondly as a member of a socially discriminated group. Dalit workers face untouchability and discrimination at the workplace both by employers and fellow workers of upper caste communities. The occupations where scheduled castes are employed should be brought within the ambit of labour legislations like Minimum Wage Act and social security coverage to provide protection for wages and working conditions.

As per 1991 census 49.06% of Scheduled Castes are agricultural labourers, compared to 19.66% belonging to other categories, which by itself is sufficient to establish the wide gap in economic status between the two. This is largely because the scheduled castes have very poor access to land and even when they are recorded as cultivators, many of them cultivate land as tenants or share croppers and have very small area of land to operate. Nearly 75% of scheduled castes primarily depend on agriculture for employment. Land and wage are the major reasons for atrocities against Dalits in rural area. This increase was observed in all heads except Dacoity, Robbery and cases under Protection of Civil Rights Act.

The National Human Rights Commission on its report on Prevention of Atrocities against Scheduled Caste recommended that cases of violence against SCs resulting from nonpayment of minimum wage should be brought within the ambit of section-3 of the SC/ ST (PoA) Act-1989 and should merit higher punishment than what is admissible under the minimum wage Act. Dalit unorganized workers are more prone to untouchability and caste discrimination by employers, and certain occupations are being denied to Dalits in the name of caste.

As per the estimate of the programme evaluation organization of the planning commission, 83% of the total numbers of bonded labours belong to SCs and STs. Bonded labour has been listed in Section-3. (1) (VI) as an atrocity under SC/ST (PoA) ACT-1989. The bonded labour system, far from disappearing, has acquired new forms. There is increasing casual and contract labour in sectors such as mining, industry, aquaculture, crusher, construction with absence of any social security benefits.

The Government supported infrastructure development programmes in rural areas undertaken by contractors are also violating the objectives of ensuring employment and labour welfare by using mechanics and avoiding labour legislations. The DRDA, Block, and Panchayats are not paying any special attention to the plight of workers engaged by contractors in government programmes.

Dalit workers hamlets have no sanitary facilities such as latrines, drinking water, electricity, drainage line, linking road, etc. The village common property and resources such as the village pond, water bodies, bathing ghats, forest, grazing lands, cremation ground, play ground, community center, etc. are inaccessible to untouchable communities in the village. Dalit women workers are victims of sexual harassment at the workplace beside, and they do not get minimum wage and equal wage. Maternity benefits and health care is highly required for Dalit working women in rural areas and urban slums. There have been complaints against rural health workers that they practice discrimination against Dalits during service delivery. There has been a visible underrepresentation of Dalits in the NGO sector, trade unions, cooperatives, media and workers organizations in the country which need to be given special attention for the effective implementation of social security measures in rural villages and urban slums.

Social security measures should create an environment for Dalits to live with dignity as human beings equal to others not as mere beneficiaries of welfare programmes. Social security measures should help them to be assertive and to enjoy all constitutional guarantees as citizens of the country who are contributing a major portion to the GDP of the country. The contribution of Dalits in nation building needs to be acknowledged and recognized by the government and civil society.

7.1. Social Security of Adivasis

About 80 million adivasis are living in different states, mostly in the interior areas, in India. Most of these areas are rich in natural resources on which adivasis traditionally depend for their livelihood, security and cultural identity. Since the colonial period, and even after the independence, the Indian state has been attacking the adivasis to continue their "eminent domain" over natural resources i.e. land, forest, water and mineral resources. Adivasis have been denied their due share in the wealth generated through exploiting their assets and have been massively displaced from their land and prohibited from accessing it. This loss of access to land has had its worse impact on women.

Adivasis have never been allowed any democratic space to fight for their livelihood rights, social security, labour rights and above all to live with dignity. According to estimates about 85 per cent of Adivasis live below the official 'poverty line'. The National Commission for Scheduled Castes and Scheduled Tribes found that 83 per cent of the total bonded labourers come from the STs. Adivasis who mostly work as forest workers are paid extremely low wages and have no social security benefits. In fact, Gujarat and Rajasthan have even exempted this employment from the provisions of the Minimum Wages Act. They are denied all other benefits such as leave, maternity benefits etc. In 1969, the National Labour Commission recommended permanent settlement and farming rights for Adivasis.

Given this historical context, social security is a very important issue for the adivasi and especially for the displaced families. Most adivais do not have a permanent occupation as they are either working as migrant labourers or contract labourers or bonded labourers. Seldom do they have any permanent address, which is a prerequisite to be included in any welfare schemes of the government.

It is thus pertinent to understand the problem of social security for the adivasi in the larger social and political context in the prevailing development paradigm. It is important to protect basic human rights and the state has to tackle the key issue of preventing direct attack on adivasi by state forces as a necessary precondition towards ensuring social security for adivasis. It is important to ensure that the inalienable rights of adivasis to the forests, lands and rivers, guaranteed to them by the International charter of UNHRC and ILO and to uphold their rights as citizens living in forest areas, as ensured by forest rights Act, 2006.

7.2. Dalit Women and Social Security

Most women work whether paid or unpaid. Despite its obvious economic and social worth, much of the work that women do remains 'invisible' in national accounting and censuses and even while defining the 'informal sector' and assessing its contribution to the GDP. Estimates based on the National Sample Survey (NSS) 1999-2000, women are said to account for one-third, about 118 million unorganised workers in India.

The non existence of social security provisions for unorganised workers therefore means that an extremely large section of women in the country remain unprotected. None of the Bills concerned with the unorganised workers that have been circulated prior to the passage of the current Act take unpaid women workers into account.

The Unorganised Workers Social Security Act, 2008, apart from excluding unpaid workers, also left out several categories of paid work where women dominate. It is important that all women workers be included in the definition of unorganised workers, including unpaid workers, domestic workers, sex workers, entertainment workers, migrant workers - seasonal and permanent, street vendors, pre-agricultural and hunter gatherer communities.

Insecurity of employment is a major vulnerability that most women face. They are engaged in seasonal in work. They are predominant in sectors where there is steady loss of employment without a corresponding creation of new avenues for work due factors such as technological changes, entrance of big domestic and multinational companies, increased imports, forced displacement and government policies. Social security provisions must ensure that women workers are guaranteed year round employment and unemployment benefits are available to all workers equally irrespective of the employment status of any other family member.

Gender based wage disparities exist across all sectors and occupations. While unorganised male workers are paid wages far below the minimum wage standards, women workers are paid even less.

All women should be entitled to social security benefits as independent citizens and not as dependents on male earning members or as part of the family/household. Social security for the unorganised workers must ensure that women are not treated as dependents on male family members and assumed that they are automatically covered by social security coverage.

Many women workers retire from paid work at an early age, due to ill health or simply because they stop getting employment. The absence of old age security provisions leaves them unprotected. Social security for unorganised workers must include a demand for provision of adequate pension to retired women workers, widows and single women and should provide for old age support.

The most productive years of a woman's life are the reproductive years. The absence of maternity entitlements often means that a woman worker has to leave her job to have a child. With the near absence of any effective primary health care system in the country, most women are forced to have children at home without any medical care. A majority of the women and their families are unable to bear the burden of hospitalization costs. Even when they opt for hospitalization, additional medical expenses and loss of employment makes women economically vulnerable. Social security for the unorganised workers must ensure that maternity entitlements including paid leave are available to all women, whether employed or not, in terms of hospital and medical expenses and these maternity entitlements include paid maternity leave of at least 12 weeks. There must be provision for financial support during childbirth so as to promote the health of mother.

The absence of child care provisions means that the burden of work on women is increased tremendously, affecting their health and work participation. Social security for unorganised workers must include childcare provisions from the point of view of women workers.

For women workers, their own health and ability to work is usually the only resource they can fall back upon. They are the most vulnerable in this regard because their health and nutrition needs are the lowest priority within the family. Women in the poorest households are the least likely to receive medical attention. Social security for the unorganised workers must ensure: health care, which provides protection during contingencies like minor and major illnesses and accidents at work and "non contingencies" such as including HIV/AIDS, special provisions for mental health and differently abled women and widespread shelters and short stay homes and other support service by the state for girls and women survivors of domestic violence, sexual assault and trafficking. Sexual harassment and violence at the workplace is a threat faced by all women workers. Social security for unorganised workers must ensure that complaint and redressal mechanisms against sexual harassment at the workplace following the Vishakha guidelines are put in place, keeping in mind the specific concerns of unorganised women workers. In general, women are usually not land or property owners. Social security for the unorganised workers must ensure that benefits are not tied to land or property and all housing schemes under social security provisions should ensure that titles are in women's name or are in joint names.

Depending solely on contribution based, social insurance types of schemes to provide old age, disability pensions will be disadvantageous for women because most women are engaged in either unpaid or low paying jobs. Most women also have many interruptions in their working life due to child birth and domestic work at home. Their capacity to contribute to such schemes, that too on a regular basis is low. Floor level social security should include food security, primary health care, adequate shelter and provision for education, especially for the girl child.

Women workers are usually at the lowest-paid end of any sector, they are usually termed as unskilled. Skill training and up gradation of skills for women workers on a widespread and continuous scale is important.

Women workers usually find themselves excluded from participation in decision making regarding the administration and implementation of labour laws, even when there is provision for equal participation of workers and employers. Social security for unorganised workers must ensure that women workers are involved adequately and proportionally at all stages including the drafting, administration and implementation of this Bill. Mechanisms for grievance redressal must be women friendly.

7.3. Migrants and Social Security

India is one of the world's largest migrant sending countries. Historically, skilled, semi-skilled, and unskilled Indian men and women have migrated to a variety of locations across the globe. While compelling individual and structural 'push' and 'pull' factors related to labour, conflict, security, and disasters underpin Indian citizens' migration overseas, equally compelling concerns draw others to India, including India's strong and stable political economy that stands out in the region. However, here is a persistence of the fundamental contradiction of globalization whereby capital and goods are exchanged under increasingly borderless conditions, but where the mobility of people is increasingly restricted under strict border controls and national security interests.

There are a huge number of in migrants in India from various countries. Among countries hosting migrants from other nations, India was placed eighth in the world in 2005, according to the United Nations Trends in Migrant Stock: A 2005 Revision. The top eight include the United States Russian Federation Germany Ukraine France Saudi Arabia Canada and India. Nepalese and Bangladeshi nationals are most likely the largest groups of inmigrants to India. However, given the porousness of India's borders and the preponderance of undocumented modes of entry into the country this figure is likely to constitute a poor approximation of the real numbers.

It has been observed in the past few decades that there is a growing importance of international migration as a source for global exchange and revenue generation. Migration is also seen as a rapid route out of poverty. Studies suggests that if global trends over the last thirty years continue, temporary migration to industrialized countries may lead to gains of as much as US$ 300 billion a year in 2025, shared equally between people in developing and developed countries.

Migrant workers face adverse, unsafe and hostile situations. They live and work in inhuman conditions and are denied human rights or labour rights. These workers and their family members deserve social security protections from the state. Cross-border migrant Indian workers are denied social security protections in the countries of destination because they are unorganised temporary workers, working as construction workers, cleaners, domestic workers, paramedical workers, guest workers for rescue operations abroad and in such other occupations in service sector and many of them are self-employed. Migrants within India are also in similar vulnerable situations. Internal migrant workers within India face similar kinds of discrimination, inequality xenophobia, remain vulnerable and are denied social security protections.

Migrant workers generate economic development and prosperity but are denied human rights and rights of social protection like medical care, old age pension, accident care and compensation, maternity entitlements, unemployment cover which is generally given to all employees in organized industry.

Moreover, due to the global economic meltdown, it is estimated that over 30 million workers lost their regular jobs and joined informal employments at much lower wages with no social security protections. The slowdown in construction, failing agriculture and excessive labour supply created a situation of all-round massive retrenchment or job losses or non availability of jobs. The worst hit are approximately 350 million unorganised interstate and intrastate migrant workers engaged in construction, domestic service, textile, transport, manufacturing, tourism and entertainment sectors and in self employments in services. The job losses in the Middle East and other developing countries compelled many Indian workers to come back.

The policy of government to withdraw from sustaining and improving health and education infrastructure worsened the situation and rendered workers more socially unprotected. The NREGA and other charity type schemes have proven to be eye wash as workers unions and people's groups are not effectively involved in decision making and their administration.

The 'Unorganized Workers Social Security Act' (UWSSA) 2008 neither shows any substantial state contribution for creating social security fund nor envisages adequate or effective provisions for medical care, pension, maternity benefit, etc. It does not provide for unemployment allowance and compensation for loss of livelihood. It does not cover unorganised cross-border temporary migrant workers. Therefore the definition of unorganised workers needs to include these 'cross border migrant workers' in under a sub-clause of definition as: Provided father that cross border migrant workers shall be considered unorganized worker for the social security protections along with their family members in India under this Act. The Act should incorporate provision of framing special social security protections to cover all adverse situations which they face and the requirements of their dependent family members in the place of origin.

7.4. Financing Social Security

Safety ranks high on the list of the universal human rights. The basic needs of human security go far beyond national security concerns to encompass all forms of economic and social insecurities which badly and often violently affect people in their day-to-day lives.

All historical experiences attest that no social progress has ever been achieved without mobilizing the capacities of the people to voice their demands, to protest and propose publicly, to contest and address the political and economic powers and policies: basic human rights, social rights and political rights are strongly inter-linked and shall be activated jointly to combat poverty effectively and develop democracy.

Unfortunately, in many countries, democratic rights are being restricted by overt and often covert militarization of the regime and the society. The extension of the arms race, the persistence of forged or fuelled nationalistic antagonisms and the development of "war policies and industries" are directly related to the degree of penetration of military interests into the political, economic and mediatic spheres, in the North as well as in the South.

Grassroots activists are daily experimenting with the relevance and the efficiency of empowering poor people to wage non-violent fights for rights in their quest for liberation from want and fear. The culture of non-violence is being promoted by the UN in a context of growing concern over the influence of various forms of terrorism on populations at large and youth in particular. Regarding the fundamental stand to reduce all forms of violence by non-violent democratic means, coherence is a key factor for credibility and efficiency.

Hence the need for extending the agenda of non-violence to the States by supporting the 10per cent Option, adopting non aggressive national defense policies, reducing arms production and arms trade, promoting "no war zones" through regional cooperation agreements.

There is a growing concern over the gross unbalance which prevails between the massive military expenditures and the meagre amounts invested in development. At the global level, the military and weaponry expenses keep increasing and exceed already 1,100 billions US dollars per year.

Thus the 10per cent Option proposes to examine rationally, the possibilities and advantages of striking a new balance within national budgets and public investments to combine sustainable defense and social development policies to better serve the security needs of the people: national security needs, by adopting defensive policies, much safer and much less expensive than offensive and wary policies; social security needs, by increasing social development investments, including all forms of social protections as a major non-violent tool to combat poverty, boost development and erase brutal inequalities.

As far as military and weaponry policies go, too few people have access to information and decisions which directly concern the lives of billions of people and the allocation of huge amounts of public money. In the same way, the control on the allocation of funds and implementation of schemes related to social development is equally required.

In this respect, the 10per cent Option is committed to enlarging the circulation of information and the involvement of social actors and representatives from the civil society at large to debate and follow-up all policies related to the security of the people and to monitor the 10per cent conversion process.

Multilateral negotiations and agreements provide the most relevant frame to conceive and conduct disarmament policies. With the worrying limitation that the vast majority of the people and the countries are so far completely dependant on the positions taken by the biggest military powers and arms producing States.

The 10 per cent Option provides readily available public financing for strategically social investments. For instance: in India it could initiate the financing of the unorganised workers social security scheme which is debated by the Parliament.

Hence the 10per cent Option offers the possibility for any country, irrespective of its size, to engage safely in an alternative approach of international influence, not based on military muscle, but on moral and political commitment to the peace and social justice agenda, and to take part into the lead towards a global new deal for human security.

References

Bharadwaj, A.N. *Problems of Scheduled Castes and Scheduled Tribes in India* [From Jammu: general review from experience by journalist and social worker of distinction]. New Delhi: Light & Life 1979.

Census of India 1961 *Study of customary rights and living and working conditions of Scavengers in two towns* [Haryana and UP]. Monog. series Vol. I, Part XI, D. 1966.

Danda, A.K. *Weaker Sections in Indian Villages*. 2 vols. New Delhi: Inter-India 1993.

Freeman, J.M. *Untouchable. An Indian Life History*. London: Allen & Unwin 1979.

8

Dalit Muslims and Christians

A large and varied body of social scientific literature establishes a fact that is now largely taken for granted, namely that like other religious communities, Muslims and Christians in India are heterogenous rather than monolithically homogenous communities. The most prominent divisions and differences have to do with the presence of multiple sects and denominations among both Muslims and Christians, with the Shia-Sunni or the Catholic-Protestant divide being the best known. However, caste refers to an institution of a different sort, one which would generally be expected to reproduce itself across and within denominational or sectarian boundaries. While scholars differ on the exact relationship between these two categories, it is generally agreed that the latter refers to an overarching pan-Indian division between the four major groupings of castes whereas jati is a more local category indicating an endogamous group with a strong network of social and kinship ties.

Common social-anthropological definitions of caste include the following features:

1. A caste is a *closed, ascriptive group* whose membership is decided by birth and is hereditary mandatory and unalterable.
2. Castes impose *rules of conduct* on their members, the most prominent being those on marriage social interaction and occupation.
3. Castes are part of a *system* in which they are both strictly separated and closely integrated in a hierarchy determined, in the original Hindu case, by notions of graded ritual purity or pollution.

Before we ask whether caste in this definitional sense exists among Muslims and Christians in India, it should be noted that the above definition is an ideal typical construct that rarely exists in reality. Even among Hindus, there is considerable regional and temporal variation in the concrete, living forms of caste, which correspond only roughly to the theoretical model. The effective question therefore is not whether some classic definition of caste can be found on the ground, but whether caste-like groups, or social divisions displaying a significant proportion of these features are present in Muslim and Christian society today.

When asked in this form, there is an overwhelming consensus on the answer – scholars are almost unanimous in their opinion that caste-like divisions exist among Muslims and Christians in India. But while this fact itself is beyond debate, there is some variation of opinion on the issues of the origins and the precise nature of caste among Muslims and Christians. On the whole, there seems to be more of a debate with regard to Muslim society than Christian society. In the case of Muslims, scholars have differing interpretations of the degree to which caste is: a) a purely Hindu 'survival' in post-conversion communities; b) a 'learnt' or newly reproduced institution due to the influence of surrounding Hindu society; and c) the product and expression of tendencies internal to Islam.

What precisely is caste-like about the caste-analogues found in Muslim and Christian society? The answer to this question is more complicated because of considerable variation in the relative importance of different aspects and features of caste in different communities and regions. While there will always be exceptions in particular cases, it is possible to arrive at the following general order of caste features, beginning with the most universal aspects found everywhere, to the most differentiated aspects on which there is too much variation to permit easy generalisation:

1. Hereditary membership conferred by birth.
2. Endogamy, usually strictly observed, but with 'hard' and 'soft' divisions.
3. Social segregation, i.e., the exclusion of lower by higher all along the hierarchy.
4. Occupational segregation and economic differentiation.

5. Specific practices of untouchability and other forms of exclusion against Dalits.
6. Belief in notions of ritual purity and pollution as the basis for caste divisions.

Of these six broad features of caste, the first two may be safely said to be universally present in Muslim and Christian society in India. The simplest way of stating this fact is to say that in India, one is never 'just' a Muslim or a Christian. The Muslim and Christian communities – like other religious communities in India · are always further subdivided into caste-like social groups to which individuals belong. Membership in these groups is determined by birth and is taken to be hereditary, so that one's parentage is always a salient feature of one's community identity. Further, the pattern of marriage relations usually follows these caste-like divisions strictly, though the degree to which this is enforced tends to vary. In general, the strictest taboos are invariably directed at the Dalit communities or those identified as such. Violations of this prohibition usually invite severe social sanctions, including in most cases the ex-communication of the erring family of the higher caste. Although such marriages are discouraged, they tend to be tolerated, particularly if they occur within the same broad class or economic status grouping.

Thus, it can be said that there is hardly any variation in these two features of caste grouping, so that they may be considered to be a routinely present aspect of Indian Muslim or Christian identity as it exists in practice.

The next two features, namely social segregation along caste lines, and hierarchization in economic and occupational terms, are also universally present, but with significant variations in the nature and extent of such hierarchical segregation. The social scientific literature of the last four decades shows that caste-like identities among Muslims and Christians are generally closely aligned with larger social, economic and political hierarchies despite local differences. Social segregation and economic hierarchies *always* follow the caste hierarchy. What can and does vary greatly, however, the distance that separates different caste groups – in some contexts the distance separating the lowest from the highest may be relatively small, in other cases quite large. It is also possible for some sections or small portions of a particular caste grouping to be at roughly the same level as lower or higher groups, but this rarely happens for the group as a whole or even for a substantial portion of the group.

The most common segregation practices, apart from endogamy, are those involving differential access to community resources, including specifically religion-related areas. Thus, access to collective worship may be actively denied to the lowest castes, or may only be granted on differential terms. As the studies described later in this chapter show, Dalit Christians generally tend to have separate churches and are served by different priests. In the case of Muslim Dalits, actual exclusion is unusual, but is at the cost of an unambiguously inferior status expressed through such practices as having to sit in the back, not being allowed to sit in front of the upper castes, and so on.

Not surprisingly, social segregation maps quite directly on to economic status hierarchies. The lower and specially the lowest caste groups among both Christians and specially Muslims find themselves left out of the networks that provide social capital, which in turn can yield opportunities for accumulating economic capital. View on such economic differentials will be discussed in detail in. Once again the pattering of difference is very stable and follows caste hierarchy, though the extent of difference between high and low may vary.

The fifth aspect of caste, specific practices of untouchability, are subject to great variation. In some instances, as with Christian communities in south India and specially Kerala, these practices seem to be virtually identical with Hindu practice. In other instances, the specific belief in or practice of untouchability may be absent, although the Dalit castes are marked out in every other way. As already noted, it is not useful to ask only whether untouchability of a particular sort is practiced or not. So, although there is a lot of variation with regard to the practice of untouchability, and many Muslim and Christian communities in many regions do not seem to have this institution, it is still true nevertheless that Dalits in these communities are at the receiving end of a variety of discriminatory and derogatory practices, as well as being at the bottom of the material status hierarchy.

Finally, beliefs about ritual purity and pollution are the most variable. They are present in some communities, but not in most; even where they are present, they are subject to change like all other aspects of society.

8.1. Caste among Dalit Muslims and Christians

If, as the above discussion has established, caste is a reality for Indian Muslims and Christians, then does caste impose the same disabilities on Dalit Christians and Dalit Muslims as are known to be imposed on Dalits of other religions? Before one proceeds to answer this question in detail, one unmistakable conclusion needs to be stressed. Regardless of whether and to what extent the caste disabilities of Dalit Muslims and Dalit Christians resemble those of Hindu or other Dalits, this survey of social scientific literature establishes beyond doubt that, compared to other castes, Dalits suffer the most from their caste identity. In short, if Muslims and Christians in India 'have' caste, then it is clear that Dalit Muslims and Dalit Christians have it the most.

To begin a detailed consideration of this question it is necessary to go back to the earliest attempts to identify the 'depressed classes' as they were known in the early twentieth century. The most significant such effort is no doubt that of the 1931 Census. This effort is all the more important since it became, in effect, the basis for the inclusion of particular Tribes and Castes in the Schedules drawn up as part of the Government of India Act of 1935 which inaugurated the 'reservations' policy in India.

The list of questions created by the then Census Commissioner Sir J.H. Hutton are not necessarily the best or the most decisive. As scholars including Lelah Dushkin and Marc Galanter have shown, some of these questions don't have clear answers, and some others which can be easily answered are not very helpful. If this were to be used,a standard for identifying Dalits today, there would be considerable variation even among Hindu castes long recognised as Dalits, leave alone among other religious communities. Despite the presence of larger groupings like 'Ashraf' and 'Ajlaf', what really matters in everyday social life and in interaction with other groups, both within the Muslim community as well as with members of other communities, is the caste-analogue. In terms of social significance, therefore, the caste-analogue matters more than other identities which may also be used.

What consequences follow if one is belongs to a caste-analogue identified as Dalit?

Compared to Muslims, there is much less ambiguity about caste practices amongs Indian Christians. And as discussed in the next chapter, a substantial proportion of the Christian community is said to be made of former Hindu untouchable castes. There is now considerable social scientific as well as NGO material available on Dalit-Non-Dalit relations among Muslims and Christians.

8.2. Caste Inequalities

The ethnographic evidence obtained via direct firsth and observation that was discussed in the previous chapter is obviously indispensable. It is only on the basis of such evidence that one can begin to investigate whether and to what extent Dalit Muslims and Christians are a distinct social group. However, such evidence has some unavoidable limitations –while it helps to establish a concrete case, it cannot be generalised at the macro level. The observed facts that have been noted in a specific case may or may not hold in other cases and contexts. Although it is possible to work towards generalisation by accumulating many local studies it is also necessary to look at evidence of a different kind that works by aggregation across large groups rather than by observing the singular case.

This chapter discusses the available macro-statistical data on caste inequalities among Muslims and Christians in India. The basic questions around which the data are organised remain the same: how do Dalit Muslims and Christians compare with a) their own community members of different castes; and b) Dalits of other religious communities? The main source of the data used here is the National Sample Survey Organisation's most recent five-yearly survey from its 61st Round, canvassed in 2004-05.

For obvious reasons state institutions are the most important sources of social statistics all around the world. Given this fact, it follows that social groups which are not recognized by the state tend to become statistically 'invisible', for the state organs that routinely collect data – the Census, other government departments and official survey organisations – do not record information on such groups. This is in fact the most discouraging aspect of studying groups like Dalit Muslims and Christians.

However, despite receiving no official recognition at the central level, Dalit Muslims and Christians have been recognised to varying degrees and in different ways by many state governments. In fact, as many as 12 major states accord recognition to sections of their Muslim and Christian populations within the Other Backward Classes (OBC) category. Ironically, this recognition creates further problems in the context of national level surveys where information on DMs and DCs may be available. As discussed in the Introduction, DMs and DCs may return themselves as OBCs because they are recognised as such in their state and region.

Apart from this, DMs and DCs also run into purely statistical problems associated with sample surveys. Because they are such a small proportion of the population, they are naturally a small proportion of the sample as well, even of a large one such as that of the NSSO's big five-yearly surveys. Hence this chapter is restricted to national level analyses, though the usual division into the rural and urban sectors is maintained throughout. For this reason no regional, gender- or occupation-specific analyses has been attempted.

Just how many DMs and DCs are there in India? There are no authoritative estimates available for the reasons mentioned above. But if some rough estimates are to be constructed, they must begin with the NSSO data. The general procedure that is followed here is to ascertain the NSSO shares or *proportions* and to apply these proportions to the *population totals* obtained from the Census.

But before we begin this process, we need to get an idea of where the NSSO stands in relation to the Census on the question of the larger categories of both religion and caste of which the DMs and DCs are subsets.

The NSSO's estimate of the population shares of the SCs for both rural and urban India exceeds the Census figures by well over three percentage points. This is broadly in keeping with the past trend as the NSSO estimates have generally tended to be higher than the Census, specially for this category. While the scholarly debate on this continues, it is reasonable to point out that this discrepancy could be due as much to conservatism on the part of the Census as to sampling errors in the NSSO survey, or non-sampling errors induced by misreporting due to confusion about the official category of the Scheduled Castes.

Going by the Census, the NSSO appears to slightly overestimate the population share of Hindus it very slightly underestimates all minorities except rural Sikhs. However the discrepancies here are very minor and well in keeping with the error margins associated with sample surveys. It should be noted in passing that Muslims on the whole tend to be underestimated the most – by almost half a percentage point in rural and a little less than one point in urban India. Christians are also marginally underestimated, more so in urban India, by about one-third of one percent. It can be seen right away that DMs are a very tiny proportion of the Muslim population, being just over half of one percent in both rural and urban India.

DMs are thus by far the least numerous Dalits of any religious community, specially if one sets aside the anomalous "Others" category. Muslims also seem to have by far the largest proportion of 'Upper' castes. Compared to Muslims, Christians seem to have a much larger proportion of Dalits. These figures are almost universally believed to be gross underestimates of the true proportion of Dalits among Indian Christians. Most scholars and activists put the proportion at between 50 and 75% percent of all Indian Christians, although it is not possible to corroborate these claims in any decisive manner due to the difficulty of the category being officially unrecognized. Since the lower bound of such 'guesstimates' seems to be 50%, it should be kept in mind that the proportion of DCs could be at least five times what the NSSO estimates show it to be.

The shares of the major caste groups in the population of the main religions of India. They show that Dalits are overwhelmingly Hindu – more than 93% in rural and 90% in urban India. In fact, Dalits are the caste category with the highest proportion of Hindus, and the other religions contribute very small proportions. Within these the share of Muslim and Christian Dalits amounts to a miniscule 1.2% in rural and 2.3% in urban India.

8.2.1. Material Status of Dalit Muslims and Dalit Christians

The rest of this chapter is devoted to a comparative assessment of the material status of DMs and DCs. In keeping with the objectives set for this chapter, the comparative analysis employs two main reference groups: a) the non-Dalit co-religionists of DMs and DCs; and b) Dalits of other religions, namely Hindus, Sikhs and Buddhists. How does the condition of the DMs and DCs compare with that of non-Dalit Muslims and Christians, and with non-Muslim and non-Christian Dalits? These are the basic questions addressed. Four main types of evidence are considered:

1) Poverty profiles of the different socio-religious groups with the main focus on DMs and DCs. Evidence of this sort mainly involves looking at the *distribution of the population of a group across the economic spectrum*. What proportion of each group is very poor, and what proportion is affluent? How do these proportions compare with the group's share in the total population.
2) Average consumption levels are the second set of criteria considered. Here the focus is not so much on the proportion of population falling in particular class segments, but on the *absolute levels of average consumption*. This involves looking at the levels of monthly percapita consumption expenditure whether in terms of averages like the median, or a broader view profiling the entire distribution via selected percentiles of MPCE. In this chapter, the three quartiles as well as the 95th percentile are considered. This helps us to get a better sense of the overall economic condition of a social group, something which averages are unable to convey on their own.
3) Occupational structure is the third dimension of comparison. This provides a rough sense of the economic condition of a social group. In both the rural and urban sectors, there are some occupational categories that indicate relatively higher economic status than others; so comparing the proportions of population of each group that fall in these categories tells us about their relative condition. For rural India, the NSSO provides a broad classification of households into the following types: a) self-employed in agriculture; b) agricultural labour; c) other labour; d) self-employed in non-agricultural activities; and e) others, which is obviously a residual category. For urban India, the categories provided are: a) self-employed; b) regular wage or salaried employment; c) casual labour; and d) others.
4) Educational status is the final criterion for comparison. This requires little explanation. The NSSO provides data on the levels

of general education ranging from 'not literate' to 'diploma holder, graduate, or above', with primary, secondary and higher secondary school levels in between. Unlike the occupational category criterion, which has the household as its unit, the unit for education is the person. This data is available from the Employment and Unemployment survey of the NSSO survey. Comparisons of proportions of population at different educational levels provides one more way of assessing the relative status of different social groups.

Two further points need to be noted. First, the Scheduled Tribes have been excluded from the following analysis since they fall outside the purview of this chapter. Second, since Buddhists are almost entirely Dalit with only a tiny proportion in the OBC and UC categories, they are included only for comparisons among Dalits, and excluded when the analysis involves other castes like the OBC and UC.

8.2.2. Poverty Profiles

This section considers relative proportions of the population that are in different economic classes as defined by MPCE. The focus is on the bottom and the top ends of the economic spectrum. The bottom is defined by the official Poverty Line, which represents the minimum level of consumption expenditure needed to meet basic nutritional norms.

The top of the economic spectrum is defined by the level of MPCE that represents the top five percent of the national population. The top 5% level may seem rather a high level to take, but this is done to offset the fact that consumption expenditure severely underestimates inequality. Because MPCE does not take account of savings, investments or accumulated wealth, it tends to understate the actual income of the rich and overstate the income of the poor. The MPCE levels of the top are thus relatively low levels and they seem to include a much larger proportion of the population than the category intuitively suggests. Thus, for example, Rs. 2500 is the 'top 5%' level of MPCE for urban India. This implies a household of 5 with a monthly expenditure of about Rs. 12,500 at 2004-05 prices!

In rural India, the Dalit Sikhs are the only group that is significantly better off than other Dalits. Less than 8% of Dalit Sikhs are in the BPL category compared to at least 30% of more for all others. Buddhists are the worst off, followed by DMs at nearly 40%. After Sikhs, DCs are the next best though they have a BPL rate of over 30%. At the other end of the spectrum, it is the DCs that are best off with about 6% in the Rs.1200 & above category. Thus, DCs in rural India have substantial numbers of poor, but they also have a small proportion in the affluent category. DMs have more in the poor and less in the affluent category than DCs, but they are broadly comparable to all other dalits except Sikhs.

DMs are by far the worst off among urban dalits. About 47% of them are in the BPL category – significantly more than Hindu dalits who are the next at about 41%. But the really striking fact is that there seem to be almost no DMs at all in the affluent category, so much so that they don't register as a significant proportion of population. DCs are better off than DMs and all other groups except the Sikhs, who are once again the best off among urban dalits.

Unsurprisingly, the DMs are the worst off compared to their OBC and UC counterparts. Their BPL population is higher and their top MPCE class population is lower than that of the other groups. Urban DMs are particularly badly off – their BPL percentage is almost 47%, and they are *completely absent* in the Rs.1200+ category. This is not a rounding problem – there are actually no DM households in this category, which does indeed appear to be a null set. This was so striking a fact that it called for re-checking; it is confirmed that of the 53 DM households in the urban sample, not one has an MPCE of more than Rs.2500. Although there are as many as 179 Muslim households in this category, none of them is from the DM category. Only one DM household has a MPCE of over Rs.2000 – and that too only just above at Rs.2026 – and only four have an MPCE of over Rs.1500. However, it should be remembered that: a) the sample size is very small – 53 is a small number; and b) there are problems with the DM category itself since it has no official status at the central level.

The differences are so great that DCs may almost be living in a different world from other Christians.In rural India, the BPL proportion for DCs is more than double that for OBCs and about four-and-half times that of the ucs. On the other hand, the DC population percentage in the top MPCE class is only one-third that of the OBCs and almost one-fifth that of the UCs.

It is at once clear that Dalits are always the group with the highest proportion of population in the BPL category in both rural and urban India, regardless of religion. Inequalities in BPL proportions are higher in urban than in rural India. The fact that Muslims have less inequality, as well as the fact that they are as a whole worse off than other communities – particularly in urban India. Once again, Dalits are always the worst off in the sense that they have a lower proportion of their population in this affluent class than their non-Dalit fellow religionists. The only exception is provided by Dalit Sikhs, who just manage to outdo their OBC counterparts in urban India. Note the absence of DMs from the urban affluent class.

The Dalits of all religions are under-represented among the top MPCE classes in both sectors, while all 'Upper' castes – with the significant exception of the Muslim UCs – are over-represented, usually quite substantially. It is noteworthy that the Hindu upper castes are more than double their proportion of population, while the Christian UCs are close behind. Interestingly, in terms of proportional under-representation, Sikh Dalits seem to be the worst off, followed by the Christian and Hindu Dalits.

8.3. Judicial Perspectives

Judicial perspectives on the status of DMs and DCs have been shaped by three main considerations:

1) the Presidential Order of 1950 (and its subsequent amendments);
2) the caste status of converts from Hinduism;
3) the specific grounds on which social groups may be included in the SC list, including questions about the nature and quantum of the admissible evidence in this regard.

These three themes are discussed below.

8.3.1. The Presidential Order of 1950

In the year 1950, the president of India issued the "Constitution Order, 1950" specifying the castes to be recognised as the Scheduled Castes by exercising the authority conferred on him under the article 341(1) of the Constitution India. The third paragraph of the order however qualifies that "notwithstanding anything contained in para 2, no person who professes a religion different from Hinduism shall be deemed to be a member of the Scheduled Castes". Subsequent amendments to the 1950 Presidential Order in 1956 and 1990 provided for the inclusion of Sikhs and Buddhists respectively within the Scheduled Caste category to avail the benefits of reservation. The main plank of this argument is that denial of SC status to DMs and DCs constitutes a violation of Articles 14 15 and 25 of the Constitution.

8.3.1.1. Caste status of converts

The original rationale for including only Hindu castes in the SC list was directly linked to the practice of untouchability and other caste sanctions against the lowest castes. Since caste as an institution was said to be native to Hinduism, not being part of the scripture or core beliefs of any other religion, only Hindu Dalits qualified to be designated as SCs. However, the later extension of this designation to Sikhs and then to Neo-Buddhists seems to have been justified on the grounds that these groups were recent converts, and their caste was still the predominant aspect of their social identity. In fact, a few Sikh castes had been included even in the first post-Independence version of the SC lists in the 1950 Presidential Order.

The remaining Dalit Sikh castes were added in 1956. The Courts seem to have been quite willing to concede the point that caste survives conversion, and that despite professing faith in a religion which has no scriptural sanction for caste distinctions, may continue to be identified and treated as a member of the original caste. While they have rejected the claim that caste may be acquired by marriage they have allowed that it is retained despite conversion and re-conversion. So the caste status of persons who have converted to other religions and are no longer practising Hindus, and even of those who were born as non-Hindus and never professed the Hindu faith, is not at issue in the courts.

8.3.1.2. Criteria and standards of evidence

These remain the most contentious issues. The extension of SC status to DMs and DCs appears to hinge on the question of evidence according to the crucial *Soosai* case. As Justice Pathak says in his judgement in this case, 'it is not sufficient to show that the same caste continues after conversion. It is necessary to establish further that the disabilities and handicaps suffered from such caste membership in the social order of its origin continue in their oppressive severity in the new environment of a different religious community. 'This distinction is related to the one that is analysed with admirable clarity by Marc Galanter, namely the distinction between caste as a unit designating a portion of the population and as an indicator of status. Justice Pathak here appears to be assenting to the use of caste as a community unit but questioning its use as a status marker. The contention here is that while castes may exist, this fact, which identifies a group as belonging to a particular caste, does not by itself allow us to come to any conclusion regarding the status of this caste relative to others. Relative status needs to be established independently of the mere fact of belonging to a particular community. The same judgement complains about the 'cursory' evidence placed before it, and about the absence of any 'authoritative and detailed' study on the condition of the DCs.

First, there is the question of how precisely caste disability is to be established. The response to this seems to be that the claimant group needs to establish, in addition to the fact of their caste identity, two further facts:

1) that they are worse off than their non-Dalit co-religionists, and that this is due to their caste status; and
2) that they are comparable in status to the Hindu, Sikh and Buddhist Dalits who are already recognised by the state as being in need of special consideration.

Whether both these criteria are to be explicitly invoked; and if so, the relative weight that is to be attached to each are questions that need to be settled at some point if the legal debate is to make any progress. Here again there seem to be two issues involved. One is that of the quality of the evidence, that is, the standards of competence and levels of expertise that it demonstrates. The second issue is that of the extent of the evidence and the related consideration of arriving at an overall judgement on a body of material that is bound to present a complex and heterogenous picture. Further clarity on these issues is perhaps only possible after the fact – that is, after a body of material is presented to the courts and they come to some judgement as to their worth on the above counts. It is certainly true that in the two decades since the *Soosai* case a lot more ethnographic and other empirical evidence has been accumulated on this issue.

One noteworthy feature of the case history on this issue is that most of it pertains to the Christian community, and cases are mostly from south India. This reflects, perhaps, the extent of mobilisation and political consciousness amongst the community in comparison to dalit Muslims, although the latter have also been organising of late. Finally, it needs to be pointed out that courts have been willing to rely on available social scientific studies, and have in fact done so without on their own whenever they have felt this material to be helpful. This is something that needs to be explicitly noted and addressed. This willingness to consider competent evidence provides ample opportunities for further action on this front.

8.3.1.3. Legal rationale for special treatment

— The state may provide special treatment for the advancement of socially and educationally backward classes of citizens or for Scheduled castes and Scheduled tribes.
— The object of Ar. 341(1) is to provide additional protection to the members of the scheduled castes, recognising the educational and economic backwardness from which they suffer.
— Criteria for inclusion of any community in the list of scheduled castes is that such a community should suffer from extreme social, educational and economic backwardness arising out of traditional practices of Untouchability

8.3.1.4. Constitutional issues

The range of constitutional issues arising from the demand of Dalit Christians and Muslims for inclusion with the Scheduled Caste category may be broadly summarised under two categories: (a) Position of those claiming SC status; and (b) Perspectives of the State on the issue concerned.

8.3.1.4.1. SC status for Dalit Christians and Muslims

— Social and educational backwardness persists even after conversion. State denies recognition of SC status only on the grounds that the concerned groups profess Islam and Christianity.

— Such benefits have been extended to converts from Hinduism to Sikhism and Buddhism even though both these religions, like Christianity and Islam, do not recognise the caste system.

8.3.1.4.2. Perspectives of the state

— The criteria adopted for determining whether a community is eligible for inclusion in the list of SC's is extreme social, educational and economic backwardness arising out of traditional practices of Untouchability. Since caste system and practices of Untouchability are a feature of Hindu society, historically the system of special representations for SC's was evolved specifically in relation to the position of these castes in Hindu society who were affected by the practice of Untouchability.

— Lack of authoritative and detailed study on the nature and extent of social disabilities, including Untouchability prevalent in the Christian community in India. Studies available at the time the Supreme or other Courts dealt with this issue did not, in the opinion of the Court, constitute adequate evidence.

— In case SC converts to Christianity are accorded the status of SCs, administrative difficulties would arise at the time of issuing caste certificates because of the difficulty, in many cases, of determining their pre-conversion caste standing. The difficulties in precise and objective determination of pre-conversion caste origin would open the floodgates for issuance of bogus SC certificates which is a cause for concern.

References

Augustine, P.A. *Social Equality in Indian Society*. New Delhi: Concept 1991.

Burman, B.K. Roy *Social Mobility Movements among Scheduled Castes and Scheduled Tribes of India*. Delhi: Government of India Press 1970.

Chandel, M.P.S. *A Social Force in Politics: Study of Scheduled Castes of UP*. New Delhi: Mittal 1990.

Chatterjee, S.K. *The Scheduled Castes in India*, 4 vol. compendium of official material by anthropologist retired from Police]. New Delhi: Gyan 1996.

Gomango, G. *Constitutional Provisions for the Scheduled Castes and Scheduled Tribes*. Bombay: Himalya 1992.

9

Caste Violence and Dalit Deprivation

The Dalit have often been in their development witnessed violent conflict, caused death, injuries, rape, property lose and impoverished their lives for generation. The caste conflict, in this sense, has long been a historical fact and continues to be an unfortunate feature of contemporary India. Moreover, history enlightens us the violent conflict has often been observable fact between the dalit minority and other dominant castes within India. It has also emphasized in the recent development debate that more people have died or suffered from violent conflict between groups within countries than in wars between countries in the past two decades and conflicts constitutes one of the most important source of deprivation, caused widespread poverty and undermined human development. If we look at the type of violence, we get to know that on an average 553 Murders, 2990 Hurt cases, 919 Rapes, 184 Kidnapping/abduction, 47 Dacoity, 127 Robbery, 456 Arson, 1485 civil right violation under OCR ACT, 6174 atrocities under atrocities Act and 12, 995 other offences were registered every year during 1990 – 2000. Consequently, the dalit, almost half of them are living under chronic poverty, widespread illiteracy, and lack of assets and denial of their basic rights such as right to food, education, health and political participation.

9.1. Conceptualization of Caste Violence

In this section we focus on some important issues related to conceptualization of the three phenomena such as caste violence and economic principles implicated in a social system, which is the major source for the caste violence and its possible impact/connections to capability failures which results human deprivation. The caste system in India has resulted in highly stratified societal structure with a hierarchy of castes. In traditional and formal sense, the caste system is based on three interrelated principles. These are predetermined social, cultural and economic rights of each caste based on birth; the unequal and hierarchical division of these rights among the castes and provision of strong social ostracism supported by social and religious ideology to maintain the Hindu social order. While the first two of them defined and laid down the framework of the caste system, the third prescribed the social mechanism of its enforcements. Third feature of caste system relating to the provision of strong ostracism for the enforcement of the system is quite important and crucial in providing the continuity of the system despite the changes in the in legal framework of social behaviour of the Hindus in contemporary India. The social ostracism normally takes the form of numerous penalties, supported by social and religious ideology. To analyse these complex effects of violent conflicts that lead to changes in people's choices and consequently affects in their functioning and freedom, Sen's *Capability Approach* could helpful us to understand the process. The complex effects of violent conflicts can change both intrinsic and instrumental aspect of human capabilities that permits people to achieve *functionings*.

The capability approach to a person's advantage is concerned with evaluating it in terms of his or her actual ability to achieve various valuable functionings as a part of living. The corresponding approach to social advantage takes the set of individual capabilities as constituting an indispensable and central part of the relevant informational base of such evaluation". The capability approach to deprivation thus evaluates people's freedom or rights according to their impact on well-being. It asks whether people are being healthy, and whether the resources necessary for this capability, such as clean water, access to medical doctors, protection from infections and diseases, and basic knowledge on health issues, are present. It asks whether people have access to a high quality education, to real political participation, to community activities, which support them to cope with struggles in daily life and which foster real friendships, to religions that console them and which can give them peace of mind. For some of these capabilities, the main input will be financial resources and economic production, but for others it can also be political practices, such as the effective guaranteeing and protection of freedom of thought, political participation, or social or cultural practices, social structures, social institutions, social norms, traditions and habits. The capability approach focuses on the information that we need to make judgments about individual well-being, social policies, and so forth, and consequently rejects alternative approaches that it considers normatively inadequate, for example when an evaluation is done exclusively in monetary terms. The capability approach alco identifies social constraints that influence and restrict both wellbeing as well as the evaluative exercises. The capability approach can be used to measure poverty or inequality, or can be used as an alternative for traditional utilitarian cost benefit analysis. It can serve as an important constituent for a theory of justice but, as Sen argues, the capability approach specifies an evaluative space and this does not amount to a theory of justice. He stresses that a theory of justice must include both aggregative considerations as well as distributive ones, whereas the capability approach does not specify an aggregative principle.

9.2. Pattern of Violent Conflicts

The conflict between the dalits and other dominant caste are not a new phenomenon. The social behaviour by the dalit contrary to the customary rules and norms or assertion in some form by them for human basic human rights- to be treated equally have invited the violence reaction and atrocities by higher caste. It is very clear from the field results that the atrocities committed on Dalits presents a pattern, which is reflective of the continuing influence of the customary rules and norms on the behaviour of the Hindu toward dalits. What has come out of this study is that discrimination and untouchability is still being practised and the traditional machanism in the form of social ostracism and numerous penalties is used by the high caste on large scale.

We present the evidence on the magnitude and pattern of atrocities against dalit based on both official statistic from 1990 to 2000 and the information from the present survey collected for the year 2000 in the eleven sample states. The nature of data however needs to be understood properly. The magnitude of atrocities is measured in terms of number of cases registered by the dalit with police under

Indian penal code, Protection of civil right act and prevention of atrocities Act. This statistics is picked up from the annual report of the SC/ST Commission and Crime in India for eleven states. Survey information is qualitative in nature, with case studies from about 550 sample villages in eleven states.

9.2.1. Evidence from Official Statistics

The officia! statistic during 1990 to 2000, indicate that a total of two and half lakh cases of various crimes were registered countrywide by the dalits. If we look at the type of crime and atrocities, we get to know that on an average: 553 Murders, 2990 Hurt cases, 919 Rapes, 184 Kidnapping/abduction, 47 Dacoity, 127 Robbery, 456 Arson, 1485 civil right violation under OCR ACT, 6174 atrocities under atrocities Act and 12, 995 other offences were registered every year by the dalits. During the latest year 2000 the break-up of the atrocities and violence include 473cases of murder, 3139 of grievous hurt, 251 cases of arson and 992 cases of rape, 631 case under PCR ACT, 6350 cases under PA Act and 12149 cases of other offences.

Of the total crimes about 94 percent is accounted by the eleven sample states. Four BIMARU states however accounted bulk of the crimes and atrocities. In fact in 2000 Uttar Pradesh, Rajasthan, and Madhya Pradesh account for about 65 percent of crimes and atrocities against SC in the country, and this is far higher than their in the total SC population in the country which is 65 percent. Southern States: Andhra Pradesh, Karnataka, Tamil Nadu and Kerala are no less good. Gujarat and Maharashtra also accounts for worst cases of crimes reported against Dalits. Uttar Pradesh tops the list of pending cases with 74303, followed by Maharashtra Rajasthan Orissa Andhra Pradesh Tamil Nadu Karnataka and Kerala. Conviction rate is very low whereas the acquittal rate is very high.After having presented the magnitude of crime and atrocities based on the official statistic we try to get insight in to the pattern of violence and atrocities based on the field survey which again the Commission have been conducted in eleven states.

9.2.1.1. Andhra Pradesh

The primary survey revealed that these crimes take numerous forms.It include Murder, Rape, Naked Parading of a Dalit woman, Social Boycott, Grievous Hurt, Beating, Attacking of Dalit Bastis,

Destruction of Properties, Causing Serious Injuries, Death in Police custody, Encroachment on Dalit lands, Bonded Labour, Forceful Eviction from House- sites, Harassment due to love relationship with Caste Hindu, Suicide due to humiliation & excessive beating by the Police, Beating up for riding a cycle; wearing nice cloths; for sitting in the Bus, Harassment of Dalits Sarpanches and Panchayat members, and Resentment and insult over winning of Dalit. Whenever Dalits have tried to organize themselves or assert their rights, there has been a backlash from the high caste feudal lords resulting in mass killings, gang rapes and arsoning of Dalit.

9.2.1.2. Bihar

Bihar represents one of the leading states in term of magnitude and intensity of violence on the dalits. Massacres after massacre and endless list yields obnoxious results- the number of Dalits killed are extremely high. The nature of atrocities that are committed on the Dalits vary in forms but there has been a single underlying logic of demeaning them and forcing them into retreat- a passive and submissive existence. They range from a macro level organized violence and repression through formation of Senas to the micro level, ban on entering village temple or discriminatory use of ghats and a forceful implementation of these discriminatory un-written rules by non-Dalit castes. The other quite commonly encountered forms of atrocity have been intentional acts designed to demean the community through challenging the notions of izzat that exists in the community. These have been the common theme in all the regions of Bihar.

9.2.1.3. Karnataka

The survey data revealed that the atrocities took number of forms like Murder, Rape, Grievous injuries, Arson, Abuse and insults, illegal occupation of Dalit lands, Bonded labour, foisting of false cases & unlawful arrests/detention by Police, Prevalence of Devadasi system, discrimination in Hotels & Tea stalls, No access to wells and other drinking water sources, Outraging the modesty of Dalit women, naked parading of Dalit Women, Forcing Dalits force to consume human waste. Brutal repression is unleashed when Dalits refuse to carry out the traditional work related to all kinds of menial and degrading jobs.

9.2.1.4. Madhya Pradesh

The field data revealed various types of atrocities being committed which include, Murder, Attempt to Murder, Rape, Arson, Hurt, Abuse; insult & beating, wrongful confinement & arrests, Attack on Dalit houses and outraging the modesty of Dalit women, Eviction from houses, Forceful driving away from villages, etc. In the recent past the atrocities against Dalits in the state have increased due to various reasons. Opening of avenues for the Dalits, has provoked the high caste to violence. Some of the sample cases provide insight in to the nature and pattern of atrocities against the dalit in M.P.

9.2.1.4.1. Maharashtra

Maharashtra, which is known for social movement, does not have good record with respect to atrocities against. The sample cases presented here throw light on the grim reality about the human rights violation of Dalits in some part of the state. In 2000 a total of 489 cases of crimes, untouchability and atrocities were registered by the dalits and this include 2 murder, 16 cases of hurt, 49 rapes, 98 cases of untouchability and 128 cases of atrocities.

9.2.1.5. Orissa

The atrocities documented during the study relate more generally to land disputes, payment of low wages, utilisation of common property resources and enforcement of caste based discrimination and untouchability. In most cases, the police or the State have had minimal role to play and never been sited as having given any justice to the Dalits. It might be said clearly that the State's responsibility to protect the dignity and livelihood of Dalits has been violated in many instances.

9.2.1.6. Punjab

The Field survey indicates that the cases of atrocities against Dalits in rural Punjab are not all that glaring. Of all the 51 villages studied, there was only one village in the Malwa region from where a case of social boycott of Dalits by the dominant castes was reported to have taken place during the last five years. Boycotting no longer works as an effective method of controlling Dalits in rural Punjab. However, there have been a few cases of "individual oriented" atrocities. Though the caste factor remains important in these cases, so far most of these cases did not lead to the involvement of the entire caste communities in the conflict. Most frequent cases of atrocities reported from rural Punjab are those of physical beatings. About 8 cases of physical beating were reported from the sample village most of those who work as attached labourers on annual contract basis do so out of some economic compulsions, invariably involving debt from the employer farmer.

9.2.1.7. Rajasthan

The Dalits in Rajasthan face far more hostile situation than in Punjab, given the feudal and deeply caste ridden character of the society.In 2000 a total of 5190 cases of crimes, untouchability and atrocities were registered by dalit. This include 48 cases of murder, 153 hurt, 128 cases of rapes and 454 cases of atrocities. This ratio of crimes against dalit was much higher than their share in the countries SC population, which was about only 5.5 percent.In fact Rajastan's share in the crime was four time higher than its share in SC population.

9.2.1.8. Tamil Nadu

The atrocities committed against Dalits are on the increase in Tamil Nadu. The raising trend in the atrocities in Tamil Nadu is closely associated with growing assertion among the dalit in the state. These atrocities are brutal in nature leading to grievous hurt and murder of dalit. They are aimed at generating scare, and fear psychosis so that Dalit would be forced to accept their subordinate status. The purpose behind most of the atrocities is to root out Dalit resistance, socially, psychologically and economically.

9.2.1.9. Uttar Pradesh

The state of U.P rank first both in term of absolute number of crimes against SC and in term of U.P.'s share of crimes against SC in the total crimes committed against SC in the country. U.P account for almost one third of the total crimes committed against the SC in the country and this ratio was much higher than the U.P. SC population's share in the total SC population in the country. In 2000 about 6600 cases of crimes were registered by the dalits with police. Theses include 302 murder, 761 cases of hurt, 346 rapes, 142 cases of arson, and 2683 cases of atrocities. The high number of cases registered under the atrocities is a grim reminder of the continuing and unabated violence and atrocities against the Scheduled Castes in the state Information from the field study in the form of sample case studies across the villages indicated cases of atrocities related to bonded labour, depriving of government housing scheme,false cases for theft,restriction on the use of public roads and discrimination in wage payments

9.2.2. Poverty and Human Deprivation

We examine the changes in achievement indicators which capture the sum total of the improvement in level of living of dalits with respect to some basic needs such as food, health,education and housing. These basic needs which capture the cumulative achievement include poverty, education, health and housing indicators.. The data on most of these indicators by social groups are available from the early 1980's to late 1990's at various points of time.

The poverty ratio for SCs and others for 1983, 1993-94 and 1999-2000 at state level.The incidence of rural poverty among the SC has declined from 58 percent 1983-84 to,48 percent in 1983-84 and further down to 35 percent. The percentage of rural Sc poor reduced at per annum rate per annum rate of 2.9% during 1983/2000, the rate of decline is however by 1.9% during 1983/93 and 4.6% during 93/2000. Due to the problem associated with 55 round this results have to be taken with lot of caution. 2 The incidence of poor among the SC urban household has also declined from 56.5 %,in 1983-84 to 49% in 1993-94 and further down to 36.6 % in 1999-2000, that is by about 2.6 % per annum during 1984/2000. The rate of decline is relatively high during the 1990's compared with the 1980's. There are however, differences in the direction and rate of change in rural and urban poverty between SC and Non-sc/st? At all India level the rural poverty has declined both SC and other group. There is however difference in the rate of decline between the two groups.Between 1983/2000 the rural poverty among the non sc/st declined at slightly higher rate as compared with Sc. In the 1980's there is not much difference in the rate of decline among the two social groups. In 1990's the poverty among the SC has declined at lower rate as compared with nonsc/st group the difference being 1.3% points.

The urban poverty among the SC has also declined by less per annum rate compared with non sc/st during the overall period and also during the two periods. The urban poverty declined at per annum rate of 2.36% for the Sc as compared to 3.91 % for non sc/st during 1984/2000. Similarly urban poverty decline at the per annum rate of 1.23 % and 4.2% during 1980's and 1990's respectively for Sc and non sc/st,as compared with 2.42% and 6.4 % for Sc and non sc/st during 1980's and 1990's respectively. Trend in disparity in poverty between SC and Non-Sc/St –1983/84—1999-2000 The objective of the government policy towards Sc is not only to improve their level of living but also to reduce the gap between them and nonsc/st group and bring them on par with the latter.

Between 1983/93 the disparity ratio and disparity index have declined by 1.96 % and 6.95 % respectively. During 1993/2000 however, both disparity ratio and disparity index have increased by 8.67 % and 1.01 % respectively. During the overall period 1983/2000 while the disparity ratio has increased by 6.64 % the disparity index declined by 16.12 percent. Thus disparity in the rural poverty between Sc and nonsc/st has increased during the 1990's both in term of disparity ratio and disparity index, the period which co-inside with liberalization of Indian economy.

Unlike disparity in rural poverty, the disparities in the urban poverty have enhanced during overall period by about 26 per cent and also during both 1980's and 1990's. The rate of increase in the disparities was higher during the 1980's as compared to the 1990's. During the overall period, 1983/2000 the disparity in poverty of Sc. and non sc/st has increased in as many as fourteen states. About ten states in the 1990's and eleven in the 1980's experienced an increase in disparity ratio.

To combine the trend in poverty and disparity, it is clear that in the case of rural poverty the decline in its incidence among the SC was accompanied by decline in disparity in 1980's.During the 1990 however,the decline in rural poverty among the Sc was associated with increase in disparity between Sc and non sc/st. In the case of urban poverty decline in urban poverty was associated with increase in disparity both during 1980's, and 1990' and the overall period between 1983/2000.

9.2.2.1. Human development

The human development has often been shown by its composite index, which basically has three key components – *longevity, knowledge and standard of living.* The composite index of HDI reveals many aspects of human condition. Beside consumption poverty, the human development is also reflected by some critical health indicators such as life expectancy and other indicators of mortality and morbidity. Life expectancy and indicator of mortality and morbidity infact capture and reflect the cumulative impact of good or bad standard of living of any population. The life expectancy estimates for 1998-99 and 1992-93 bring out the situation of SC vis-à-vis the non SC/ST. In 1992-93 the LE was 62, 63 and 58 years for all India average, Others and SCs respectively. Thus in 1992-93 the LE of SCs was lower compared with non SC/STs by about five years and four years compared to the all India average.

Malnutrition is generally considered a common disseminator of deprivation that reduces child survival. Taking the health status of women in 1998-99, among SC women, about 33 per cent women suffered from anemia as compared to only 15 percent among non SC/ST.

The nutritional status of women and children brings out the disparities between SC and non-SC/ST women and children. The indicator of undernourishment of the children is much higher for SC children - 54 per cent for SC and 44 per cent for non SC/ST. Similarly, undernourishment reflected in terms of stunting was 52 per cent for SC children and 43 per cent non SC/ST children. In case of wasting as indicator of undernourishment, however the difference is minimum. The indicators of nutritional status of women also bring out similar disparities between Sc and nonsc/st.These include height below 145 centi meter and Body mass index. The values of both indicators are generally higher for SC women –17 and 42 per cent for Sc women as compared with 12 and 32 per cent for non SC/ST women respectively.

The poor nutritional status, higher undernourishment, and higher incidence of anemia among children and women are culminated in higher incidence of mortality among the SC children, which is one of the important indicators of health status. Among the measures of mortality, the IMR is generally considered as the most sensitive and important indicator of health status of a population, which is determined by the leaving standard.

REFERENCES

Burman, B.K. Roy The problem of Untouchables. In Romesh Thapar (ed.) *Tribe, Caste and Religion in India*. Delhi: Macmillan 1977.

Das, D.P. *The Untouchable Story.* New Delhi: Allied 1975.

Desai, A.R. *Caste and Communal Violence in India*. Bombay: Popular 1985.

Dushkin, L. Scheduled Caste politics. In J.M. Mahar (ed.) *The Untouchables in Contemporary India*. Tucson: University of Arizona Press 1972.

Gokhale, J. *From Concessions to Confrontation: the Politics of an Indian Untouchable Community*. Bombay: Popular Prakashan 1993.

10

Dalits and Millennium Development Goals

In order to address the issues of poverty, hunger and development, 189 countries under the aegis of United Nations adopted and endorsed Millennium Development Goals (MDGs) through Millennium Declaration in September 2000. Millennium Development Goals (MDGs), representing global partnership, grew from the commitments and targets established at several world summits held in the 1990s. As a response to the world's development challenges and call of the civil society movements, the MDGs aim at halving poverty, providing universal education, reducing maternal and child mortality, overcoming gender inequalities, and combating AIDS and other diseases. Set for achieving by the year 2015, the MDGs are an agreed set of goals, which could be realised if all actors work together towards fulfilling their commitments seriously.

10.1. Millennium Development Goals

There are eight Millennium Development Goals (MDGs), addressing to the world's main development challenges, need to be achieved by 2015. The MDGs are drawn from the actions and targets contained in the Millennium Declaration. The 8 MDGs break down into 18 quantifiable targets that are measured by 48 indicators. The Millennium Development Goals:

— Synthesise, in a single package, many of the most important commitments made separately at the international conferences and summits of the 1990s;

— Recognise explicitly the interdependence between growth, poverty reduction and sustainable development;

— Acknowledge that development rests on the foundations of democratic governance, the rule of law, respect for human rights and peace and security;

— Are based on time-bound and measurable targets accompanied by indicators for monitoring progress; and

— Bring together, in the eighth Goal, the responsibilities of developing countries with those of developed countries, founded on a global partnership endorsed at the International Conference on Financing for Development in Monetary, Mexico in 2002, and again at the Johannesburg World Summit on Sustainable Development in August 2003.

10.1.1. MDGs: Targets, Indicators and Progress

10.1.1.1. Goal 1: Eradicate extreme poverty and hunger

— *Target 1:* Halve, between 1990 and 2015, the proportion of people whose income is less than one dollar a day

  — *Indicator 1:* Proportion of population below $ 1 purchasing power parity (PPP) per day poverty head count ratio

  — *Indicator 2:* Poverty Gap Ratio

  — *Indicator 3:* Share of poorest Quintile in National Consumption

— *Target 2:* Halve between 1990 and 2015, the proportion of people who suffer from hunger.

  — *Indicator 4:* Prevalence of underweight children under five years of age.

  — *Indicator 5:* Proportion of population below minimum level of dietary energy consumption

10.1.1.1.1. Progress

Global poverty rates are falling, led by Asia. But millions more people have sunk deep into poverty in sub - Saharan Africa, where the poor are getting poorer. Since 1990, millions more people are chronically hungry in sub - Saharan Africa and in Southern Asia, where half the children under age 5 are malnourished.

10.1.1.2. Goal 2: Achieve universal primary education

— *Target 3:* Ensure that, by 2015, children everywhere, boys and girls alike, will be able to complete a full course of primary school

— *Indicator 6:* Net enrolment ratio in primary education

— *Indicator 7:* Proportion of pupils starting grade 1 who reach grade 5.

— *Indicator 8:* Literacy rate of 15-24 year olds.

10.1.1.2.1. Progress

Five developing regions are approaching universal enrolment. But in sub-Saharan Africa, less than two thirds of children are enrolled in primary school. Other regions, including Southern Asia and Oceania, also have a long way to go. In these regions and elsewhere, increased enrolment must be accompanied by efforts to ensure that all children remain in school and receive a high-quality education.

10.1.1.3. Goal 3: Promote gender equality and empower women

— *Target 4:* Eliminate Gender disparity in Primary and secondary education, preferably by 2015, and in all levels of education no later than 2015

— *Indicator 9:* Ratio of girls to boys in primary, secondary and tertiary education Indicator 10: Ratio of literate women to men, 15-24 year olds Indicator 11: Share of women in wage employment in the non – agricultural sector Indicator 12: Proportion of seats held by women in national parliament.

10.1.1.3.1. Progress

The gender gap is closing in primary school enrolment in the developing world. This is a first step towards easing long-standing inequalities between women and men. Though progress is being made, women still lack equal representation at highest levels of government, holding only 16 per cent of parliamentary seats worldwide.

10.1.1.4. Goal 4: Reduce child mortality

— *Target 5:* Reduce by two thirds, between 1990 and 2015, the under –five mortality rate

  — *Indicator 13:* Under five mortality rate

  — *Indicator 14:* Infant mortality rate

  — *Indicator 15:* Proportion of 1-year-old children immunized against measles.

10.1.1.4.1. Progress

Death rates in children under age 5 are dropping. But not fast enough. Eleven million children a year — 30,000 a day — die from preventable or treatable causes. Expanding existing programmes that promote simple and low-cost solutions could save most of these lives.

10.1.1.5. Goal 5: *Improve maternal health*

— *Target 6:* Reduce by three quarters, between 1990 and 2015, the maternal mortality ratio

  — *Indicator 16:* Maternal mortality ratio (MMR)

  — *Indicator 17:* Proportion of births attended by skilled health personnel

10.1.1.5.1. Progress

More than half a million women die each year during pregnancy or childbirth. Twenty times that number suffer serious injury or disability. Some progress has been made in reducing maternal deaths in developing regions, but not in the countries where giving birth is most risky.

10.1.1.6. Goal 6: Combat HIV/AIDS, malaria and other diseases

— *Target 7:* Have halted by 2015 and begun to reverse the spread of HIV / AIDS

  — Indicator 18: HIV Prevalence among Pregnant Women Aged 15 –24 Years

  — *Indicators 19:* Condom use rate of the contraceptive prevalence rate

- *Indicator 19:* Condom use at last high – risk - sex
- *Indicator 19:* Contraceptive Prevalence Rate
- *Indicator 20:* Ratio of School Attendance of Orphans to School Attendance of non-orphan aged 10-14 years

— *Target 8:* Have halted by 2015 and begun to reverse the incidence of malaria and other major diseases

- *Indicator 21:* Prevalence and Death Rates associated with Malaria
- *Indicator 22:* Proportion of population in Malaria-risk Areas using Effective Malaria Prevention and Treatment Measures Indicator 23: Prevalence and Death Rates Associated with Tuberculosis Indicator 24: Proportion of Tuberculosis Cases Detected and Cured under directly observed treatment short course (DOTS)

10.1.1.6.1. Progress

AIDS has become the leading cause of premature death in sub-Saharan Africa and the fourth largest killer worldwide. In the European countries of the Commonwealth of Independent States (CIS) and parts of Asia, HIV is spreading at an alarming rate. Though new drug treatments prolong life, there is no cure for AIDS, and prevention efforts must be intensified in every region of the world if the target is to be reached. Ninety per cent of malaria deaths occur in sub-Saharan Africa, where prevention and treatment efforts are being scaled up. Tuberculosis is on the rise, partly as a result of HIV/AIDS, though a new international protocol to detect and treat the disease is showing promise.

10.1.1.7. Goal 7: Ensure environmental sustainability

— *Target 9:* Integrate the principles of sustainable development into country policies and programmes and reverse the loss of environmental resources

- *Indicator 25:* Proportion of Land Area Covered by Forest
- *Indicator 26:* Ratio of Area Protected to Maintain Biological Diversity to surface Area.

— *Indicator 27:* Energy use (Kg oil equivalent) per $ 1 GDP (PPP)
— *Indicator 28:* Carbon Dioxide emissions per capita and Consumption of Ozone-depleting Cholorofluoro Carbons (CFCs) (ODP Tons) .
— *Indicator 29:* Proportion of Population Using Solid Fuels

— *Target 10:* Halve, by 2015, the proportion of people without sustainable access to safe drinking water and basic sanitation
— *Indicator 30:* Proportion of population with sustainable access to an improved water source, urban and rural
— *Indicator 31:* Proportion of Population with access to improved sanitation, urban and rural

— *Target 11:* By 2020, to have achieved a significant improvement in the lives of at least 100 million slum dwellers
— *Indicator 32:* Proportion of Households with access to secure tenure

10.1.1.7.1. Progress

Most countries have committed to the principles of sustainable development. But this has not resulted in sufficient progress to reverse the loss of the world's environmental resources. Achieving the goal will require greater attention to the plight of the poor, whose day-to-day subsistence is often directly linked to the natural resources around them, and an unprecedented level of global cooperation. Access to safe drinking water has increased, but half the developing world still lacks toilets or other forms of basic sanitation.

10.2. Millennium Development Goals and Indian Dalits

The Planning Commission of India, in its Tenth Five Year Plan document, has outlined India's human development goals and targets for the next 10 years. These are related to and are more ambitious than the MDGs. These targets were fixed by the erstwhile government in the centre. There is new government in the Centre now. This new government has resolved to work to fulfil its commitments mentioned in the commonly accepted National Common Minimum Programme (NCMP).

The Millennium Declaration adopted by the Government of India in September 2000 reaffirmed its commitment to the right to development, peace, security and gender equality to the eradication of many dimensions of poverty and to overall sustainable development. The head of the country at the General Assembly of the United Nations pledged to adopt new measures and join efforts in the fight against poverty, illiteracy, hunger, lack of education, gender equality, infant and maternal mortality, disease and environmental degradation. The Tenth year plan rightly took the note of the MDGs and included a number of targets to be achieved during the plan period.

There are improvements in the lives of people over the years. This has been possible due to the planned implementation of programmes, despite the enormous and complex problems and diversities.

All the monitor-able indicators and progress towards achieving MDGs in India paints a rosy picture as far as presented data is concerned. However, the ground realities are something different. Looking at dalits and adivasi groups, their situation has not really changed. Today's dalits and Adivasis are living in distressed conditions. Though National Food for Work Programme and National Employment Guarantee Act (NREGA), 2005 has been introduced in selected 150 and 200 districts respectively, but its implementation status is not very progressive.

The above is also true in for Millennium Development Goals. While the Indian government is claiming that things are on the track, but for Dalits and Adivasis, there is not much to cheer about. In a state like Uttar Pradesh only 7.2 percent of the amount earmarked has been utilised under the National Food for Work programme. Even NREGA seems to be very progressive, but its accessibility to dalits and adivasi groups is still a distant dream.

The word Dalit has its origin in Pali, a pre-Sanskrit language and it means the deprived. This term is used as an act of confident assertion, rejecting nomenclature of Harijan, the 'children of God'. Dalit Panthers, a radical movement of Dalit youth in the seventies used this term for the first time for those who were Scheduled Castes and Scheduled Tribes, neo-Buddhist, the working-people, the land-less and poor peasants, women, and all those who are being exploited politically, socially, economically, and in the name of religion. The term Dalit does not refer to a caste. It symbolises unity of all those who suffered at the hands of iniquitous Brahmanism, which is the basis of Hindutva. It is a symbol of change and revolution. Dalits believe in humanism. However, the term is usually seen today in a much narrower context of referring only to Untouchables and Adivasis communities of the past.

10.2.1. Dalits: Social and Economic Context

In 2001, the Scheduled Castes and Scheduled Tribes constituted 24.4 percent of India's population. The population of Scheduled Castes and Scheduled Tribes as per the 2001 census was 166.67 million and 84.32 million respectively.

Dalits today not only constitute numerically an important section of the Indian society but also represent a community still struggling to break out of the centuries of mental bondage of the oppressive and hegemonic Brahmanical/Hindutva order and inhuman existence. Social injustice, cultural and economic deprivation and exclusion of Scheduled Castes, Scheduled Tribes and other backward classes have a historical legacy. They also had special privileges and powers in cultural, economic, political, legal and administrative fields, which were sanctified by the religious scriptures.

Right to education and gaining knowledge, right to vocation or choose employment and right to good habitations, which form three principles needs for Human Development, were officially denied to the Dalits and Adivasis. Stories of Shambhuka Vadh and chopping of thumb of Adivasi child Eklavya indicate this denial. This denial resulted in the lack of not only Human Development among the Dalits and Adivasis, but also prevented any significant technological changes in the means of production involving the labouring classes.

The colonial rule brought about certain basic changes in the economic structure and sowed the seeds of capitalism. For the first time crime and punishment were de-linked with caste and social status. Legal ownership and tenancy backed up by courts operating on definition of legal private property was firmly established. This resulted in emergence of individuals in every caste who could get education, a little bit of land and some access to new opportunities.

In other areas also, the law opened some possibilities for advancement and change to the lower castes, but it did not provide, any special leverage for the lowly, and hence tended to strengthen the then existing distribution of resources.

Independent India inherited the same social, legal and administrative structure set up by the British with complete dominance of the higher castes in all spheres. The post-independence India has basically seen the consolidation and strengthening of the hold of the minuscule upper castes elite in the emerging new economic and social order.

10.2.1.1. The scheduled castes

According to the 2001 Census, the Scheduled Castes population in India stands at 166,635,700 persons which constitute 16.2 per cent of the country's population. Of the total Scheduled Castes population, 79.8 per cent live in rural areas and 20.2 per cent live in urban areas. The sex ratio of 936 females per thousand males is slightly higher than national average of 933 sex ratios.

The largest proportion of population of the Scheduled Castes to total population of the State is found in Punjab followed by Himachal Pradesh and West Bengal. In Andhra Pradesh, Karnataka and Pondicherry proportion of SCs population is exactly equal to the National average of 16.2 per cent. The smallest concentration of the Scheduled Castes population is in the North-eastern Adivasi States such as Mizoram followed by Meghalaya and Arunachal Pradesh. The highest percentage of Scheduled Castes population to the total SCs population of the country is reported in Uttar Pradesh followed by West Bengal and Bihar Andhra Pradesh and Tamil Nadu. In fact, more than 57 per cent of total SCs population inhabit in these five States.

At the district level, there are only 22 districts where the SC population is 30 per cent or more as per the 2001 Census. In majority of the districtsthe concentration of SC population to the total population is between 10 to 20 per cent. In Nagaland, Lakshadweep, Andaman and Nicobar Islands, no Scheduled Caste is notified.

10.2.1.2. The scheduled tribes

The total population of the Scheduled Tribes in India stands at 84,326,240 persons as per the 2001 Census. They constitute 8.2 per cent of the total population of the country. Out of their total population in the country, 91.7 per cent were living in rural areas, whereas, only 8.3 per cent from urban areas. The sex ratio of Scheduled Tribes population was 978 females per thousand males. The sex ratio among Scheduled Tribes population is higher than that of the total population of the country as well as that of SCs. The proportion of the Scheduled Tribes to the total population of the States/Union territories is highest in Mizoram and Lakshadweep followed by Nagaland Meghalaya. Within the major states Chhattisgarh has the highest percentage of Scheduled Tribes population followed by Jharkhand and Orissa. These proportions are in the lowest in Uttar Pradesh Bihar Tamil Nadu and Kerala. Madhya Pradesh accounts for the highest percentage of Scheduled Tribes population to total STs population of the country followed by Maharashtra Orissa, Gujarat, Rajasthan, Jharkhand and Chhattisgarh. In fact, 68 per cent of the country's Scheduled Tribes population lives in these seven States.

In a little over half of the total number of 543 districts, STs accounted for less than 5% of the total population. On the other hand, in 75 districts the share of STs to total population was 50% or higher. In Haryana, Punjab, Chandigarh, Delhi and Pondicherry, no Scheduled Tribe is notified.

As the first decade of the 21st Century unfolds, Millennium Development Goals (MDGs) and the Millennium Campaign around these Goals is gaining the centre stage in the development debate of United Nations, Governments and international development agencies. The formulation of the MDGs has been contested. These goals have been the subject of a serious debate, relating to the very relevance and significance of the MDGs. On the positive side, the MDGs have been portrayed as 'a development manifesto for ordinary citizens around the world: time-bound, measurable, pocketbook issues that they can easily understand – and more importantly, with adequate data, the Goals seek to hold their governments and the international community accountable for their achievement'. The MDGs have been criticised for sidelining the critical and important issues of human rights and for ignoring inequitous international economic structure, which is antagonistic to the achievement of the MDGs themselves.

A pragmatic approach to the MDGs, based on a critical assessment of the issues involved, demands situating the emergence of MDGs as the culmination of a historical process, caught between two streams within the United Nations system – two streams, simultaneous but mutually contradictory. Centring on the various Human Rights Conventions and based on the series of Global summits over the 1990's, this approach put forth a strong human right-focused perspective on Social development. The policies and economic strategies promoted by the World Bank, IMF and WTO today often contradict important UN Conventions on development and human rights, and undermine the UN's commitment to the MDGs.

The 2003 Human Development Report of UNDP provides a sort of a semi-mid-term review of the progress of the implementation of MDGs by various countries. The major point that emerges from the review is the fact that even in successful cases of MDGs implementation; certain groups have been excluded or left behind. "In Brazil, China, India and Mexico overall progress has been excellent. But some areas and groups are not benefiting enough, while wealthy segments of the population continue to surge ahead..."

The groups, so excluded or left behind, have been identified as women, ethnic and racial minorities and rural inhabitants. This includes Dalits and Adivasi in India. They are also termed as special social groups. Though it is heartening to see the question of gender finding mention routinely, there is hardly a mention of Dalits or Adivasis, who still continue to be the most excluded communities of the country. This chapter has hardly taken any notice of the conditions of the Dalits and Adivasis vis-à-vis MDGs. Successive reports by the National Commission for Scheduled Castes and Scheduled Tribes, National Commission for Human Rights, National Commission for Women, National Minority Commission, Planning Commission's Working Groups on Scheduled Castes and Scheduled Tribes, Government of India Task Force on Scheduled Castes and Scheduled Tribes, Ministry of Social Justice and Empowerment, and the Millennium Development Goals India Country report 2005 by Government of India, and many other studies and reports in their equivocal voice have said that in this country, dalits have tended to be excluded and have lagged behind other sections of population in literally every dimension of human and social development.

10.2.2. Poverty and Dalits

Since the inception of development planning in India, the main concern of the development strategy has been to improve the standard of living of its people. This was sought to be achieved by raising economic growth, particularly by investing larger share of resources in industry. However, by the late 1960s it had become quite clear that growth had not percolated down to the poor to the desired extent and millions of them were still living in deplorable conditions. This was particularly the case of certain sections of the society, viz. the Scheduled Castes and the Scheduled Tribes.

The persistence of poverty in India despite achieving increase in per capita income levels over the successive five - year plans has remained a matter of concern for the policy makers. Quantification of poverty based on certain minimum consumption standards has evolved in the official circles in India since 1970s. The Planning Commission uses poverty line, based on per capita consumption expenditure, as the criterion to determine the persons living below the poverty line. The latter is obtained from the large sample surveys of household consumer expenditure conducted by the National Sample Survey Organization every five years.

Based on the same Surveys, it is possible to estimate the proportion of people living below the poverty line for different social groups viz. SCs, STs, etc. It may be mentioned that the poverty ratios for SCs and STs have not been estimated for all the States.

At the all-India level the poverty ratio for the rural areas was 37.3 percent in 1993-94 and it declined to 27.1 percent by 1999-2000. The corresponding ratios for the urban households were 32.4 percent and 23.65 percent respectively. The poverty ratios for SCs and STs were significantly higher both in 1993-94 and 1999-2000.

It may be observed that as against 27 percent of all population living below the poverty line in the rural areas in 1999-2000, 36 percent of SC population and 46 percent of ST population lived below the poverty line. There was a decline in the poverty ratio of 27% for all population, 25% for SCs and 12% for STs as compared to 1993-94. This implies that the poverty ratio declined faster for all population than for SCs and STs, though between the SCs and STs, the decline has been more rapid in the case of former. However, there is significant difference between the rural and the urban areas. In the rural areas the proportion of SC population living in poverty is lower than poverty ratio of ST population. As a result the ratio of people living in poverty for SCs and STs to (all) population below poverty line has changed significantly.

It may also be observed that the poverty ratio has declined faster in the case of SCs than for STs. This is true of both the rural as well as of the urban areas. There are large variations in the proportion of population living below the poverty line across the States. In the rural areas of Bihar, close to 70 percent of the SCs and STs lived below the poverty line in 1993-94; similarly over 70 percent of the ST population in Orissa was below the poverty line. Even in better-off States like Maharashtra, the poverty ratio for the SCs and the STs was over 50 percent both in the rural as well as the urban areas in that year. On the other hand around one fourth of the SCs and ST population in the rural areas of Punjab lived in poverty. In 1999-2000, over 70 percent of the ST population in rural Orissa and over 70 percent of the SC population in urban Orissa lived below the poverty line. The proportion of SC and ST population living in poverty in rural areas of Bihar was close to 60 percent in that year. On the other around one-eighth of Punjab's SC and ST population was below the poverty line. It may be mentioned that the proportion of all population living below the poverty line in most of the States is significantly lower than the proportion of SC and ST population living below the poverty line. There are a few exceptions mainly in the urban areas, particularly for the Adivasis.

10.2.2.1. Dalits below the Poverty Line

One of the measures to analyse the state of the poor persons is the income gap ratio (IGR). It essentially measures the difference between the poverty line and the average consumption of the people living below the poverty line and can be expressed symbolically as

$$IGR = Pl - P^* / Pl$$

where IGR = Income Gap Ratio

Pl = Poverty Line

P* = Average Consumption of people below poverty line

Though the poverty ratio between the SCs, STs and the total population varies significantly, the income gap ratio in most of the States is not significantly different between SC, ST and All-population. This is true both of rural and the urban areas. This would seem to suggest that while the chances of SCs and STs being poor are significantly higher than that of the total population in most of the states, the condition of the poor as reflected in the consumption pattern of the Surveys conducted by the NSSO in 1993-94 and 1999-2000 and measured by the income-gap ratio is unlikely to be very different for SCs, STs and all population.

It may further be mentioned that this assertion needs to be examined further in detail as it could have policy implications for anti-poverty programmes. Although there has been a reduction in the incidence of poverty among all sections of society including Scheduled Castes, the reduction was comparatively lesser in case of Scheduled Castes in Urban areas. But the situation is strikingly worse in case of urban Scheduled Caste population. Their housing and economic empowerment would be the main areas of concern although education, health and safe drinking water for the urban SC population, which mostly dwells in the slums, are not far behind.

Collating some of the facts in different government reports and correlating them with the major Goals and Targets of MDGs can indeed be revealing - as to how far, after more than 50 years of planning, the socio-economic status of dalits has significantly lagged behind that of others, vis-à-vis the goals of the MDG.

Though the official data on poverty suggest a reduction in the percentage of population below the poverty line, there is a reason for presuming that the incidence of hunger is increasing. The proportion of the rural population accessing less than 1800 kcal/day exceeds 30 percent. This is indeed cause for concern for larger dalits and adivasi community. There are several incidences of starvation deaths experienced in the state of Uttar Pradesh in recent days, which has been raised by NACDOR and its community based organization, but action in favour of the community like Musahar and Saharia is still inactive. Maternal and foetal under-nutrition is resulting in the birth of babies with low birth weight. This has serious consequences for the future intellectual capital of India.

10.2.3. Dalits and Educational Status

In India, the crude literacy rate of Scheduled Castes increased from 10.27 in 1961 to 45.20 in 2001 registering an increase of 34.9

percentage points in the last forty years. The crude literacy of Scheduled Tribes was 8.53% in 1961, which increased to 38.41% in 2001 registering an increase of 29.88 percentage points in the last forty years.

The Effective Literacy Rate for SCs in 2001 Census is 54.69 and in 1991 Census was 37.41 registering an increase of 17.28 percentage points between 1991 and 2001. The effective literacy rate for STs in 2001 Census is 47.1 and in 1991 Census was 29.6 registering an increase of 17.5 percentage points in the last ten years. The literacy percentage of SC/ST when compared with the literacy percentage of other communities other than SCs /STs during 1991 and 2001 reflects that the literacy gap has decreased from 20.28 in 1991 to 14.12 in 2001 in respect SCs and from 28.09 in 1991 to 21.71 in 2001 in respect of STs to other than SC/ST. The reduction in the literacy gap between the SCs and STs and others is a positive sign, yet the gap is quite large and sustained effort is required to bridge this.

10.2.3.1. Literacy

The performance of literacy rate of Scheduled Castes in 2001 in states of Bihar, Jharkhand and Uttar Pradesh and that of Scheduled Tribes in states of Andhra Pradesh, Arunachal Pradesh, Bihar, Gujarat, J and K, Jharkhand, Karnataka, Madhya Pradesh Orissa, Rajasthan, Tamil Nadu, Uttar Pradesh, West Bengal and Dadra and Nagra Haveli is below 50%. Among the SCs the proportion of literates in 1991 was the highest in Kerala and the lowest was in Bihar. The pattern was similar in 2001 with the literacy rate being 82.7% in Kerala and the lowest 28.5% in Bihar, thereby showing a narrowing of gaps. As far as STs are concerned, Mizoram had the highest literacy rates in 1991 and 89.3% in 2001. This was the lowest in 19.4% in Rajasthan in 1991 and 28.2% in Bihar in 2001

10.2.3.2. Enrolment

Enrolment of SC and ST students has increased in all categories in Primary, Upper Primary, Secondary/Senior Secondary and Higher Education levels during the period 1995-96 to 2002-2003/2001-02. More so, percentage increase of ST enrolment is faster than that of SC enrolment.

Gross Enrolment Ratio: GER is defined as the percentage of enrolment in Primary and Upper Primary to the estimated child population in the age group 6 to below 11 years and 11 to below 14 years respectively. Enrolment in these stages includes underage and over-age children.

Dropout Rates: The data on dropout rate for the period 1996-97 to 2002-03 indicate decreasing trend and the decrease in percentage points. There is an improvement for SCs and STs in all categories of school education.

10.2.3.3. Drop outs

Drop out rates for All India fell during 1996-97 to 2002-03 by 5.3% for all children in Class I to V, although it fell by 1.3% for SCs and 5.2% for STs. The drop out rates increased in 2002-03 as compared to 1996-97 of scheduled castes in Madhya Pradesh, Meghalaya, Tamil Nadu, Uttar Pradesh, Dadar Nagar Haveli and Delhi and that of scheduled Tribes increased in Bihar, Madhya Pradesh, Meghalaya, Uttar Pradesh, West Bengal and Daman and Diu shows the quality of education is on decline in the above stated States/UTs.

10.2.3.4. Gender Inequality

The 1991 Census revealed the great disparity between SC women illiteracy rate and that of the general population. The SC female dropout rate at every stage of education is higher than that of either SC boys or the general female population.

10.2.4. Health status among SCs and STs

The National Health Policy-2002 recognizes that access to and benefits from, the public health system have been very uneven between the better endowed and the more vulnerable sections of society.

10.2.4.1. Total fertility rate

At the National level the Total Fertility Rate is higher among SC and STs as compared to others. In the States of Bihar, Haryana, J and K, M.P, Rajasthan, Sikkim and Uttar Pradesh the TFR among SCs is more than the average TFR among SCs at national level. It is further observed that in the States of Bihar, Delhi, Gujarat, Haryana, J and K,

Madhya Pradesh, Sikkim, and Uttaranchal the TFR among SCs is greater than 3 children whereas it is more than 4 in Rajasthan and Uttar Pradesh.

10.2.4.2. Neo natal, infant and child mortality rate

In 1998-99, the infant mortality rate among SCs was 83 and among STs were 84.2 against others of 67.6 per 1000 live births. According to NFHS II data, the neo natal mortality, Infant mortality, child mortality and under-five mortality is higher for SCs and STs at all India level compared with total mortality rates and mortality rates for others respectively.

10.2.4.3. Working population

'Work Participation Rate' is defined as the percentage of total workers to total population. The Work Participation Rate at All India level is highest among the Scheduled Tribes being 49.1 percent followed by Scheduled Castes and General population. The picture is somewhat similar in all the States/UTs where the Scheduled Tribes have much higher WPR followed by the Scheduled Castes. Among the Scheduled Castes, Andhra Pradesh has recorded the largest WPR being 50.5 followed by Himachal Pradesh Tamil Nadu and Karnataka.

Although the Scheduled Tribes and the Scheduled Castes appear to be doing well in the employment front, an in-depth examination of the data in terms of the availability of work throughout the year and the type of activity provides clearer picture of the deprivation. According to Census definition a Worker is categorised as 'Main Worker' if she/he has worked for 6 months or more, otherwise she/he is considered to be a 'Marginal Worker'.

While 80 percent of the workers among the general population are main workers, the share of main workers among Scheduled Castes is 73 percent and that among Scheduled Tribes is 69 percent. The situation is similar in the states with Jharkhand having the largest proportion of marginal workers among the Scheduled Castes and J and K and Orissa among the Scheduled Tribes.

Type of Economic activity: It will be interesting to look at the type of economic activities pursued by the different categories of population.

From the statement it comes out that an overwhelming proportion of Scheduled Tribes are engaged in basic agriculture work; only about 18 percent of the Scheduled Tribes are engaged in nonagricultural sectors, as against 34 percent among SCs and 47 percent among general population. This is mainly because more than 90 percent of the population lives in rural area. Although, the share of Scheduled Caste employees in all the Groups of services has increased from 1991 to 2001, yet there is still a shortfall in Group A and Group B. In Group C, it is at the desired level and in Group D it is 21.24% against a reservation of 15%.

10.2.4.4. Maternal Health

The National rural Health Mission seeks to provide effective healthcare to rural population throughout the country with special focus on 18 states, which have weak public health indicators and / or weak infrastructure. It has a key components provisions of a female health activist in each village. But the selection criteria for these Female health personnel are not pro SCs / STs. The minimum criteria of education standards do not suit for SCs / STs especially in underserved and un-served areas.

10.2.4.5. Combating Diseases

Comparing the institutional delivery at the country level, it is observed that indicators for both SCs and STs are less than others. Anaemia among SC and ST women is more compared to the women of other communities. It is also seen that at national the full vaccination among SC and ST infants is less compared to others. At national level Anaemia among SC and ST children is more than that prevalent among others. At national level the unmet need for limiting is more for SCs compared with unmet need for limiting among others. The same is true for unmet need among SCs with regard to spacing.

It was also observed that TB generally prevails among SCs and minorities. It is now well established that TB can be deadly when occurring in a patient of HIV/AIDs, especially due to the advent of new and drug resistant forms of the disease. The scenario for them does not look very bright, especially due to the fact that these populations have the least access to even basic healthcare.

10.2.4.6. Access to Water, Sanitation and Basic Amenities

According to the data on electricity based on Houses and households' amenities data, Census of India 2001, 55.8 percent of the households in the country have access to electricity. The extent of attainments and deprivation among SCs, STs vis- à- vis 'General' with regard to availability of electricity.

The 1991 figures excludes Jammu and Kashmir. The figures of 2001 excludes Mao-Maram, Paomata and Purab sub division of Senapati district of Manipur in 2001.

Though during the decade 1991-2001, the access to availability of electricity among the households of General, SCs and STs population increased by 13.3, 16.2 and 13.7 percent points respectively, still both the SCs and STs households were still deprived in comparison to General households. The criteria of 10 percent households using electricity was adopted based on the input given by Power Ministry for a village to be considered as electrified. At All India level, percentages are as follows:

The deprivation is clearly reflected among SCs and STs villages as compared to other villages.

Electrification in SCs households: Barring a few States namely JandK, Arunachal Pradesh, Mizoram, Daman and Diu where percentage of SC household electrification is more than the General category households, in most of the States the proportion of electrified household is less in SC category. Incidentally, these are also the States that have low level of overall household electrification. Thus, we can see that the States having low level of electrification have larger disparity between General and SC Category.

Electrification in STs Households: Overall 36.5% of ST households in the country have access to electricity. Barring the States of Uttar Pradesh and Sikkim, in all other States the percentage of electrified households is less in ST category compared to General Category.

ST population largely reside in forest, hilly and remote areas of the country, where rural electrification has not been able to penetrate much because it becomes difficult to sustain the commercial operation of electric supply as compared to the densely populated plain areas.

This is also one of the reasons for low household electrification in ST category compared to SC or General Category.

Status of drinking water supply to Scheduled Castes and Scheduled Tribes are coupled with inadequacy of available data. According to the Report of Census of India 2001, out of total 53.69 million urban households, the SCs and STs households are 7.808 million and 2.328 million respectively.

In India 45.2 percent households among the general population are having drinking water source within premises whereas only 27.0 percent Scheduled Castes and 15.2 percent Scheduled Tribes households have this facility. As regards availability of drinking water sources within premises at the state level, Punjab have 89.3 percent households among the general population followed by Lakshadweep Chandigarh Delhi and Kerala. Except Goa Maharashtra and Gujarat states, in rest of the states, the percentage of households having drinking water source within premises is below 50 percent. In case of Scheduled Castes households, the drinking water source within premises in Punjab, Delhi, Goa, Chandigarh and Kerala are 77.8 %, 56.9 %, 53.8 %, 53.0 % and 52.5 % households respectively.

Among the Scheduled Tribes households the situation is very discouraging, as compared to the General and Scheduled Caste households. Goa, Uttar Pradesh, Sikkim, and Uttaranchal have been reported 48.4 %, 47.2 %, 44.5 % and 44.0 percentages respectively have drinking water source within the premises. The remaining major states have reported less than 40 per cent households are having drinking water source within premises. While analysing, the data at Rural/Urban level, the scenario in general is much better in case of urban areas compared to rural areas. The SCs and STs are better compared to General population. The General households in Manipur, have drinking water source near premises followed by, Chhattisgarh Tamil Nadu Jharkhand and Himachal Pradesh. In remaining major states the percentage of households having drinking water source near premises were below 50 percent. While comparing the state level data for Scheduled Castes households, 74.5% households are having drinking water source near premises in Tamil Nadu followed by Pondicherry Chhattisgarh Manipur Bihar Jharkhand Andhra Pradesh Himachal Pradesh Madhya Pradesh Uttar Pradesh Karnataka Daman and Diu Tripura Orissa and West Bengal respectively. In rest of the states, less than 50 per cent households are having drinking water source near their premises.

There are eighteen states where General households are having drinking water source away premises higher than the national average 14.4 percentage. Of these states, Manipur leads the table in which 27.4 % households are having drinking water source away from their premises followed by other states. In case of Scheduled Castes Population 34.2% households are having drinking water source away from their premises in Orissa followed by Madhya Pradesh (28.3%), Jharkhand Karnataka Rajasthan Assam Haryana Tripura Uttaranchal Meghalaya Andhra Pradesh and Manipur Sikkim Kerala Chhattisgarh Mizoram Jammu and Kashmir Bihar and West Bengal. There are thirteen states where Scheduled Caste households are having drinking water source away from their premises were below the national average of 19.5 percent. A total of 28.2 % households among the Scheduled Tribes are having drinking water source away from their premises in comparison to 19.5 % and 14.4% among the Scheduled Castes and General households respectively.

The above discussions indicate that the gap between General, Scheduled Castes and Scheduled Tribes population in relation to drinking water source is high.

10.2.4.7. Sanitation

As per the 2001 Census data, 23.7 percent of Scheduled Castes households have latrine facility within premises as compared to 42.3 per cent general households. Among the Scheduled Tribes only 17 per cent households have latrine facilities. There are eighteen states where Scheduled Castes households and sixteen states where Scheduled Tribes households are have latrine facility below the national average at 36.4 percent. Of these states, Orissa Bihar Chhattisgarh Jharkhand Madhya Pradesh are the states where only less than 15 percent households are have latrine facility among Scheduled Castes households. On the other hand Orissa Chhattisgarh Madhya Pradesh Jharkhand Rajasthan Andhra Pradesh and Bihar are the states where less than 15 percent households are have Latrine facility among STs households. As regards, households with connectivity for waste-water outlet, 50.6 percent of general households, 42.9 percent of SCs households and 21.8 percent of STs Households have access to this facility in India.

10.2.4.8. Housing

Housing is one of basic requirements for human survival. For a normal citizen, owning a house provides significant economic security and dignity in society. For a shelter less person, possession of a house brings about a profound social change in his existence, endowing him with an identity, thus integrating him with his immediate social milieu. As per the 2001 Census, 57.7 percent of general households have permanent houses, whereas 42.8 percent SCs households and only 24.4 percent STs Households possessed permanent houses. The condition of housing for the Scheduled Castes in Orissa (19.5 percent), Chhattisgarh West Bengal BiharJharkhand Madhya Pradesh Uttar Pradesh and all the North-eastern states except Mizoram are below the national average. The condition of housing for STs is pre-dominantly Adivasi states are pitiable. Chhattisgarh has only 8.2 percent of their Adivasi households living in permanent houses followed by Jharkhand and Orissa.

10.3. Global Partnership for Dalit's Development

Today, in 2005, the scenario has undergone in amazing transformation. Telecommunication sector in India has witnessed a dramatic transformation on almost all the fronts and has achieved national recognition as the key driver for development and growth.

Prior to 1999, there were very few private operators in the field. With the announcement of National Telecom Policy (NTP) 1999, a large number of private operators have been given licenses.

The government vision is to use information technology as a tool for raising the living standards of the common man and enriching their lives towards this end an ambitious programme of PC and Internet penetration to the rural and under served urban areas has been taken up.

However a huge gap still exists between the development assistance required to meet the MDGs and what the developed countries have pledged so far. The accessibility level of IT among SC / ST is negligible in rural areas and extremely low in urban areas. Unfortunately there are no data available in this regard, but looking at the socio economic profile discussed in the report, it can be safely presumed that accessibility level of IT among SC / ST is extremely low both in rural and urban areas.

The connection between discrimination, poverty and hunger is evident. Social and economic indicators across South Asia reflect the fact that Dalits and indigenous people remain at the bottom of the society when it comes to education, income, employment, health, etc. The data mentioned above also justifies this in the Indian Context. In countries with a poor human rights record or ineffective protection of the poor and discriminated groups, international companies and investors have a particular responsibility to avoid violation of human rights and labour conventions and to contribute with affirmative action.

Discrimination against Dalits is often hidden to outsiders, but it is deeply engrained in the Indian society and it cuts across all sectors and livelihood areas. Dalits are also excluded and marginalised in the labour market, resulting in low income or lack of income and accompanying poverty.

Recent surveys reveal that international companies in India hardly employ any Dalits, although they constitute between 18-20% of the population. At the same time evidence is growing that it is unprofitable for business to enter into a system with widespread discrimination and not seek to address it. The caste system itself runs against efficient and rational operations.

Some examples are: A notion of purity and pollution, segregation of living / working areas; prohibitions on where to move and how to act in front of an upper caste person; Dalits are often denied access to public places, such as tea-shops and restaurants, and to public resources such as water taps, wells, and public grounds. The allocation of labour on the basis of caste is a fundamental part of the caste system. Dalits are forced to undertake certain types of work, the most menial, dirty and degrading work for a very low pay or meagre payment in kind. In the private sector, Dalits have a low employment record in proportion to their share of the total population - both in the rural areas and in the middle class occupations in the cities. The perception that Dalits should be restricted to their traditional low status occupation is widespread, and those who have obtained educational qualifications find it difficult to get work. Discrimination also includes fewer career opportunities and lower wages for Dalits.

Some companies may claim that there is no discrimination within their operations as they have a general policy of 'non discrimination'. In a society with systemic and engrained discrimination; special measures are need to be introduced in a big way, before any claims to existence of 'non discriminatory environment' can be made.

A country Risk Assessment on India made for companies by the HR and Business project identifies caste discrimination as a critical human rights issue in the country - which cuts across all major rights areas – and therefore constitutes a high risk factor for companies.

One particularly critical area for companies trading with and investing in India relates to the supplier or sub-contracting chain. Bonded labour, forced labour and child labour are widespread – it is estimated that 40 million people are kept in bondage and slavery working under horrifying conditions in for example agricultural, textile and handicraft production sectors. The reason for getting into bondage is poverty. Poor families with little or no income and no access to means of productions obtain loans from landlords and employers to cover basic living expenses and ensure daily survival. Due to high rates of interest and extremely low wages people are caught in forced labour sometime for generations. This area must be of special concern to companies with suppliers and sub-contractors in India.

10.3.1. Role of Private Sector

There is a strong need to eliminate caste discrimination in the labour market. It require interventions from international organisations, national organisations and government in association with the organisations of the Dalits develop guidelines to be adhered by all doing business in India and South Asia. This necessitates urgent action from the corporate world to reorient its policies so that they are just, fair and fit the constitutional morality of the country.

10.4. Agenda for the Future

The level of development in a society determines the quality of life enjoyed by its people. Development measures affect day to day life intimately and the degree of access on an individual or group to basic amenities and services reflect its relative status in the society. Therefore, the constitutional commitments to ensure equality in social relations can at once be tested through distributional aspects of development. This is much more in case of Dalits than in any other group for the simple reason that they under the oppressive stronghold of caste based social order compelled to live in a sub-human existence.

There are many areas where action agenda really need to focus. These areas are:

1) Adequate investment of public resources
   a. Government shall commit substantial funds as per norms set for the Special Component Plan and Tribal Sub Plan.
   b. Immediate reversal of budgetary trends of reducing allocations to the Dalits
   c. Financial stringency and other competitive commitments not to affect or dilute government spending on the developmental schemes of Scheduled Castes and Scheduled Tribes
2) Checking non-utilisation, wrong utilisation and diversion of earmarked, allocated or committed funds for the development of Scheduled Castes and Scheduled Tribes
3) Improvement in Development Planning by :
   a. Priority needs of Dalits – targeting 8 MDGs and their 18 targets
   b. Targeted interventions in the traditional occupation having large participation from the Scheduled Castes and Scheduled Tribes.
   c. Serious efforts to identify the extremely vulnerable sections within the Dalits and creating schemes catering to their requirements.
   d. Health issues of the Dalits are specifically addressed
   e. Scheduled Castes and Scheduled Tribes women to be focus of gender budgeting
   f. Attention to Dalit child labour and schemes to liberate them
   g. Innovative schools addressing needs of the Dalits

h. Ensuring in built component for dalits in Employment Generation Programmes such as NREGA

4) Adequate Monitoring of Development Plans
5) Responsive Delivery Mechanism
6) Sensitisation of Civil Society, development organisations, NGOs and community based organisations
7) Participatory formulation of Development Policies, Planning, and Schemes.
8) Awareness and Educational Programme among the Dalits
9) Mobilisation of Dalits for Advocacy and Lobbying
10) Education of the Dalit elected representative from Panchayat to Parliament

There is however, a need to focus on some core areas such as Land and agrarian reforms. The existing agrarian reform legislation should not be undermined to serve the interests of large landholdings of landlords and agribusiness. This land Reform would be helpful in achieving the attainment of three major goals namely MDGs 1, MDGs 7 and MDGs 8. The Land Acquisition Act should be amended or new legislation adopted, to recognize a justifiable right to resettlement and rehabilitation for all displaced or evicted persons, including those without formal land titles and including women Minimum wage legislation and the Employment Guarantee Act should be fully enforced. Decisive action must be taken against widespread evasion, particularly for agricultural labour and the informal sector. The focus should be given for effective implementation of national Rural Guarantee Act 2005 in favour of Scheduled Castes and Scheduled Tribes in selected 200 district of India.

The MDGs Campaign offers an excellent opportunity to demand from Central and state Governments for a White paper on the implementation of Special Component Plans (SCP) and Tribal Sub Plan (TSP) by every department and creates mechanisms to ensure that proper implementation of SCP and TSP becomes a powerful instrument in the manifold empowerment of Dalit communities in India.

The Right to Information Act should be respected in relation to all programmes, including making publicly available all information on entitlements. Corruption must be challenged at all levels of the system and all public officials and shop licensees held accountable for any diversion of resources.

It is important to acknowledge that SCs / STs have representations from Panchayat to Parliament proportionate to their share in the population. They could be the most powerful voice in advocacy and lobbying efforts with the government to ensure achievements of MDGs vis-à-vis dalits and Adivasis. Currently there are more than 2.5 lakh Panchayats in India having same number of elected Dalit Panchayat members who represent the interests of the Dalits. They, however, being in minority in all Panchayats and also due to non-existing support structure are unable to take up the cause of the Dalits boldly.

It has been the experience of National Conference of Dalit Organisations (NACDOR), a confederation and a network of more than 300 grass root Dalit organisations across the country that schemes and programme need stake building by the beneficiaries.

Though, the focus has been targeted under MDGs – Gender equality, but Dalits women have remained out of this target in Govt. interventions. It is a well known fact that majority of the victims of the poverty come from SCs / STs Communities and hence the children of these communities face are highly marginalised in the context of MDGs. However unless the children of SCs / STs are specially targeted they will remains ignored vis-à-vis MDGs / NDGs / NCMP.

The government of India passed important legislation which is the 'Scheduled Castes and Scheduled Tribes (Prevention of Atrocities) Act - 1989'. One of the main aims of this legislation is to ensure that government officials protect the rights of the Dalits. In case they fail to do so, they are liable to be penalised for their inaction. Often the above act is not used / the police and the state machinery try to dissuade / obstruct the victims from seeking redressal under the above Act.

Even though the basic perspective of this chapter has restricted itself to dalits and the MDGs campaign in India, the Millennium Development campaign offers also to forums such as the South Asian Dalit Forum on MDGs to take up the above perspectives at the South Asian, Asian and even global level. A Dalit-focused approach to

MDGs is bound to offer innumerable benefits not only to dalits, but also to the very success of the Millennium Development Campaign. The above programmes, however, urgently requires a mass mobilisation, and action from community groups. There is an urgent need of canvassing the MDGs / NDGs / CMP target from Parliament to Panchayat level. This become all the more important as the government of India as decided to implement three important programmes such as NREGA, NRHM and Right to Education covering at least seven MDGs.

References

Bhowmik, K.L. (ed.) Development of Scheduled Communities. 1985 Conference papers on tribals. *Current Anthropological and Archaeological Perspectives*, Vol. 6. New Delhi: Inter-India Publications 1988.

Corrie, B.D. A human development index for the Dalit child in India, *Social Indicators Research* 34, 1995: 395-409.

Freeman, J.M. The consciousness of freedom amongst India's Untouchables. In D.K. Basu & R. Sisson (eds) *Social and Economic Development in India*. New Delhi: Sage 1986.

Joshi, B. Recent developments in inter-regional mobilization of Dalit protest in India, *South Asia Bulletin* 7, 1987: 86-96.

Massey, J. *Down Trodden: The Struggle of Indian Dalits for Identity, Solidarity and Liberation*. Geneva: WCC Publications 1997.

11

Dalit Rights Movement

The word dalit means broken or downtrodden in Sanskrit and was "used as far back as 1931 in journalistic writing". Popularised by Dr. B.R. Ambedkar in the 1920s and 30s, and later by the Dalit Panthers movement in the 1970s, the term became a new secular identity for millions of those formerly known as 'untouchables' in India. Today, modern dalit identity is in a discursive competition with various religious identities for control of between one-fourth and one-fifth of India's billion-person population, which is classified as scheduled caste (SC).

Compared to the rhetorical calls by Trailokya Bauddha Mahasangha, Sahayak Gana (TBMSG) activists to work towards a time when "all India will be Buddhist," the above quote provides a stark secular-focused contrast to Indian social activists' penchant for citing religious ideals in order to galvanise the identity of followers.

Yet, it was the life and legacy of Dr. B.R. Ambedkar that laid the foundation for this competition to win the hearts and minds of dalits. As both a social reformer from within the government, and then later a cultural reformer from the outside, Dr. Ambedkar's life itself represented a balancing between these two, not incompatible, identities. While many people outside the Indian sub-continent are familiar with Mahatma Gandhi, few who live outside of India know much about Dr. Ambedkar, or about the movement he helped spawn. Both his political significance as the foremost representative of the Mahar 'untouchable' community in Maharashtra, and the religious importance he played in changing the social identity and spiritual commitments of that particular community of dalits through a revival of Buddhism, are unrivaled throughout India's long historical development. Though his life narrative is so compelling that Indians of all persuasions have appropriated his image, like other low-caste social reformers, both before and after him, Dr. Ambedkar struggled to create intra-caste bonds; bonds that were lacking even among the lowest of caste groupings who were divided and aggrieved.

Dr. Bhimrao Ramji Ambedkar affectionately known by his followers as Babasaheb, overcame the cultural and economic impasses of being born an 'untouchable' Mahar, one of three lowest-caste segments of Maharashtra society, in late 19th Century Hindu-dominated India. Breaking through countless stereotypes, Ambedkar was taught early of the importance of education, and he used the social cleavages that the British administrative policy provided to transcend his socially prescribed role. Rising to the post of Law Minister in Nehru's first independent Indian cabinet, he was appointed chairman of the drafting committee for the new constitution. In it can be seen Ambedkar's push to get social change codified legalistically.

But despite this important legal success, Dr. Ambedkar slowly began to realise that structural reform was only one means to his larger goal of social change in India. Increasingly frustrated that change was not coming to his people fast enough, he began to believe that social revolution was necessary, which could come only from actively critiquing the cultural structure of Hinduism, as opposed to attempting to change it from within. Or should we pursue justice for a particular group, knowing that this pursuit may increase conflict rather than resolve it?. Gradually coming to believe the answer to these questions was a resounding commitment to pursue justice, Dr. Ambedkar began to focus more on societal rather than structural change.

Ambedkar's identity evolved throughout his life to one of social activist, and the evolution of his growth and thought can be seen clearly in his prolific writings. During the latter part of his career, Ambedkar increasingly began to see religion as a valuable means to realise change through socio-cultural critique. As an answer to his discontent with the structural violence imposed by the caste system, religion provided a vehicle to restructure social discourse and remake the foundational values of the social system. It was also with a life-long desire to understand religion that Ambedkar conditioned his analysis of caste.

This, he believed, was the best solution for the Mahar 'untouchables' that he now led.

But Ambedkar saw religion as a social vehicle as much as others saw it for its soteriological commitments to explain life. For Ambedkar choice of religions was a means to social change in the present. By changing religious traditions he, as well as each individual, could change society. Declaring Hinduism the root cause of dalit suffering Ambedkar challenged the orthodox beliefs of Indian culture head on, and was either reviled or loved for this audacity. These acts created support, criticism and fierce debate. Gandhi, upon hearing Ambedkar speak, was once said to have remarked, "religion is not like a horse or a cloak, which can be changed at will. It is a more integral part of one's self than one's own body".

Yet, while Gandhi criticised the idea of a choice in religion, Ambedkar studied all the world's faiths in order to find the one, which would best fit his 'untouchable' communities' needs. The act of choosing his religion was, for Ambedkar, the cement of a re-positioned identity which was both personal and collective. As the answer to many of the needs of his 'untouchable' community, it was an act of social protest and self-help rolled into one. If his more outwardly social protests brought spite from Brahmins, his re-positioned identity as a Buddhist would bring him deification among his own 'untouchable' community—something he himself was said to be uncomfortable with. On October 14, 1956, on the 2500 anniversary of the Buddha's Nirvana, Ambedkar led a mass conversion of 'untouchable' Hindus to Buddhism. This was the culminating act of his now re-positioned identity and in writing his own vows upon taking refuge Ambedkar ensured that he had created what some religious scholars have since called "neo-Buddhism". As the ultimate *upaya* Buddhism itself was to give new hope and confidence to thousands of dalits. However, as Ambedkar died only six months after his controversial conversion, it is not completely clear what form of institutionalisation his Buddhism would have taken.

The above leadership narrative provides a common grounding for both secular and religiously inclined dalit rights activists. Yet, depending on the specifics of the story that is emphasised, one can see divergences in social movement organisation. At the same time, future activists will continue to argue as to which void Ambedkar's narrative fills—a clarion call for secular rights or a human need for ultimate meaning? As Taylor, Bougie, and Caouette have argued, lack of a collective cultural identity is the most socially damaging and difficult to overcome aspect of a group's identity. It seems that Ambedkar's emphasis on the role of religion in society is an implicit acknowledgement of this argument and an attempt to reconstruct a new version of this collective cultural identiThe role of cultural collective identity is not merely for group members to have a shared cultural history.

Ambedkar was a pragmatist, studying under John Dewey at Columbia University, eager to develop a healthy collective cultural identity for those he considered his people—the downtrodden of society. Religious narrative structures were used as a vehicle to attempt to re-deploy a self-aware collective cultural identity. But his use of both secular and religious narrative structure as a means is telling. Ambedkar had a modern understanding of religion, which emphasised that belief was not only about ends, but also a means of social interpretation. Unfortunately, Ambedkar's Buddhist followers have failed to openly and fully explore the social and political resources of both the secular and religious narratives they have at their disposal. Despite the fact that Ambedkar dalit activists' discourse seems to strategically use one or the other these narrative structure to support their cause and build support, an analysis of the social positions that each creates has been lacking. Secular attempts to focus on Ambedkar's injunction to "educate, organise, agitate" have failed to see the added value that creating a new religious identity can bring to oppressed groups' aspirations, not to mention the added value religious institutions bring to attempts at mass mobilisation. Though preaching an inclusive and voluntary belief system, converted dalits often fail to realise their emphasis on religious-based explanation sidelines broadbased rights-based opportunities for mobilisation. Further, each side of this spectrum of activism has seen the other side as problematic for maintaining their own base of support within the dalit community. In other words, followers of Ambedkar's religious narrative see secular rights talk as problematic since it relies too much on outside notions of liberty, democracy, fraternity, and agency while followers of Ambedkar's secular narrative see religious rhetoric as backward and pre-modern.

11.1. Secular Versus Religious Activism

The religious narratives of dalit assertion focus on leaving the Hindu-fold, which is seen as the root cause of the dalit social condition. In doing so, the individual re-asserts him/her self and re-positions their identity as coming from a religiously converted worldview, as opposed to coming from a certain caste which is seen as a partitioning of society that has been too long sanctified by the hierarchical system now called Hinduism. As such, the religious framework of conversion as a means to social justice fosters a sort of dualistic identity among dalits by empowering dalits not only as newly self-reliant through the experience of conversion, but also as one that has been victimised in an all too recent past.

In particular, the combination of liberation and victimisation is problematic for mobilising widespread international support. Conversion as the living out of theology's connection to praxis does not have the same universal appeal as a narrative structure which equates dalit rights with human rights. Despite a new identity as Buddhist the converted dalit cannot completely divorce him/her self from the psychological legacy and mobilising power of past experiences of injustice. This dual identity has both advantages and disadvantages for newly converted dalits as they attempt to achieve social justice. The secular frame of social justice, by comparison, presents a more unified conception of dalit identity as first and foremost human.

While this more materialist perspective on social justice places Dr. B.R. Ambedkar near the end of a long line of important low-caste social thinkers, it also downplays any religious proclivities as subordinate to secular humanism. Simultaneously, this secular frame presents a belief that the problems of dalits can only be cured with the help of the unified action of outside intervention, advocacy, and political agitation, taking the onus for change off the individual and placing it on the collective. From this view, the root causes of a lack of social justice, as contextual and unchangeable by any one individual, are confused by any attempt to focus attention on any sacred ultimate. It is therefore, assumed from this secular perspective that the root causes of a lack of social justice must be approached from a religiously neutral position of secular re-humanisation of the oppressed. As a consequence the concepts of reconciliation and healing are often overlooked by these secular humanists in a rush to realise the equitable society.

The secular narrative and social position of dalits as oppressed victim predominates among dalit social actors partly because of the slow, but steady, success of this narrative structure's ability to build transnational support and advocacy networks. Bob argues convincingly that "organising" and "rhetorical" changes among dalit activists led to increased success of a dalit rights as human rights frame of contention in the late 1990s. While the secular narrative structure has allowed activists to conflate dalit rights with human rights, it has also disempowered many religiously inclined dalits through its aversion to religious language and frames. In short, there is a cultural divide between Western post-enlightenment rights thinking and traditional thoughts rooted in local contexts that value ritualistic and institutional expressions of culture.

This is not to say that the dialectic between secular versus religious narratives can be explained simply by arguing that a post-colonial clash of civilisations or cultures is either the genesis of the divergence, or the solution to unifying these different worldviews. Rather, noticing this cultural divide does signal the risky footing one stands on if advocating either a strongly secular narrative structure to combat caste or a strongly religious one.

As Ganguly concisely puts it: "The modernising desire to first reify caste as a relic of times past, and then to annihilate it, is truly alive and well". This secular bias away from the traditional is neither the best nor most effective way to create social change. Instead, it often leads to sensational excitement outside of India, while faltering in the local context. The bias among secular dalit rights organisations, which disregard the conversion perspective so prevalent among Indian Ambedkarite Buddhists, serves as a case in point. Beyond the academic community, however, a secular rights-based focus also creates a number of limitations and paradoxes for activists.

DANRIA, the organisation portrayed in the second short vignette that began this piece provides a prime example of the dialectical problems that secular activists face in approaching their religiously-grounded counterparts. The DANRIA leaders desire to engage Ambedkar Buddhists, but within a frame of the strictly secular. At a DANRIA planning meeting in May 2007 Ambedkar Buddhist representatives from the TBMSG attempted to develop linkages with the work and resources of DANRIA members, and DANRIA members continually made it clear that their work was to support secular dalit education and empowerment. Partly due to how religion is understood in a postreformation West, such interactions revolve around a judgment that equates support for religious-based organisations as support for the propagation of that religion. In this dance of assumptions and commitments, Ambedkar Buddhists try to re-frame their contention to fit the desires of secular activists, while secular activists assume religious organisations' exclusive goals and underestimate their ability and opportunities to mobilise.

Secular narrative structures of dalit contention present benefits to go along with the limitations, which they pose. They bring pragmatism to an often-disorganised array of activist decisions and goals. Through an unequivocal support for humanity and secular humanism these narrative structures provide grounding for international mobilisation which bridges religious and cultural difference. The International Commission for Dalit Rights' (ICRD's) mission statement demonstrates this tendency to both symbolically and pragmatically bridge these aspects of difference within the dalit movement: "Eliminating rights-based human need and fulfilling freedom and democracy is necessary to achieve effective national and global development policies and programs, and to alleviate discrimination and extreme poverty."

In place of a strong religious commitment, the secular narratives that such organisations profess, are often founded on an enduring faith in ideology. In interviewing Chadra Bhan Prasad, the only dalit writer for a major Indian weekly and a dalit rights activist who tends towards the secular end of the dalit movement's narrative structure, it was immediately evident that he was not even familiar with TBMSG, one of the major purveyors of the religious narrative of Ambedkar and dalit rights in Maharashtra. Now arguing that capitalism is the only thing that will save the dalit, Prasad draws an interesting comparison to the Ambedkar Buddhist activists of the TBMSG who see the solution for dalits as coming through the dharma.

This secular narrative structure implies that religious commitment can be sidelined in favour of an underlying, and more basic, commitment to humanism—an assumption, which runs deep in the dalit rights movement. One ICRD dalit activist even stated: "Despite the fact that many different dalit groups employ different strategies, our goal is the same." The idea that dalit activists' deploy diverging strategies despite common goals posits not only that dalit activists have one collective identity, but also that this collective's social justice concerns are all the same.

11.2. Future of Dalit Activism

Inherent in the promise of these two worldviews is a sort of grounded pragmatism. The mobilisation experience, social networks, and common purpose of religious activists, is something that secular dalit right activists can and must tap into. The following reaction to the celebratory Buddhist conversions of October 2, 2006 by a keen observer of the Ambedkar movement underscores the issues at stake when this connection between secular and religious narrative structures goes unattended and unanalysed:

> 'What do they mean: All India will become Buddhist?... These people *need to* live in a world with Muslims and Hindus and all the rest. Dr. Ambedkar wanted to reconstruct the Buddhist tradition so it met the needs of his time. But can the Ambedkarites do the same with Ambedkar's own ideas? Nagaloka [TBMSG's University] should be teaching comparative religion… They need to say what they are for, and leave aside what they are against.'

The seeming incongruence of dalit identities as either victim or as self-aware Buddhist leaves conceptions of social justice, citizenship, and community vague and unbounded. Hence this lack of balance cries for a syncretism between these often competing narrative frames of social justice—an integrated religious/secular focus on individual rights that does not overlook the importance of individuals' spiritual worldview in creating social justice. Such a mix of transnational and local strategies for contention redefines the transnational and highlights the need to critically analyse the role of such activists' narratives in the wider global society.

References

Mendelsohn, O. & Vicziany, M. *The Untouchables. Poverty, Pollution and the State in Modern India*. Cambridge: CUP 1998.

Michael, S.M. (ed.) *Dalits in Modern India. Vision and Values*. New Delhi: Vistaar 1999.

Mukerjee, H.N. *Gandhi, Ambedkar and the Extirpation of Untouchability*. New Delhi: People's 1982.

Roy, A.K. *New Dalit Revolution*. Patna: 1980.

Santoshi, H. *Daliton Mein Dalit*. New Delhi: Nav Sahitye Academy 1990.

12

Laws to Protect Dalit Rights in India

After Independence, to fulfill the Constitution provisions, the Indian Government has passed various legislations to enforce the abolishment of 'untouchability' and remove the barriers of caste discrimination impeding the socio-economic progress of the Dalits. This included the Protection of Civil Rights (Anti-Untouchability) Act, 1955 and various land reform laws to redistribute land to the landless, a large and disproportionate percentage of whom were and still are Dalits. Later years saw the passage of the Bonded Labour (Abolition) Act, 1976, Employment of Manual Scavengers and Construction of Dry Latrines (Prohibition) Act, 1993, Jogini Act No. 10, and the Scheduled Castes/Scheduled Tribes (Prevention of Atrocities) Act, 1989 & Rules, 1995. The central and state governments also established SC/ST Welfare Departments soon after Independence. In the early 1990s, the Central Government passed legislation establishing the National Commission for SC/ST and the National Human Rights Commission.

There is no doubt that none of these would have been possible without the interventions made by Dr. Ambedkar, to ensure that Independent India would be based on a democratic constitution that guaranteed equality, fundamental rights and dignity to all regardless of caste. Had he succumbed to his contemporary dominant-caste nationalists who pressured him to settle these matters internally, Dalits would be much worse off than they are today.

The much acclaimed affirmative actions by the Governments, in the form of the Constitutional provisions, powerful Legislations, Judicial Activism and the existence of Human Rights Mechanisms –

National Human Rights Commission (NHRC), Scheduled Caste and Scheduled Tribes (Dalits) Commission, National Commission for Women are not able to protect Dalits from the heinous crime of untouchability.

Any small attempt of Dalits, to "assert their rights or their resistance against the violence" unleashed on Dalits, is viewed as an act of Disobedience and creation of a Law and Order problem. This results in brutal attack on Dalits, by the state machinery, especially the police. The Dalits are at the receiving end, both by the dominant caste and by the state police force, which is also very much dominated by the dominant caste persons. Crimes and atrocities on Dalits have ever been increasing over the past few years. The National Crimes Record Bureau recorded only 8,500 crimes against Dalits in 1997 but the 'Minor Studies Series' puts the figure at between 55,000 and 65,000 per year. There has been a sudden spurt from around 18,000 per year in 1993. The Report states that over 250 people have been killed in caste clashes in TamilNadu since 1995. Eighty-six were killed in 1997 alone. Of the total of 167,000 cases of crime against the Scheduled Castes and Scheduled Tribes framed between 1995 and 1996, only 4,322, a paltry 2.6% resulted in conviction. Chopping of heads of Dalits, maiming limbs, chasing them from their inhabitations and looting their properties, still persist. Dalits are prevented from contesting in local body elections and in case elected, not recognized and allowed to function as leaders of village body Panchayats. More than that the people in power still have no real concern for the emancipation of the dalits.

The Indian Government sounded increasingly irrational as it shouted itself hoarse to deny a problem that everybody else can plainly see. Similar to its predecessors in the Nationalist Movement who opposed Dr. Ambedkar for raising the specific concerns of the Dalits with regard to Independence in the Round Table Conference, the then BJP Government was opposed to the efforts of Dalits who seek the support of the United Nations in the context of the World Conference Against Racism in strengthening India's own constitutional obligations to abolish 'untouchability' and caste-based discrimination. As on date, courts have to intervene and order district collectors to make it possible for dalits to rightfully partake in the temple functions.

Either the constitution or the legislations or the judiciary or the other Human Rights mechanisms in the form of Human rights commissions at various levels from the states to the center are not providing effective safeguards and guarantees to ensure Dalits rights. Even the most powerful instrument currently available in defense of Dalits rights, namely SC/ST (Prevention of Atrocities) Act 1989, hardly provide effective safeguards for protection and promotion of Dalit Human Rights. Article 17 of the Indian constitution proclaims that the practice of untouchability is abolished. Denial of temple entry, prohibiting access to common water sourecs, denial of share in the common property of villages, separate burial grounds, prevalence of two separate glass system in tea stall, are some of the inhuman forms of manifestations of untouchability that exist even today.

Caste discrimination cannot end without concrete social, educational and economic changes. The irony is that dalits, comprising 16% of India's population, suffer from a disease, even more pathetic than the practice of untouchability – the ideological dominance of the upper castes who control not only social, economic and political power in the country but even knowledge and opinion. Even the personal experience of being discriminated against does not become an issue unless 'permitted' by the experts and the state. To disbelieve them is a necessary precondition for dalit assertion. The Dalits have been in dark in exercising their political rights viz the denial of rights to contest the village local body election. The village Melavalavu in Madurai District evinced the murder of the Dalit Panchayat President and other six Dalits by the Dominant Caste, for they could not assimilate the winning of a post in election by a Dalit.

The correlation between quality education and emancipation is well established globally. How then can we justify that 50% of dalit children (64% dalit girl children) are pushed out of the school system before they can complete even primary education? How do we ensure a strong nation, assuming that dalits are part of the nation, when we cannot even ensure basic education to 16% of our population?

The current government statistics of murder, rape and assault that dalits are subjected to paint a horrible picture if extended to a history of 3000 years. We have reason to believe that approximately 21,90,000 dalits have been murdered, 32,85,000 raped and over 7,50,00,000 assaulted. The violence perpetrated on dalits cannot be rooted out until long term economic, social and political measures, such as land reforms, are firmly implemented. The helplessness of dalits gets magnified by the general apathy of bureaucrats and especially of the police force to rush to their help. Even when dalits are attacked by caste hindus it is always the dalits who bear the brunt of the violence. The Keezha-vanmani burning decades ago or the recent killings in Melavalavu and the routine massacres in Bihar and the significant lack of conviction will always remain as indelible stains on our democracy. Unless dalits too get social positions, especially in the police force, the administrative institutions will be always against the dalits.

All these things are what the government and othe s have to do for the emancipation of the dalits. But this would not be enough at all. The awareness of the dalits themselves is most essenctioal requirement. Any amount of eduction or awareness programs cannot result in the assertion of the dalits. Instead it has to come from within. Waiting for somethjng to hapaen outside to help themcome out of their pitiable state may be a pipe dream. An even more serious question is whether the state that represents a certain class and caste culture, can be entrusted with the responsibility of education, especially for dalit children. Education, if perceived as a tool of empowerment, needless to add, cannot be trusted in the hands of state agencies. The oneness of all sects of dalits and their inner force to break the shackles are the need of the day.

The Scheduled Castes and Scheduled Tribes are the two most disadvantaged segments of the weaker sections of our society. Atrocities are committed on them on account of their economic dependence on non-SC/ST landowners, educational backwardness and social discrimination. The Scheduled Castes suffer from the stigma of untouchability. Age-old caste prejudices and practice of untouchability against them lead to commission of atrocities.

For ensuring alround development of SC and ST and to protect them from all types of exploitation a number of safeguards have been provided in the Constitution of India. Under Article 15 no citizen shall on grounds only of religion, race, caste, sex, place of birth or any of them, be subject to any disability, liability, restriction or condition with regard to (a) access to shops, public restaurants, hotels and places of public entertainment; or (b) the use of wells, tanks, bathing ghats, roads and places of public resort maintained wholly or partly out of State funds or dedicated to the use of general public. "Untouchability" stands abolished under Article 17 and its practice in any form is forbidden and punishable under law. Traffic in human beings and forced labour are prohibited under Article 23 of the Constitution of India. Special enactments have been made by the Central and State Governments to protect SC and ST from all forms of exploitation. The SC and ST constitute major bulk of agricultural and other types of labour and majority of the bonded labour also belong to SC and ST. The Minimum Wages Act, 1948, provides for fixing minimum wages for different types of labour and the Bonded Labour System (Abolition) Act, 1976, provides for abolition of the bonded labour system and for release and rehabilitation of freed bonded laborers.

There are two important legislations related to Article 17, viz., The Protection of Civil Rights Act, 1955 (PCRA), and The Scheduled Castes and the Scheduled Tribes (Prevention of Atrocities) Act, 1989 (PAA). Initially the Untouchability (Offences) Act, 1955, had been enacted to abolish the practice of untouchability and social disabilities arising out of it against members of the Scheduled Castes. it was amended in 1977 and is now known as the Protection of Civil Rights Act, 1955. Under the revised Act the practice of untouchability was made both cognizable and non-compoundable and stricter punishment was provided for the offenders. To check the commission of atrocities on SC and ST, The Scheduled Castes and the Scheduled Tribes (Prevention of Atrocities) Act, 1989, came into force on 31-1-90. The Act, inter alia, specifies some types of offences as atrocities, provides or imposition of stricter penalties for the guilty and setting up of Special Courts for speedy trial of such cases. The crimes under the PCRA were brought under the purview of the PAA as the latter provides for stricter punishment to the offenders. The salient features of the PCRA and the PAA have been discussed in detail in the First Annual Report of the Commission. The trend of cases under the PCRA and the PAA over the last two years, the working of the various provisions of these Acts by the Central and State Governments, the steps taken to check occurrence of such cases, the provision of monetary relief/rehabilitation measures to victims of atrocities, the setting up of Special Courts for speedy trial of such cases and the nature of their disposal have been discussed in this chapter.

Under Article 338 of the Constitution the commission is required to inquire into specific complaints with respect to the deprivation of rights and safeguards of SC and ST. It is also the duty of the Commission to investigate and monitor all matters relating to the safeguards provided for SC and ST under the Constitution or under any law or any order of the Government. The present Report presents an account of the work done by the Commission during 1993-94 in dealing with specific cases of complaints and on-the-spot enquiries into cases of untouchability offences and atrocities.

12.1. Protection of Civl Rights Act, 1955

The Twelfth Annual Report of the Ministry of Welfare on the Protection of Civil Rights Act, 1955, for the year 1991 was laid on the Table of Lok Sabha on 24-2-94 and that of Rajya Sabha on 4-3-94. The Report provides information regarding the number of cases registered during 1991, the nature of their disposal at the police and the Court levels and the trend in registration of cases from year to year. A comparative analysis of the number of cases registered during three years from 1989 to 1991 indicates that though the number of cases registered increased from 3,700 during 1989 to 3,730 during 1990, it came down to 3,406 during 1991 indicating a decrease of 9.51% in registration of cases over the previous year. As compared to 1990 the decrease in reporting of cases during 1991 was marked in Rajasthan (207:107), Karnataka (807:722), Madhya Pradesh (463:384) and Uttar Pradesh (357:296) while during the same period an increase was noticeable in Andhra Pradesh (203:365), Maharashtra (257:340), Tamil Nadu (787:861) and Gujarat (172:209).

Majority of the cases were reported from Tamil Nadu (861) followed by Karnataka (722), Madhya Pradesh (384), Andhra Pradesh (365), Maharashtra (340), Uttar Pradesh (296), Gujarat (207) and Rajasthan (107) while no cases were reported from Assam, Punjab and Chandigarh. It is significant that majority of the cases were reported from the southern States. The total number of 1,948 cases reported from Andhra Pradesh (365), Karnataka (722) and Tamil Nadu (861) constituted 57.2% of the total number of cases registered in the country during 1991.

Measures taken by the State Governments/UT Administrations for effective implementation of the provisions of the PCR Act have not been quite encouraging. Special Courts to try cases registered under the Act were reportedly not set up in Assam, Gujarat, Haryana, Jammu & Kashmir, Kerala, Maharashtra, Orissa, Punjab, Tripura, West Bengal and the Union Territories of Chandigarh, Dadra & Nagar Haveli, Delhi and Pondicherry. The proposal to set up such courts was being considered by the State Governments of Goa and Uttar Pradesh. For taking preventive action in checking untouchability offences, untouchabilty-prone areas/districts were identified only by four States, viz., Gujarat, Maharashtra, Tamil Nadu and Uttar Pradesh. No State Government had conducted any periodical survey about the working of the Act during 1991 as envisaged under the Act.

During 1993-94 a sum of Rs.4,40,05,584 was released by the Ministry of Welfare as grants-in-aid to 14 States and one U.T. for implementation of the PCR Act. It is observed that no grant-in-aid was released to the Governments of Rajasthan and Uttar Pradesh and the U.T.Adm. of Dadra & Nagar Haveli during 1993-94 on account of the fact that these Governments could not utilise the grants released to them during 1992-93 and so did not seek further grants during 1993-94. The Commission is deeply concerned that these State Governments did not appreciate the need and urgency for implementation of the PCR Act, 1955, and did not come forward for availing of grants-in-aid from the ministry of Welfare.

The implementation of the provisions of the PAA by the State Governments/UT Administrations has not been quite satisfactory. Though Section 14 of the Act provides for setting up of Special Courts for speedy trial of atrocity cases, only Andhra Pradesh and Rajasthan have set up such Special Courts to exclusively deal with atrocity cases.

The achievements of the Special Courts set up in Andhra Pradesh and Rajasthan are also not known as no evaluation study has been conducted to assess their impact. The Commission recommends that the Ministry of welfare may get sample studies conducted by the Tribal Research. Institutes, Universities and other research organisations to evaluate the working of the Special Courts dealing with atrocity cases and suggest remedial measures to overcome the problems faced by these courts for ensuring speedy trial of these cases. In order that atrocity cases get priority over other cases and delay is minimised in awarding punishment to the guilty the Commission further recommends that the remaining State Governments/UT

Administrations may set up Special Courts exclusively to deal with atrocity cases.

A positive step to check occurrence of atrocities is to identify atrocity-prone areas and take preventive measures so that incidents of atrocities do not occur. Section 21 of the PAA enjoins upon the State Governments/UT Administrations to conduct periodic surveys of the working of the Act with a view to suggesting measures for better implementation of the provisions of the Act and for identification of areas where SC and ST persons are likely to be victims of atrocities so as to take preventive action to check occurrence of such crimes. According to the information available with the Ministry of Welfare only eight States had identified 69 districts and villages in such districts as atrocity-prone and sensitive areas. Eleven districts each in Bihar and Gujarat, five in Haryana, six each in Karnataka and Maharashtra, seven in Madhya Pradesh, eight villages in three districts of Punjab and twenty districts in Uttar Pradesh have been identified under this category. In order that timely preventive measures could be taken to check incidents of atrocities resulting in loss of life and property it is desirable that all the State Governments/UT Administrations conduct periodic surveys and identify atrocity-prone areas for taking preventive measures.

Atrocities resulting in death or permanent incapacitation or grievous hurt to SC/ST victims, destruction of their property due to arson or otherwise and social ostracization imposed on them by the dominant caste people hit them hard. To mitigate the financial and other hardships faced by SC/ST victims of atrocities monetary relief and rehabilitation facilities are provided to them by the concerned State Government/UT Administration. Section 21(2) (iii) provides for the State Governments to take measures for economic and social rehabilitation of victims of atrocities. Barring a few States like Gujarat, Karnataka, Kerala and Orissa other State Governments have not revised the scale of monetary relief paid to victims of atrocities since 1981. The Governments of Jammu & Kashmir, Punjab and West Bengal have not adopted any scale of monetary relief for victims of atrocities. In its First Annual Report the Commission had stressed that the scale of relief needed to be revised as done by the Government of Gujarat and at least Rs.1 lakh provided to the family of an SC/ST person killed in a case of atrocity, particularly if the deceased was an earning member or physically fit to earn. The Commission also recommended that the States which had not prescribed any scale of monetary relief and rehabilitation facilities to SC/ST victims of atrocities might do so without further delay. These recommendations of the Commission are reiterated.

During 1993-94, an amount of Rs.2,66,13,316 was released by the ministry of welfare to 10 States and one Union Territory for implementation of the PAA. No grants were released to Goa, Himachal Pradesh, Madhya Pradesh, Orissa, Punjab, Tamil Nadu and Pondicherry as the grants-in-aid released to them during the previous year were not fully utilised and no proposals were received from them seeking further financial assistance from the Ministry of Welfare. The position was alike during 1992-93 as States like Maharashtra, Orissa, Punjab and Tamil Nadu did not avail of any grants from the Ministry of welfare for implementation of the PAA. Apathy on the part of some of the States/Union Territories in utilising the grants-in-aid from the Centre does not indicate a healthy trend. The Commission urges that sincere efforts be made by all States/UTs for availing of the grants from the Ministry of Welfare and for ensuring proper utilisation of the amount in implementation of the PCRA and the PAA.

The total number of atrocity cases in the country during 1992 was 22,049. It may be observed that since the promulgation of the PAA there had been progressive increase in the number of atrocity cases from 19,422 during 1989 to 21,245 during 1990 and 22,424 during 1991. But during 1992 the number of such cases decreased to 22,049 indicating a marginal decrease of 1.7% over the previous year.

12.2. The Scheduled Castes and Scheduled Tribes (Prevention of Atrocities) Act, 1989 265

An Act to prevent the commission of offences of atrocities against the members of the Scheduled Castes and the Scheduled Tribes, to provide for Special Courts for the trial of such offences and for the relief and rehabilitation of the victims of such offences and for matters connected therewith or incidental thereto.

Be it enacted by Parliament in the Fortieth Year of the Republic of India as follows:

Chapter I : Preliminary

1. Short title, extent and commencement

(1) This Act may be called the Scheduled Castes and the Scheduled Tribes (Prevention of Atrocities) Act, 1989.

(2) It extends to the whole of India except the State of Jammu and Kashmir.

(3) It shall come into force on such date as the Central Government may, by notification in the Official Gazette, appoint.

2. Definitions

(1) In this Act, unless the context otherwise requires,-

(a) "atrocity" means an offence punishable under Section 3;

(b) "Code" means the Code of Criminal Procedure, 1973 (2 of 1974);

(c) "Scheduled Castes and Scheduled Tribes" shall have the meanings assigned to them respectively under clause (24) and clause (25) of Article 366 of the Constitution;

(d) "Special Court" means a Court of Session specified as a Special Court in section 14;

(e) "Special Public Prosecutor" means a Public Prosecutor specified as a Special Public Prosecutor or an advocate referred to in section 15;

(f) words and expressions used but not defined in this Act and defined in the Code or the Indian Penal Code (45 of 1860) shall have the meanings assigned to them respectively in the Code, or as the case may be, in the Indian Penal Code.

(2) Any reference in this Act to any enactment or any provision thereof shall, in relation to an area in which such enactment or such provision is, not in force, be construed as a reference to the corresponding law, if any, in force in that area.

Chapter II : Offences of Atrocities

3. Punishments for offences of atrocities-

(1) Whoever, not being a member of a Scheduled Caste or a Scheduled Tribe:

(i) forces a member of a Scheduled Caste or a Scheduled Tribe to drink or eat any inedible or obnoxious substance;

(ii) acts with intent to cause injury, insult or annoyance to any member of a Scheduled Caste or a Scheduled Tribe by dumping excreta, waste matter, carcasses or any other obnoxious substance in his premises or neighborhood;

(iii) forcibly removes clothes from the person of a member of a Scheduled Caste or a Scheduled Tribe or parades him naked orwith painted face or body or commits any similar act which is derogatory to human dignity;

(iv) wrongfully occupies or cultivates any land owned by, or allotted to, or notified by any competent authority to be allotted to, a member of a Scheduled Caste or a Scheduled Tribe or gets the land allotted to him transferred;

(v) wrongfully dispossesses a member of a Scheduled Caste or a Scheduled Tribe from his land or premises or interferes with the enjoyment of his rights over any land, premises or water;

(vi) compels or entices a member of a Scheduled Caste or a Scheduled Tribe to do 'begar' or other similar forms of forced or bonded labor other than any compulsory service for public purposes imposed by Government;

(vii) forces or intimidates a member of a Scheduled Caste or a Scheduled Tribe not to vote or to vote to a particular candidate or to vote in a manner other than that provided by law;

(viii) institutes false, malicious or vexatious suit or criminal or other legal proceedings against a member of a Scheduled Caste or a Scheduled Tribe;

(ix) gives any false or frivolous information to any public servant and thereby causes such public servant to use his lawful power to the injury or annoyance of a member of a Scheduled Caste or a Scheduled Tribe;

(x) intentionally insults or intimidates with intent to humiliate a member of a Scheduled Caste or a Scheduled Tribe in any place within public view;

(xi) assaults or uses force to any woman belonging to a Scheduled Caste or a Scheduled Tribe with intent to dishonor or outrage her modesty;

(xii) being in a position to dominate the will of a woman belonging to a Scheduled Caste or a Scheduled Tribe and uses that position to exploit her sexually to which she would not have otherwise agreed;

(xiii) corrupts or fouls the water of any spring, reservoir or any other source ordinarily used by members of the Scheduled Caste or the Scheduled Tribes so as to render it less fit for the purpose for which it is ordinarily used;

(xiv) denies a member of a Scheduled Caste or a Scheduled Tribe any customary right of passage to a place of public resort or obstructs such member so as to prevent him from using or having access to a place of public resort to which other members of public or any section thereof have a right to use or access to;

(xv) forces or causes a member of a Scheduled Caste or a Scheduled Tribe to leave his house, village or other place of residence, shall be punishable with imprisonment for a term which shall not be less than six months but which may extend to five years and with fine.

(2) Whoever, not being a member of a Scheduled Caste or a Scheduled Tribe:

(i) gives or fabricates false evidence intending thereby to cause, or knowing it to be likely that he will thereby cause, any member of a Scheduled Caste or a Scheduled Tribe to be convicted of an offence which is capital by the law for the time being in force shall be punished with imprisonment for life and with fine; and if an innocent member of a Scheduled Caste or a Scheduled Tribe be convicted and executed in consequence of such false or fabricated evidence, the person who gives or fabricates such false evidence, shall be punished with death;

(ii) gives or fabricates false evidence intending thereby to cause, or knowing it to be likely that he will thereby cause, any member of a Scheduled Caste or a Scheduled Tribe to be convicted of an offence which is not capital but punishable with imprisonmentfor a term of seven years or upwards, shall be punishable with imprisonment for a term which shall not be less than six months but which may extend to seven years or upwards and with fine;

(iii) commits mischief by fire or any explosive substance intend ing to cause or knowing it to be likely that he will thereby cause damage to any property belonging to a member of a Scheduled Caste or a Scheduled Tribe shall be punishable with imprisonment for a term which shall not be less than six months but which may extend to seven years and with fine;

(iv) commits mischief by fire or any explosive substance intend ing to cause or knowing it to be likely that he will thereby cause destruction of any building which is ordinarily used as a place of worship or as a place for human dwelling or as a place for custody of the property by a member of a Scheduled Caste or a Scheduled Tribe, shall be punishable with imprisonment for life and with fine;

(v) commits any offence under the Indian Penal Code (45 of 1860) punishable with imprisonment for a term of ten years or more against a person or property on the ground that such person is a member of a Scheduled Caste or a Scheduled Tribe or such property belongs to such member, shall be punishable with imprisonment for life and with fine;

(vi) knowingly or having reason to believe that an offence has been committed under this Chapter, causes any evidence of the commission of that offence to disappear with the intention of screening the offender from legal punishment, or with that intention gives any information respecting the offence which he knows or believes to be false, shall be punishable with the punishment provided for that offence; or

(vii) being a public servant, commits any offence under this section, shall be punishable with imprisonment for a term which shall not be less than one year but which may extend to the punishment provided for that offence.

4. Punishment for neglect of duties

Whoever, being a public servant but not being a member of a Scheduled Caste or a Scheduled Tribe, wilfully neglects his duties required to be performed by him under this Act, shall be punishable with imprisonment for a term which shall not be less than six months but which may extend to one year.

5. Enhanced punishment for subsequent conviction

Whoever, having already been convicted of an offence under this Chapter is convicted for the second offence or any offence subsequent to the second offence, shall be punishable with imprisonment for a term which shall not be less than one year but which may extend to the punishment provided for that offence.

6. Application of certain provisions of the Indian Penal Code

Subject to the other provisions of this Act, the provisions of section 34, Chapter III, Chapter IV, Chapter V, Chapter V-A, section 149 and Chapter XXIII of the Indian Penal Code (45 of 1860), shall, so far as may be, apply for the purposes of this Act as they apply for the purposes of the Indian Penal Code.

7. Forfeiture of property of certain persons

(1) Where a person has been convicted of any offence punishable under this Chapter, the Special Court may, in addition to awarding any punishment, by order in writing, declare that any property, movable or immovable or both, belonging to the person which has been used for the commission of that offence, shall stand forfeited to Government.

(2) Where any person is accused of any offence under this Chapter, it shall be open to the Special Court trying him to pass an order that all or any of the properties, movable or immovable or both, belonging to him, shall, during the period of such trial, be attached, and where such trial ends in conviction, the property so attached shall be liable to forfeiture to the extent it is required for the purpose of realization of any fine imposed under this Chapter.

8. Presumption as to offences

In a prosecution for an offence under this Chapter, if it is proved that

(a) the accused rendered any financial assistance to a person accused of, or reasonably suspected of committing, an offence under this Chapter, the Special Court shall presume, unless the contrary is proved, that such person had, abetted the offence;

(b) a group of persons committed an offence under this Chapter and if it is proved that the offence committed was a sequel to any existing dispute regarding land or any other matter, it shall be presumed that the offence was committed in furtherance of the common intention or in prosecution of the common object.

9. Conferment of powers

(1) Notwithstanding anything contained in the Code or in any other provision of this Act, the State Government may, if it considers it necessary or expedient so to do,-

  (a) for the prevention of and for coping with any offence under this Act, or

  (b) for any case or class or group of cases under this Act, in any district or part thereof, confer, by notification in the Official Gazette, on any officer of the State Government, the powers exercisable by a police officer under the Code in such district or part thereof or, as the case maybe, for such case or class or group of cases, and in particular, the powers of arrest, investigation and prosecution of persons before any Special Court.

(2) All officers of police and all other officers of Government shall assist the officer referred to in sub-section (1) in the execution of the provisions of this Act or any rule, scheme or order made thereunder.

(3) The provisions of the Code shall, so far as may be, apply to the exercise of the powers by an officer under sub-section (1).

Chapter III : Externment

10. Removal of person likely to commit offence-

(l) Where the Special Court is satisfied, upon a complaint or a police report that a person is likely to commit an offence under Chapter II of this Act in any area included in 'Scheduled Areas' or 'Tribal areas' as referred to in Article 244 of the Constitution, it may, by order in writing, direct such person to remove himself beyond the limits of such area, by such route and within such time as may be specified in the order, and not to return to that area from which he was directed to remove himself for such period, not exceeding two years, as may be specified in the order.

(2) The Special Court shall, along with the order under sub-section (1), communicate to the person directed under that sub-section the grounds on which such order has been made.

(3) The Special Court may revoke or modify the order made under sub section (1), for the reasons to be recorded in writing, on the representation made by the person against whom such order has been made or by any other person on his behalf within thirty days from the date of the order.

11. Procedure on failure of person to remove himself from area and enter thereon after removal

(1) If a person to whom a direction has been issued under Section 10 to remove himself from any area-

(a) fails to remove himself as directed; or

(b) having so removed himself enters such area within the period specified in the order, otherwise than with the permission in writing of the Special Court under sub-section (2), the Special Court may cause him to be arrested and removed in police custody to such place outside such area as the Special Court may specify.

(2) The Special Court may, by order in writing, permit any person in respect of whom an order under section 10 has been made, to return to the area from which he was directed to remove himself for such temporary period and subject to such conditions as may be specified in such order and may require him to execute a bond with or without surety for the due observation of the conditions imposed.

(3) The Special Court may at any time revoke any such permission.

(4) Any person who, with such permission, returns to the area from which he was directed to remove himself shall observe the

conditions imposed and at the expiry of the temporary period for which he was permitted to return or on the revocation of such permission before the expiry of such temporary period shall remove himself outside such area and shall not return thereto within the unexpired portion specified under Section 10 without a fresh permission.

(5) If a person fails to observe any of the conditions imposed or to remove himself accordingly or having so removed himself enters or returns to such area without fresh permission the Special Court may cause him to be arrested and removed in police custody to such place outside such area as the Special Court may specify.

12. Taking measurements and photographs, etc. of persons against whom order under section 10 is made-

(1) Every person against whom an order has been made under Section 10 shall, if so required by the Special Court, allow his measurements and photographs to be taken by a police officer.

(2) If any person referred to in sub-section (1) when required to allow his measurements or photographs to be taken, resists or refuses to allow the taking of such measurements or photographs, it shall be lawful to use all necessary means to secure the taking thereof.

(3) Resistance to or refusal to allow the taking of measurements or photographs under sub-section (2) shall be deemed to be an offence under section 186 of the Indian Penal Code (45 of 1860).

(4) Where an order under section 10 is revoked, all measurements and photographs (including negatives) taken under sub-section (2) shall be destroyed or made over to the person against whom such order is made.

13. Penalty for non-compliance of order under section 10

Any person contravening an order of the Special Court made under Section 10 shall be punishable with imprisonment for a term which may extend to one year and with fine.

Chapter IV : Special Courts

14. Special Court

For the purpose of providing for speedy trial, the State Government shall, with the concurrence of the Chief Justice of the High Court, by notification in the Official Gazette, specify for each district a Court of Session to be a Special Court to try the offences under this Act.

15. Special Public Prosecutor

For every Special Court, the State Government shall, by notification in the Official Gazette, specify a Public Prosecutor or appoint an advocate who has been in practice as an advocate for not less than seven years, as a Special Public Prosecutor for the purpose of conducting cases in that Court.

Chapter V : Miscellaneous

16. Power of State Government to impose collective fine

The provisions of Section 10-A of the Protection of Civil Rights Act, 1955 (22 of 1955) shall, so far as may be, apply for the purposes of imposition and realization of collective fine and for all other matters connected therewith under this Act.

17. Preventive action to be taken by the law and order machinery

(1) A District Magistrate or a Sub-divisional Magistrate or any other Executive Magistrate or any police officer not below the rank of a Deputy Superintendent of Police may, on receiving information and after such enquiry as he may think necessary, has reason to believe that a person or a group of persons not belonging to the Scheduled Castes or the Scheduled Tribes, residing in or frequenting any place within the local limits of his jurisdiction is likely to commit an offence or has threatened to commit any offence under this Act and is of the opinion that there is sufficient ground for proceeding, declare such an area to be an area prone to atrocities and take necessary action for keeping the peace and good behavior and maintenance of public order and tranquillity and may take preventive action.

(2) The provisions of Chapters VIII, X and XI of the Code shall, so far as may be, apply for the purposes of sub-Section (1).

(3) The State Government may, by notification in the Official Gazette, make one or more schemes specifying the manner in

which the officers referred to in sub-Section (1) shall take appropriate action specified in such scheme or schemes to prevent atrocities and to restore the feeling of security amongst the members of the Scheduled Castes and the Scheduled Tribes.

18. Section 438 of the Code not to apply to persons committing an offence under the Act

Nothing in Section 438 of the Code shall apply in relation to any case involving the arrest of any person on an accusation of having committed an offence under this Act.

19. Section 360 of the Code and the provisions of the Probation of Offenders Act not to apply to persons guilty of an offence under the Act

The provisions of Section 360 of the Code and the provisions of the Probation of Offenders Act, 1958 (20 of 1958) shall not apply to any person above the age of eighteen years who is found guilty of having committed an offence under this Act.

20. Act to override other laws

Save as otherwise provided in this Act, the provisions of this Act shall have effect notwithstanding anything inconsistent therewith contained in any other law for the time being in force or any custom or usage or any instrument having effect by virtue of any such law.

21. Duty of Government to ensure effective implementation of the Act

(1) Subject to such rules as the Central Government may make in this behalf, the State Government shall take such measures as may be necessary for the effective implementation of this Act.

(2) In particular, and without prejudice to the generality of the foregoing provisions, such measures may include,-

(i) the provision for adequate facilities, including legal aid, to the persons subjected to atrocities to enable them to avail themselves of justice-

(ii) the provision for travelling and maintenance expenses to wit nesses including the victims of atrocities, during investigation and trial of offences under this Act;

(iii) the provision for the economic and social rehabilitation of the victims of the atrocities;

(iv) the appointment of officers for initiating or exercising super vision over prosecutions for the contravention of the provisions of this Act;

(v) the setting up of committees at such appropriate levels as the State Government may think fit to assist that Government in formulation or implementation of such measures;

(vi) provision for a periodic survey of the working of the provi sions of this Act with a view to suggesting measures for the better implementation of the provisions of this Act;

(vii) the identification of the areas where the members of the Scheduled Castes and the Scheduled Tribes are likely to be subjected to atrocities and adoption of such measures so as to ensure safety for such members.

(3) The Central Government shall take such steps as may be necessary to co-ordinate the measures taken by the State Governments under sub-Section (1).

(4) The Central Government shall, every year, place on the table of each House of Parliament a report on the measures taken by itself and by the State Governments in pursuance of the provisions of this Section.

22. Protection of action taken in good faith

No suit, prosecution or other legal proceedings shall lie against the Central Government or against the State Government or any officer or authority of Government or any other person for anything which is in good faith done or intended to be done under this Act.

23. Power to make rules

(1) The Central Government may, by notification in the Official Gazette, make rules for carrying out the purposes of this Act.

(2) Every rule made under this Act shall be laid, as soon as may be after it is made, before each House of Parliament, while it is in session for a total period of thirty days which may be comprised

in one session or in two or more successive sessions, and if before the expiry of the session immediately following the session or the successive sessions aforesaid, both Houses agree in making any modification in the rule or both Houses agree that the rule should not be made, the rule shall thereafter have effect only in such modified form or be of no effect, as the case may be; so, however, that any such modification or annulment shall be without prejudice to the validity of anything previously done under that rule.

12.3. THE SCHEDULED CASTES AND SCHEDULED TRIBES (PREVENTION OF ATROCITIES) RULES, 1995

In exercise of the powers conferred by sub-Section (1) of Sec. 23 of the Scheduled Castes and the Scheduled Tribes (Prevention of Atrocities) Act. 1989 (33 of 1989), the Central Government hereby makes the following rules, namely:

1. Short title and commencement

(1) These rules may be called the Scheduled Castes and the Scheduled Tribes (Prevention of Atrocities) Rules, 1995.

(2) They shall come into force on the date of their publication in the Official Gazette.

2. Definitions

In these rules. unless the context otherwise requires,

(a) "Act" means the Scheduled Castes and the Scheduled Tribes (Prevention of Atrocities) Act, 1989 (33 of 1989).

(b) "dependent", with its grammatical variations and cognate expressions, includes wife, children, whether married or unmarried, dependent parents, widowed sister, widow and children of pre-deceased son of a victim of atrocity;

(c) "identified area" means such area where State Government has reason to believe that atrocity may take place or there is an apprehension of re-occurrence of an offence under the Act or an area prone to victim of atrocity;

(d) "Non-Government Organization" means a voluntary organization engaged in the welfare activities relating to the scheduled castes and the scheduled tribes and registered under the Societies Registration Act.- 1860 (21 of 1860) or under any law for the registration of documents of such Organization for the time being in force;

(e) "Schedule" means the Schedule annexed to these rules;

(f) "Section" means Section of the Act;

(g) "State Government", in relation to a Union territory, means the Administrator of that Union territory appointed by the President under Art. 239 of the Constitution;

(h) words and expressions used herein and not defined but defined in the Act shall have the meanings respectively assigned to them in the Act.

3. Precautionary and preventive measures.-

With a view to prevent atrocities on the Scheduled Castes and the Scheduled Tribes the State Government shall,-

(i) identify the area where it has reason to believe that atrocity may take place or there is an apprehension of reoccurrence of an offence under the Act ;

(ii) order the District Magistrate and Superintendent of Police or any other officer to visit the identified area and review the law and order situation;

(iii) if deem necessary, in the identified area cancel the arm licenses of the persons, not being member of the Scheduled Castes or Scheduled Tribes, their near relations, servants or employees and family friends and get such arms deposited in the Government Armory;

(iv) seize all illegal fire-arms and prohibit any illegal manufacture of fire-arms;

(v) with a view to ensure the safety of person and property, if deem necessary, provide arms licenses to the members of the Scheduled Castes and the Scheduled Tribes;

(vi) constitute a high power State-level committee, district and divisional level committees or such number of other committees as deem proper and necessary for assisting the Government in implementation of the provisions of the Act.

(vii) set up a vigilance and monitoring committee to suggest effective measures to implement the provisions of the Act;

(viii) set up Awareness Centers and organize Workshops in the identified area or at some other place to educate the persons belonging to the Scheduled Castes and the Scheduled Tribes about their rights and the protection available to them under the provisions of various Central and State enactments or rules, regulations and schemes framed thereunder;

(ix) encourage Non-Government Organizations for establishing and maintaining Awareness Centers and organizing Workshops and provide them necessary financial and other sort of assistance;

(x) deploy special police force in the identified area;

(xi) by the end of every quarter, review the law and order situation, functioning of different committees, performance of Special Public Prosecutors, Investigating Officers and other Officers responsible for implementing the provisions of the Act and the cases registered under the Act.

4. Supervision of prosecution and submission of report

(1) The State Government on the recommendation of the District Magistrate shall prepare for each District a panel of such number of eminent senior advocates who has been in practice for not less than seven years, as it may deem necessary for conducting cases in the Special Courts. Similarly, in consultation with the Director-Prosecution in charge of the prosecution, a panel of such number of Public Prosecutors as it may deem necessary for conducting cases in the Special Courts, shall also be specified. Both these panels shall be notified in the Official Gazette of the State and shall remain in force for a period of three years.

(2) The District Magistrate and the Director of prosecution in charge of the prosecution shall review at least twice in a calendar year, in the month of January and July, the performance of Special Public Prosecutors so specified or appointed and submit a report to the State Government.

(3) If the State Government is satisfied or has reason to believe that a Special Public Prosecutor so appointed or specified has not conducted the case to the best of his ability and with due care and caution, his name may be, for reasons to be recorded in writing, denotified.

(4) The District Magistrate and the Officer-in-charge of the prosecution at the District level, shall review the position of cases registered under the Act and submit a monthly report on or before 20th day of each subsequent month to the Director of Prosecution and the State Government. This chapter shall specify the actions taken/proposed to be taken in respect of investigation and prosecution of each case.

(5) Notwithstanding anything contained in sub-rule (1) the District Magistrate or the Sub-Divisional Magistrate may, if deem necessary or if so desired by the victim of atrocity engage an eminent Senior Advocate for conducting cases in the Special Courts on such payment of fees as he may consider appropriate.

(6) Payment of fee to the Special Public Prosecutor shall be fixed by the State Government on a scale higher than the other panel advocates in the State.

5. Information to Police Officer in-charge of a Police Station

(1) Every information relating to the commission of an offence under the Act, if given orally to an officer in-charge of a police station shall be reduced to writing by him or under his direction. and be read over to the informant, and every such information, whether given in writing or reduced to writing as aforesaid, shall be signed by the persons giving it, and the substance thereof shall be entered in a book to be maintained by that police station.

(2) A copy of the information as so recorded under sub-rule (1) above shall be given forthwith, free of cost, to the informant.

(3) Any person aggrieved by a refusal on the part of an officer in charge of a police station to record the information referred in sub-rule (1) may send the substance of such information, in writing and by post, to the Superintendent of Police concerned who after investigation either by himself or by a police officer not below the rank of Deputy Superintendent of Police, shall make an

order in writing to the officer in-charge of the concerned police station to enter the substance of that information to be entered in the book to be maintained by the police station.

6. Spot inspection by officers

(1) Whenever the District Magistrate or the Sub-Divisional Magistrate or any other executive Magistrate or any police officer not below the rank of Deputy Superintendent of Police receives an information from any person or upon his own knowledge that an atrocity has been committed on the members of the Scheduled Castes or the Scheduled Tribes within his jurisdiction he shall immediately himself visit the place of occurrence to assess the extent of atrocity, loss of life, loss and damage to the property and submit a report forthwith to the State Government.

(2) The District Magistrate or the sub-Divisional Magistrate or any other executive Magistrate and the Superintendent of Police, Deputy Superintendent of Police after inspecting the place or area on the spot,-

(i) draw a list of victims, their family members and dependents entitled for relief;

(ii) prepare a detailed report of the extent of atrocity, loss and damage to the property of the victims;

(iii) order for intensive police patrolling in the area;

(iv) take effective and necessary steps to provide protection to the witnesses and other sympathizers of the victims;

(v) provide immediate relief to the victims.

7. Investigating Officer

(1) An offence committed under the Act shall be investigated by a police officer not below the rank of a Deputy Superintendent of Police. The investigating officer shall be appointed by the State Government, Director-General of Police, Superintendent of Police after taking into account his past experience, sense of ability and justice to perceive the implications of the case and investigate it along with right lines within the shortest possible time.

(2) The investigating officer so appointed under sub-rule (1) shall complete the investigation on top priority within thirty days and submit the report to the Superintendent of Police who in turn will immediately forward the report to the Director-General of Police of the State Government.

(3) The Home Secretary and the Social Welfare Secretary to the State Government, Director of Prosecution the officer-in-charge of Prosecution and the Director-General of Police shall review by the end of every quarter the position of all investigations done by the investigating officer.

8. Setting up of the Scheduled Castes and the Scheduled Tribes Protection Cell

The State Government shall set up a Scheduled Castes and the Scheduled Tribes Protection Cell at the State headquarter under the charge of Director of Police, Inspector-General of Police. This Cell shall be responsible for,

(i) conducting survey of the identified area;

(ii) maintaining public order and tranquillity in the identified area;

(iii) recommending to the State Government for deployment of special police force or establishment of special police post in the identified area;

(iv) making investigations about the probable causes leading to an offence under the Act;

(v) restoring the feeling of security amongst the members of the Scheduled Castes and the Scheduled Tribes;

(vi) informing the nodal officer and special officer about the law and order situation in the identified area;

(vii) making enquiries about the investigation and spot inspections conducted by various officers;

(viii) making enquiries about the action taken by the Superintendent of Police in the cases where an officer in-charge of the police station has refused to enter an information in a book to be maintained by that police station under sub-rule (3) of rule 5;

(ix) making enquiries about the wilful negligence by a public servant;

(x) reviewing the position of cases registered under the Act, and

(xi) submitting a monthly report on or before 20th day of each subsequent month to the State Government, nodal officer about the action taken proposed to be taken, in respect of the above.

9. Nomination of Nodal Officer

The State Government shall nominate a nodal officer of the level of a Secretary to the Government preferably belonging to the Scheduled Castes or the Scheduled Tribes, for coordinating the functioning of the District Magistrates and Superintendent of Police or other officers authorized by them investigating officers and other officers responsible for implementing the provisions of the Act. By the end of the every quarter, the nodal officer shall review,-

(i) the reports received by the State Government under sub-rules (2) and (4) of rule 4, rule 6, Cl. (xi) of rule 8.

(ii) the position of cases registered under the Act;

(iii) law and order situation in the identified area;

(iv) various kinds of measures adopted for providing immediate relief in cash or kind or both to the victims of atrocity or his or her dependent;

(v) adequacy of immediate facilities like rationing, clothing, shelter, legal aid, travelling allowance, daily allowance and transport facilities provided to the victims of atrocity of his/her dependents;

(vi) performance of non-Governmental organizations, the Scheduled Castes and the Scheduled Tribes Protection Cell, various committees and the public servants responsible for implementing the provisions of the Act.

10. Appointment of a Special Officer

In the identified area a Special Officer not below the rank of an Additional District Magistrate shall be appointed to co-ordinate with the District Magistrate, Superintendent of Police or other officers responsible for implementing the provisions of the Act, various committees and the Scheduled Castes and the Scheduled Tribes Protection Cell.

The Special Officer shall be responsible for:

(i) providing immediate relief and other facilities to the victims of atrocity and initiate necessary measures to prevent or avoid re-occurrence of atrocity;

(ii) setting up an awareness center and organizing workshop in the identified area or at the District headquarters to educate the persons belonging to the Scheduled Castes and the Scheduled Tribes about their rights and the protection available to them under the provisions of various Central and State enactments or rules and schemes, etc. framed therein;

(iii) coordinating with the non-governmental organizations and providing necessary facilities and financial and other type of assistance to non-governmental organizations for maintaining centers or organizing workshops.

11.Travelling allowances, daily allowance, maintenance expenses and transport facilities to the victim atrocity, his or her dependent and witnesses

(1) Every victim of atrocity or his/her dependent and witnesses shall be paid to and for rail fare by second class in express / mail/ passenger train or actual bus of taxi fare from his / her place of residence or actual bus or taxi fare from his /her place of residence or place of stay to the place of investigation or hearing of trial of an offence under the Act.

(2) The District Magistrate or the Sub-Divisional Magistrate or any other Executive Magistrate shall make necessary arrangements for providing transport facilities or reimbursement of full payment thereof to the victims of atrocity and witnesses for visiting the investigating officer, Superintendent of Police/ Deputy Superintendent of Police, District Magistrate or any other Executive Magistrate.

(3) Every woman witness, the victim of atrocity or her dependent being a woman or a minor, a person more than sixty years of age and a person having 40 per cent or more disability shall be entitled to be accompanied by an attendant of her/ his choice. The attendant shall also be paid travelling and maintenance expenses

as applicable to the witness or the victim of atrocity when called upon during hearing, investigation and trial of an offence under the Act.

(4) The witness, the victim of atrocity or his/her dependent and the attendant shall be paid daily maintenance expenses for the days he/she is away from the place of his/her residence or stay during investigation, hearing and trial of an offence, at such rates but not less than the minimum wages, as may be fixed by the State Government for the agricultural laborers.

(5) In additional to daily maintenance expenses the witness' the victim of atrocity (or his/her dependent) and the attendant shall also be paid diet expenses at such rates as may be fixed by the State Government from time to time.

(6) The payment of travelling allowance, daily allowance, maintenance expenses and reimbursement of transport facilities shall be made im mediately or not later than three days by the District Magistrate or theSub-Divisional Magistrate or any other Executive Magistrate to the victims, their dependents/attendant and witnesses for the days they visit the investigating officer or in-charge police station or hospital authorities or Superintendent of Police, Deputy Superintendent of Police or District Magistrate or any other officer concerned or the Special Court.

(7) When an offence has been committed under Sec. 3 of the Act, the District Magistrate or the Sub-Divisional Magistrate or any other Executive Magistrate shall reimburse the payment of medicines, special medical consultation, blood transfusion, replacement of essential clothing, meals and fruits provided to the victim(s) of atrocity.

12. Measures to be taken by the District Administration

(1) The District Magistrate and the Superintendent of Police shall visit the place or area where the atrocity has been committed to assess the loss of life and damage to the property and draw a list of victim, their family members and dependents entitled for relief.

(2) Superintendent of Police shall ensure that the First Information Report is registered in the book of the concerned police station and effective measures for apprehending the accused are taken.

(3) The Superintendent of Police, after spot inspection, shall immediately appoint an investigation officer and deploy such police force in the area and take such other preventive measures as he may deem proper and necessary.

(4) The District Magistrate or the Sub-Divisional Magistrate or any other Executive Magistrate shall make arrangements for providing immediate relief in cash or in kind or both to the victims of atrocity, their family members and dependents according to the scale as in the schedule annexed to these Rules. Such immediate relief shall also include food, water, clothing, shelter, medical aid, transport facilities and other essential items necessary for human beings.

(5) The relief provided to the victim of the atrocity or his /her dependent under sub-rule (4) in respect of death, or injury to, or damage to propertyshall be in addition to any other right to claim compensation in respect thereof under any other law for the time being in force.

(6) The relief and rehabilitation facilities mentioned in sub-rule (4) above shall be provided by the District Magistrate or the Sub-Divisional Magistrate or any other Executive Magistrate in accordance with the scales provided in the Schedule annexed to these rules.

(7) A report of the relief and rehabilitation facilities provided to the victims shall also be forwarded to the Special Court by the District Magis trate or the Sub-Divisional Magistrate or the Executive Magistrate or Superintendent of Police. In case the Special Court is satisfied that the payment of relief was not made to the victim or his/her dependent in time or the amount of relief or compensation was not sufficient or only a part of payment of relief or compensation was made, it may order for making in full or part the payment of relief or any other kind of assistance.

13. Selection of Officers and other State Members for completing the work relating to atrocity

(1) The State Government shall ensure that the administrative officers and other staff members to be appointed in an area prone to atrocity shall have the right aptitude and understanding of the problems of the Scheduled Castes and posts and police station.

(2) It shall also be ensured by the State Government that persons from the Scheduled Castes and the Scheduled Tribes are adequately represented in the administration and in the police force at all levels, particularly at the level or police posts and police station.

14. Specific responsibility of the State Government

The State Government shall make necessary provisions in its annual budget for providing relief and rehabilitation facilities to the victims of atrocity. It shall review at least twice in a calendar year, in the month of January and July the performance of the Special Public Prosecutor specified or appointed under Sec. 15 of the Act, various reports received, investigation made and preventive steps taken by the District Magistrate,Sub-Divisional Magistrate and Superintendent of Police, relief and rehabilitation facilities provided to the victims and the reports in respect of lapses on behalf of the concerned officers.

15. Contingency Plan by the State Government

(1) The State Government shall prepare a model contingency plan for implementing the provisions of the Act and notify the same in the Official Gazette of the State Government. It should specify the role and responsibility of various departments and their officers at different levels, the role and responsibility of Rural/ Urban Local Bodies and Non-Government Organizations. Inter alia this plan shall contain a package of relief measures including the following:

(a) scheme to provide immediate relief in cash or in kind or both;

(b) allotment of agricultural land,and house-sites;

(c) the rehabilitation packages;

(d) scheme for employment in Government or Government undertaking to the dependent or one of the family members of the victim;

(e) pension scheme for widows, dependent children of the deceased, handicapped or old age victims of atrocity;

(f) mandatory compensation for the victims;

(g) scheme for strengthening the socioeconomic condition of the victim;

(h) provisions for providing brick/stone masonry house to the victims;

(i) such other elements as health care, supply of essential commodities, electrification, adequate drinking water facility,burial/cremation ground and link roads to the Scheduled Castes and the Scheduled Tribes.

(2) The State Government shall forward a copy of the contingency plan or a summary thereof and a copy of the scheme, as soon as may be, to the Central Government in the Ministry of Welfare and to all the District Magistrates, Sub-Divisional Magistrates, Inspectors-General of Police and Superintendents of Police.

16. Constitution of State-level Vigilance and Monitoring Committee

(1) The State Government shall constitute high power vigilance and monitoring committee of not more than 25 members consisting of the following:

(i) Chief Minister/Administrator-Chairman (in case of a State under President's Rule Governor-Chairman).

(ii) Home Minister, Finance Minister and Welfare Minister-Members (in case of a State under the President's Rule Advisors-Members);

(iii) all elected Members of Parliament and State Legislative As sembly and Legislative Council from the State belonging to the Scheduled Castes and the Scheduled Tribes- Members

(iv) Chief Secretary, the Home Secretary, the Director-General of Police, Director/ Deputy Director, National Commission for the Scheduled Castes and the Scheduled Tribes-Members;

(v) the Secretary in-charge of the welfare and development of the Scheduled Castes and the Scheduled Tribes- Convener.

(2) The high power vigilance and monitoring committee shall meet at least twice in a calendar year, in the month of January and July to review the implementation of the provisions of the Act, relief and rehabilitation facilities provided to the victims and other matters connected therewith, prosecution of cases under the Act, rule of

different officers/agenciesresponsible for implementing the provisions of the Act and various reports received by the State Government.

17. Constitution of District Level Vigilance and Monitoring Committee

(1) In each district within the State, the District Magistrate shall set up a vigilance and monitoring committee in his district to review the implementation of the provisions of the Act, relief and rehabilitation facilities provided to the victims and other matters connected therewith, prosecution of cases under the Act, role of different officers /agencies responsible for implementing the provisions of the Act and various reports received by the District Administration.

(2) The district level vigilance and monitoring committee shall consist of the elected Members of the Parliament and State Legislative Assembly and Legislative Council, Superintendent of Police, three-group 'A' Officers, Gazetted Officers of the State Government belonging to the Scheduled Castes and the Scheduled Tribes, not more than 5 non-official members belonging to the Scheduled Castes and the Scheduled Tribes and not more than 3 members from the categories other than the Scheduled Castes and the Scheduled Tribes having association with Non-Government Organizations. The District Magistrate and District Social Welfare Officer shall be Chairman and Member-Secretary respectively.

(3) The district level committee shall meet at least once in three months.

18. Material for Annual Report

The State Government shall every year before the 31st March, forward the report to the Central Government about the measures taken for implementing provisions of the Act and various schemes/plans framed by it during the previous calendar year.

REFERENCES

D'Souza, V. Does urbanism desegregate Scheduled Castes? Evidence from a District in Punjab, *Contributions to Indian Sociology* 11, 1977: 219-39.

Galanter, M. *Competing Equalities: Law and the Backward Classes in India.* Berkeley: University of California Press 1984.

Khosla, D. *Myth and Reality of the Protection of Civil Rights Law: a Case of Untouchability in Rural India.* Delhi: 1987.

Kshirsagar, R.K. *Untouchability in India: Implementation of Law and Abolition.* New Delhi: Deep & Deep 1986.

Pundir, J.K. Law and the Weaker Sections. In I.N. Tiwary et al. (eds) *Challenges and Alternatives.* U.P. Political Science Association 1980.

13

Kathmandu Dalit Declaration

by *International Consultation on Caste-Based Discrimination*

Establishing Dalit Rights in the Contemporary World: the Role of Governments, the United Nations and the Private Sector, November 29 – December 1 2004, Kathmandu, Nepal

The Participants to the International Consultation on Caste-Based Discrimination:

Recognising that caste discrimination affects, in its most severe forms, at least 260 million people worldwide and is particularly acute in South Asia, Africa, and Japan,

Recalling the terms of the Universal Declaration of Human Rights according to which all human beings are born free and equal in dignity and rights and are entitled to the rights and freedoms therein without distinction of any kind, including race, colour, sex, language, religion, social origin, birth or other status,

Recalling the terms of the Vienna Declaration and Programme of Action of the World Conference on Human Rights according to which it is the duty of States, regardless of political, economic and cultural system, to promote and protect all human rights and fundamental freedoms,

Recalling the condemnation of discrimination against persons of Asian and African descent and indigenous and other forms of descent in the Durban Declaration and Programme of Action of the World Conference against Racism, Racial Discrimination, Xenophobia and Related Intolerance,

Recalling also General Recommendation XXIX on descent-based discrimination of the Committee on the Elimination of Racial Discrimination,

Recognising the relevance of the Discrimination Convention, 1958 and its accompanying Recommendation for Dalit Human Rights,

Highlighting the reinforcing relationship between poverty, landlessness, and caste discrimination,

Affirming the need for the full implementation of the Millennium Development Goals as key mechanisms for the elimination of extreme poverty and the fulfilment of other rights-based human needs.

Fully Supporting Resolution 2004/17 of the U.N. Sub-Commission on the Promotion and Protection of Human Rights to appoint two Rapporteurs with the task of preparing a comprehensive study on discrimination based on work and descent,

Supporting also the U.N. Sub-Commission Norms on the Responsibilities of Transnational Corporations and Other Business Enterprises with Regard to Human Rights,

Conscious of the difficulties faced by Nepal's Dalits who represent a significant sector of Nepal's population and economy, and who are being caught in the crossfire of the conflict being waged in the country,

Recommend that concerned governments, international and national human rights bodies, U.N. and aid agencies, the European Union, donor countries, international financial institutions, the private sector, and non-governmental organisations adopt the following measures:

To Governments in Caste-Affected Countries

Concerned governments must act to uphold their constitutional principles and international treaty obligations and work toward the full enjoyment of rights by all citizens, regardless of caste or descent.

In particular, we call on concerned governments to:

Constitutional, Legislative and Judicial Measures

1. Ensure that all necessary constitutional, legislative and administrative measures, including appropriate forms of affirmative action and public education programs, are in place to prevent, prohibit and redress caste-based discrimination, and that

such measures are respected and implemented by all state authorities at all levels.

2. Establish a program and timetable to enforce the abolition of "untouchability", segregation, manual scavenging and similar practices. In both public and private sectors, Dalits and other outcaste communities should have full access to employment opportunities; agricultural land; credit; adequate housing; health; and common property resources, such as forest and water resources.

3. Ensure that, where they exist, national human rights institutions, women's commissions, minority commissions and Dalit commissions can act independently and effectively in protecting the interests of all people affected by caste discrimination by providing adequate financial, statutory and personnel support.

4. Take special measures to guarantee that members of Dalit and other outcaste communities enjoy the rights to vote, stand for election and have due representation in government and legislative bodies, revenue administration, the police, and the judiciary.

5. Ensure greater participation by Dalits in civil administration. Priority should be given to the administration of justice, particularly in key institutions such as the police and the judiciary.

6. End the culture of impunity for atrocities against Dalits through strict enforcement of relevant penal codes and legislation.

7. Monitor and publicize the extent to which existing laws and rulings to end caste discrimination, including untouchability, have been implemented.

8. Repeal national security and anti-terrorism laws that are contrary to the due process norms of international law.

9. Uphold human rights obligations, even in the face of national security concerns.

10. Ensure that Dalit human rights defenders are able to carry out their mandates effectively without any illegal or arbitrary interference or intimidation by the government or other forces in society.

11. Take the necessary steps to secure equal access to the justice system for all members of descent-based communities, including by providing legal aid, facilitating of group claims and

encouraging non-governmental organisations to defend individual and peoples' rights.

12. Reform criminal justice systems to ensure that Dalits at the local level have an independent complaints mechanism freely available to them in cases of police torture, other abuses or general failures to uphold justice.
13. Implement the recommendations of national HR institutions and other relevant national commissions on measures to eliminate caste-based discrimination.

Gender equity and violence against women

14. Take adequate measures to address abuses particular to Dalit women and girls who suffer multiple discrimination on the basis of caste, class and gender.
15. Take action to eradicate trafficking, forced and ritual prostitution of Dalit girls and women; take measures to address sexual exploitation and domestic violence, including early marriage and sexual violence in marriage, against Dalit women and girls.
16. Amend discriminatory laws regarding birth and marriage registration, and citizenship laws that confer citizenship to children solely on the basis of their father's identity.

Media and public wwareness

17. Take special affirmative measures to promote due representation in the mass media of members of Dalits and other disadvantaged groups, including women.
18. Carry out sensitisation campaigns and awareness-raising programs with media representatives.
19. Liaise with media outlets to profile and publicize abuses faced by caste-affected communities, including acts of violence, discriminatory social and customary practices and exploitation of labour.

Policy reform and access to land, education, health, housing and common resources

20. Enact land reform legislation that includes land distribution

clauses to counter the pervasive landlessness of Dalits, a majority of whom are dependent on agriculture for their livelihood.

21. Amend and enforce existing land reform legislation to prevent land alienation and ensure development of land belonging to Dalits through, among other things, greater access to credit and markets.

22. Introduce measures to combat homelessness and discrimination in tenancy, particularly in urban areas.

23. With the involvement of and input from civil society organisations, launch nationwide public awareness campaigns regarding legal prohibitions on caste discrimination.

24. Enlist the support of school teachers, social workers, law enforcement officials, government employees, the private sector and other relevant actors to undertake active training and sensitization programs against caste discrimination.

25. Ensure the inclusion of all Dalit children in free, full-time formal quality education from primary level until the completion of elementary level.

26. Introduce mid-day meal schemes in all public schools and ensure non-discriminatory access.

27. Ensure greater participation by Dalits and other outcaste communities in educational institutions after finishing elementary education.

28. Introduce social justice and human rights education, including principles of non-discrimination, in public schools

Employment

29. Enact equality laws that prohibit public and private employer discrimination on the basis of caste.

30. Take necessary steps to remove the customary constraints on leaving traditional caste-based occupations and promote more gainful alternative employment opportunities for Dalits.

31. Enact and enforce legislation guaranteeing decent work, a living wage, labour rights, and access to land for Dalits and other exploited or oppressed communities, particularly in the informal economy

Development planning and implementation

32. Ensure that government programs are designed in consultation with Dalits and other marginalized communities at both the state and central government levels.
33. Pay particular attention to the needs of Dalit and other outcaste communities in the devising and implementation of strategies and plans to achieve the Millennium Development Goals (MDGs).
34. Include Dalit groups and other civil society groups in discussions on priorities for engagement with the World Bank and Asian Development Bank.
35. Allocate adequate funding for programs for the socio-economic and educational support of communities that have faced discrimination on the basis of caste or descent.

International

36. Strongly support initiatives to promote and enhance the fight against caste discrimination in all relevant United Nations and related fora, including U.N. human rights bodies, the International Labour Organisation (ILO), the United Nations Development Programme (UNDP), the United Nations Fund for Women (UNIFEM), the United Nations Children's Fund (UNICEF), the World Bank, the Asian Development Bank and the International Monetary Fund.
37. Support efforts at the 61st session of the U.N. Commission on Human Rights in 2005 to adopt the draft decision contained in resolution 2004/17 of the Sub-Commission on the Promotion and Protection of Human Rights to appoint two Rapporteurs with the task of preparing a comprehensive study on discrimination based on work and descent.
38. Ratify (or accede to) and fully implement provisions of the U.N. International Convention on the Elimination of All Forms of Racial Discrimination (ICERD).
39. Implement without delay recommendations contained in CERD's General Recommendation XXIX on descent-based discrimination, including those on the administration of justice, civil and political rights, economic and social rights, the right to education, and the dissemination of hate speech.

40. Promote the call for the appointment of a Special Rapporteur on Caste Discrimination by the U.N. Commission on Human Rights.
41. Ratify and implement the provisions of the International Covenant on Civil and Political Rights the International Covenant on Economic, Social and Cultural Rights (ICESCR), the U.N. Convention against Torture and Other Cruel, Inhuman or Degrading Treatment or Punishment the Convention on the Elimination of All Forms of Discrimination Against Women and the Convention on the Rights of the Child. Cooperate fully with the treaty bodies set up to monitor these covenants and conventions.
42. Review and make effective time-bound action plans for the implementation of all ILO Conventions and domestic laws pertaining to labour rights, bonded and child labour, and manual scavenging.

National Human Rights Institutions and Other National Commissions

43. Ensure affected community representation, including women, in the membership and staff of national human rights institutions, women's commissions, minority commissions, and Dalit commissions.
44. Create a core group of NGOs to assist in the commissions' work and ensure Dalit NGO representation in this group.
45. Ensure that the Asia Pacific Forum of National Human Rights Institutions (APFNHRI) discusses specific strategies to fight caste discrimination. The NGO Forum of the APFNHRI should include representation from caste-affected communities.

To U.N. Human Rights Bodies

46. Take every opportunity to raise the issue of caste and descent-based discrimination with relevant governments and encourage enactment and implementation of laws against the violations of human rights of members of Dalit communities, including laws prohibiting manual scavenging, bonded labour, caste-based violence and other abusive practices.

Commission on human rights and its special procedures

47. The Commission on Human Rights should adopt the draft decision contained in the resolution 2004/17 of the Sub-Commission on the Promotion and Protection of Human Rights to appoint two Rapporteurs with the task of preparing a comprehensive study on discrimination based on work and descent, and call upon States to extend all necessary cooperation to the Rapporteurs.
48. The Special Rapporteur on Contemporary Forms of Racism should continue to raise the issue of caste discrimination in their reports, make specific recommendations to concerned governments, and continue to request government invitations for official visits to the respective countries.
49. All relevant Special Rapporteurs should pay particular attention to the plight of Dalits in a manner relevant to their respective mandates.
50. The Commission on Human Rights should appoint a Special Rapporteur on Caste Discrimination and declare in a resolution that caste-based discrimination is prohibited by international law, and call upon all concerned States to the take necessary measures for its elimination.
51. Support the U.N. Norms on the Responsibilities of Transnational Corporations and Other Business Enterprises with Regard to Human Rights and promote its development into an international instrument that is binding on companies in order to ensure, within their sphere of influence, their accountability and liability with regard to the realisation of human rights.

Sub-commission on the promotion and protection of human rights

52. The Sub-Commission's prospective Rapporteurs on discrimination based on work and descent should be provided with all the necessary support and resources required to carry out their mandate.
53. Subject to confirmation of the Rapporteurs' mandate by the Commission on Human Rights, priority should be given to the formulation of the requested Principles and Guidelines for the Elimination of Discrimination Based on Work and Descent.

Human rights treaty monitoring bodies

54. Treaty monitoring bodies - in particular the Committee on the Elimination of Racial Discrimination, the Committee on the Rights of the Child, the Committee on Economic, Social and Cultural Rights, the Committee on the Elimination of Discrimination Against Women, the Human Rights Committee, and the Committee Against Torture. Should pay attention to human rights violations against Dalits.

To the United Nations and its Specialized Agencies

55. The Secretary-General of the United Nations and the United Nations High Commissioner for Human Rights should help ensure that all U.N. agencies working in caste-affected countries pay particular attention to the issue of caste violence and discrimination.
56. Assess the impact of existing programs in caste-affected countries with regard to caste discrimination.
57. All U.N. agencies should build partnerships with Dalit organisations and establish consultative mechanisms to seek Dalit NGO input into project design and evaluation.
58. In its programs on HIV/AIDS, the UNDP should ensure that Dalit children are not discriminated against in their access to health and education.
59. All U.N. agencies should implement affirmative action measures in order to proportionately employ Dalits, including women, in all development activities.
60. In its forthcoming Global Report on non-discrimination as one the four fundamental labour rights, the ILO should conduct a thorough analysis of the impact of caste discrimination on labour.
61. Undertake assessments of UN recruitment policy and practice in relevant country offices to ensure non-discrimination of Dalits and other caste affected and marginalised groups.

To Bilateral Aid Agencies

62. Promote the inclusion of marginalized groups such as Dalits into the consultation and design of programs.

63. Provide political and financial support for programs of the United Nations and regional bodies to assist countries seeking to eradicate caste discrimination.
64. Provide assistance for Dalit groups at the community level to participate in the planning of infrastructure and other government programs to ensure equal access by Dalits.
65. Take every opportunity to raise the issue of caste discrimination with caste-affected country officials, and encourage enactment and implementation of relevant laws against caste-based abuses.
66. Support civil society initiatives, including those led by Dalit organisations, that seek to eliminate caste-based discrimination.
67. Implement affirmative action measures in order to proportionately employ Dalits, including women, in all development activities.

6. To the European Union.

68. Open up political and human rights dialogue with caste-affected countries on caste discrimination and ensure the effectiveness of EU Human Rights policy in this respect by ensuring that the issue forms a central part of Ministerial-level dialogues.
69. Ensure that caste-discrimination and its consequences are effectively analyzed and included in EU country strategy papers, reports, recommendations, resolutions, mid-term reviews and communications on affected countries.
70. Ensure that EU development programmes in affected countries are designed to assist national Governments to counter existing inequalities and specifically eradicate caste discrimination, and monitor the results.
71. The EU must promote and support initiatives to address caste-based discrimination in all relevant United Nations fora, including the adoption of the U.N.
72. Include references to and recommendations for the elimination of caste-based discrimination in all relevant EU statements, resolutions, working papers, declarations and programs of action pertaining to relevant agenda items in the United Nations Commission on Human Rights, the General Assembly's Third Committee, and in the follow up to the World Conference against

Racism, Racial Discrimination, Xenophobia and Related Intolerance.

73. As part of its policies on corporate social responsibility, encourage and provide incentives for private companies with EU origin operating in caste-affected countries to adopt and implement the Ambedkar Principles.

74. Assess the impact of trade, investment relations, and cooperation programs between EU and caste-affected countries on those suffering from caste discrimination. Formulate recommendations to make these programmes non-detrimental and more beneficial to Dalits.

To Donor Countries

75. Fulfil commitments made under Millennium Development Goal 8 to build a global partnership for development.

76. Fulfil the human rights obligations of international cooperation as found in the Universal Declaration of Human Rights, the U.N. Charter and the ICESCR, toward the promotion of economic, social and cultural rights in developed and developing countries.

77. Be mindful that the obligation of States to protect economic, social and cultural rights extend also to their participation in international organisations, where they act collectively, such as the World Trade Organisation and international financial institutions.

To the World Bank and Asian Development Bank

78. Incorporate an analysis of caste exclusion into Corporate Social Development Strategies. For policy-based lending ensure that Poverty and Social Assessments (PSIA), carried out before loans are approved, include investigations of how the proposed policy changes will affect Dalit men and women, and their livelihoods.

79. As part of their commitment to good governance, the World Bank and Asian Development Bank, as well as other international lending institutions, should, together with the governments concerned, establish an ongoing dialogue with Dalit NGOs and representatives of other marginalized groups at all stages of the decision-making process.

80. In the design of infrastructure programs, the World Bank and Asian Development Bank should ensure that concerned governments consult with Dalit and other marginalized groups, particularly women, to promote access to water, food, sanitation, land, rural transport, irrigation and social infrastructure.
81. With regard to basic services in health and education, the World Bank and Asian Development Bank should design an accountability framework that allows Dalit and other civil society groups to monitor access to these services.

The Private Sector including Transnational Corporations

82. All companies investing in or operating in caste-affected countries should support and implement the U.N. Norms on the Responsibilities of Transnational Corporations and Other Business Enterprises with Regard to Human Rights, as well as sign the more general Global Compact, and implement changes in their business practices consistent with its principles.
83. Companies from OECD countries, should also implement the OECD Guidelines for Multinationals and other Enterprises, whilst all companies should implement the principles contained in the ILO Tripartite Declaration.
84. Adopt specific policies pertaining to human rights and ensure that, within your sphere of influence, these principles are also implemented by all suppliers and business partners.
85. Ensure that infrastructure investments are carried out in consultation with marginalized groups, including Dalits, and prioritise access of these groups to the fruits of these investments.
86. Ensure compliance with nationally mandated affirmative action programs. Where no such programs exist, companies should voluntarily institute and implement affirmative action programs for Dalits.
87. As a specific development of the above, adopt and implement the Ambedkar Principles. The Ambedkar Principles are employment principles to assist foreign investors to address caste discrimination in South Asia.

TO NON-GOVERNMENTAL ORGANISATIONS

88. Include documentation on caste-based abuses and analysis of caste-based discrimination in reporting on caste-affected countries. Where appropriate, include critical assessments of the effectiveness of national policies and legislation addressing caste discrimination.
89. Pay particular attention to the intersection of gender, class and caste discrimination as it affects Dalit and other outcaste women.
90. Give due attention to the nexus between caste discrimination and other forms of human rights violations such as torture, gender-based violence, modern forms of slavery including child and bonded labour, denial of equal treatment before the law, and deprivations of livelihood, food, water, healthcare, education, housing and land.
91. Plan for the reduction and elimination of caste-based discrimination and violence through development programming and monitor the impact of such programs.
92. Implement public awareness-raising and education campaigns to promote positive change in public attitudes and practices vis-à-vis members of communities affected by caste discrimination.
93. Lobby and provide information to relevant U.N. bodies to increase their attention to the plight of Dalits and other caste-affected communities, and encourage the creation of social, economic, cultural and political programs to help overcome historic discrimination.
94. Lobby governments to implement CERD General Recommendation XXIX as well as recommendations addressed to them following consideration of state reports by CERD.
95. Translate into national languages and disseminate widely CERD General Recommendation XXIX and CERD's country-specific recommendations.
96. Provide CERD and other relevant human rights treaty bodies with information on caste-based discrimination and encourage them to review the implementation of ICERD and other relevant instruments even when governments fail to comply with their reporting obligations.

97. Raise awareness among international aid agencies, the private sector, transnational corporations, and governments on the prevalence of caste discrimination and recommend appropriate interventions similar to those outlined in this chapter.
98. Develop and implement staff policies that will ensure the maximum participation of Dalits at all levels within domestic and international NGOs. Ensure that Dalits, including women, are involved in all stages of relevant projects, including planning, implementation, monitoring and evaluation.

Bibliography

Agarwal, L.B. *The Harijans in Rebellion*. Bombay: Taraporewala 1934.

Alte, I.D. *Rural Employment of Scheduled Castes*. New Delhi:Deep & Deep 1992.

Ambedkar, B.R. *What Congress and Gandhi Have Done to the Untouchables*. Bombay: Thacker 1945.

Augustine, P.A. *Social Equality in Indian Society*. New Delhi: Concept 1991.

Bailey, F.G. *Caste and the Economic Frontier*. Manchester: MUP 1957.

Berreman, G. *Hindus of the Himalayas: Ethnography and Change*. Berkeley: University of California Press 1963 .

Berreman, G.D. *Caste and Other Inequities*. Meerut: Folklore Institute 1979.

Beteille, A. *The Backward Classes in Contemporary India*. Delhi: OUP 1992 .

Bhai, N. *Harijan Women in Independent India*. Delhi: BR Publishing 1986.

Bharadwaj, A.N. *Problems of Scheduled Castes and Scheduled Tribes in India* [From Jammu: general review from experience by journalist and social worker of distinction]. New Delhi: Light & Life 1979.

Bharti, I. Bihar's most wretched, *Economic & Political Weekly* Sept 22, 1990: 2124-25.

Bhave, S. *Pan on Fire: Eight Dalit Women Tell Their Story*. New Delhi: 1988.

Bhowmik, K.L. (ed.) Development of Scheduled Communities. 1985 Conference papers on tribals. *Current Anthropological and Archaeological Perspectives*, Vol. 6. New Delhi: Inter-India Publications 1988.

Burman, B.K. Roy *Social Mobility Movements among Scheduled Castes and Scheduled Tribes of India*. Delhi: Government of India Press 1970.

Burman, B.K. Roy The problem of Untouchables. In Romesh Thapar (ed.) *Tribe, Caste and Religion in India*. Delhi: Macmillan 1977.

Census of India 1961 *Study of customary rights and living and working conditions of Scavengers in two towns* [Haryana and UP]. Monog. series Vol. I, Part XI, D. 1966.

Centre for Social Studies, Surat (ed.) *Caste, Caste Conflict and Reservation*. Delhi: Ajanta 1985.

Chalam, K.S. Caste and economic reform, *Seminar* 471, Nov. 1998: 33-37.

Chandel, M.P.S. *A Social Force in Politics: Study of Scheduled Castes of UP*. New Delhi: Mittal 1990.

Chandra, V. *Handbook on Scheduled Castes and Scheduled Tribes*. New Delhi: Office of the Commissioner for SC&ST 1968.

Chatterjee, S.K. *The Scheduled Castes in India*, 4 vol. compendium of official material by anthropologist retired from Police]. New Delhi: Gyan 1996.

Corrie, B.D. A human development index for the Dalit child in India, *Social Indicators Research* 34, 1995: 395-409.

D'Souza, V. An operational definition of backward groups in India, *Indian Journal of Agricultural Economics* 13, 1958; 33-45.

D'Souza, V. Does urbanism desegregate Scheduled Castes? Evidence from a District in Punjab, *Contributions to Indian Sociology* 11, 1977: 219-39.

Danda, A.K. *Weaker Sections in Indian Villages*. 2 vols. New Delhi: Inter-India 1993.

Das, D.P. *The Untouchable Story.* New Delhi: Allied 1975.

Desai, A.R. *Caste and Communal Violence in India*. Bombay: Popular 1985.

Desai, I.P. *Water facilities for the Untouchables in rural Gujerat*. Occasional Monographs No. 8. New Delhi: ICSSR 1973.

Dushkin, L. Scheduled Caste politics. In J.M. Mahar (ed.) *The Untouchables in Contemporary India*. Tucson: University of Arizona Press 1972.

Freeman, J.M. The consciousness of freedom amongst India's Untouchables. In D.K. Basu & R. Sisson (eds) *Social and Economic Development in India*. New Delhi: Sage 1986.

Freeman, J.M. *Untouchable. An Indian Life History*. London: Allen & Unwin 1979.

Galanter, M. *Competing Equalities: Law and the Backward Classes in India*. Berkeley: University of California Press 1984.

Galanter, M. Pursuing equality. An assessment of India's policy of compensatory discrimination for disadvantaged groups. In D.K. Basu & R. Sisson (eds) *Social and Economic Development in India*. New Delhi: Sage 1986.

Ghosh, S.K. *Protection of Minorities and Scheduled Castes*. New Delhi: Ashish 1980.

Gokhale, J. *From Concessions to Confrontation: the Politics of an Indian Untouchable Community*. Bombay: Popular Prakashan 1993.

Gomango, G. *Constitutional Provisions for the Scheduled Castes and Scheduled Tribes*. Bombay: Himalya 1992.

Gupta, S.K. *Scheduled Castes in Modern Indian Politics: Their Emergence as a Political Power*. New Delhi: Munshiram Manoharlal 1985.

Jain, P.C., Jain Shashi & Bhatnagar, Sudha *Scheduled Caste Women* [Muzaffarnagar District, UP]. Jaipur: Rawat 1997.

Jeffery, P. *et al.* Contaminating states: midwifery, childbearing and the state in rural North India. In H. Afshar (ed.) *Women, State and Ideology*. Basingstoke: Macmillan 1987.

Jones, K. *Socio-Religious Reform Movements in British India*. Cambridge: CUP 1989.

Joshi, B. Recent developments in inter-regional mobilization of Dalit protest in India, *South Asia Bulletin* 7, 1987: 86-96.

Kamble, J.R. *Rise and Awakening of the Depressed Classes in India*. New Delhi: National 1979.

Karlekar, M. *Poverty and Women's Work: a Study of Sweeper Women in Delhi*. Delhi: Vikas 1982.

Khosla, D. *Myth and Reality of the Protection of Civil Rights Law: a Case of Untouchability in Rural India*. Delhi: 1987.

Kshirsagar, R.K. *Untouchability in India: Implementation of Law and Abolition*. New Delhi: Deep & Deep 1986.

Massey, J. *Down Trodden: The Struggle of Indian Dalits for Identity, Solidarity and Liberation*. Geneva: WCC Publications 1997.

Mendelsohn, O. & Vicziany, M. *The Untouchables. Poverty, Pollution and the State in Modern India*. Cambridge: CUP 1998.

Michael, S.M. (ed.) *Dalits in Modern India. Vision and Values*. New Delhi: Vistaar 1999.

Mukerjee, H.N. *Gandhi, Ambedkar and the Extirpation of Untouchability*. New Delhi: People's 1982.

Pundir, J.K. Law and the Weaker Sections. In I.N. Tiwary et al. (eds) *Challenges and Alternatives*. U.P. Political Science Association 1980.

Roy, A.K. *New Dalit Revolution*. Patna: 1980.

Santoshi, H. *Daliton Mein Dalit*. New Delhi: Nav Sahitye Academy 1990.

Tripathi, R.S. & Tiwari, P.D. (eds) *Dimensions of Scheduled Caste Development in India*. New Delhi: Uppal 1991.

Tuinmin, H. *The Political Economy of Untouchability*. Unpubl. thesis, University of New South Wales, Sydney, 1984.

Vidyarthi, L.P. & Mishra, N. *Harijan Today. Sociological, Economics, Political, Religious and Cultural Analysis*. New Delhi: Classical 1977.

Zelliot, E. *From Untouchable to Dalit: Essays on Ambedkar Movement*. New Delhi: Manohar 1992.

Index